Hello to All That

Hello to All That

a memoir of war, zoloft, and peace

john falk

henry holt and company, new york

Henry Holt and Company, LLC
Publisher since 1866
115 West 18th Street
New York, New York 10011

Henry Holt® is a registered trademark of Henry Holt and Company, LLC.

Library of Congress Cataloging-in-Publication Data
Falk, John.
    Hello to all that : a memoir of war, Zoloft, and peace / John Falk.—1st ed.
        p.   cm.
    ISBN 0-8050-7218-7
    EAN 987-0-8050-7218-1
    1. Falk, John—Mental health.   2. Depression, Mental—Patients—
United States—Biography.   3. Journalists—Bosnia and Hercegovina—Biography.
4. Sertraline.   I. Title.

RC537.F34 2005
616.85'27'0092—dc22
[B]   2004054286

Henry Holt books are available for special promotions and premiums.
For details contact: Director, Special Markets.

First Edition 2005

Designed by Fritz Metsch

Printed in the United States of America

1 2 3 4 5 6 7 8 9 10

To my parents, Arthur and Joanne Falk,
who only grow stronger with time

"The unexamined life is not worth living."—Plato

"The unlived life is not worth examining."—Alfred E. Neuman

contents

Hello to All That

Tabula Rasa

August 3, 1993

The plane was a Luftwaffe C-130 packed with tons of food aid, en route to Sarajevo. The German Air Force had issued parachutes to give us a fighting chance in case we were shot down, but the other passengers thought it was a waste. "Just means our bodies will burn faster," bitched a distinctly American voice. I was cheered.

Actually, I didn't get it. Yeah, the parachutes were uncomfortable. Yeah, we looked like idiots. But I was a war correspondent, flying into my first war zone and, if I had to wear a giant silver diaper to get it done, so be it. I was going in.

About forty minutes into the flight from the coast of Croatia, a German sergeant ordered us to buckle up, barking about ground fire at the airport. "Be ready to disembark immediately," he yelled over the engines as we flew through a cloud bank that obscured everything below. I stared out the window anyway; I couldn't help it. When Sarajevo revealed itself, I wanted to see everything. It was ugly; it was grim; it was war. But at the time, I admit it, it was exciting to me.

I knew more about the siege of Sarajevo than many, having read up in graduate school. Sarajevo was a city of almost half a million tucked away in a valley dominated on all sides by mountains and steep hillsides where approximately ten thousand Serb soldiers armed with the latest weaponry were dug in. Their aim was to kill as many as they could of the lightly armed, mostly Muslim inhabitants in the city below. So far, they had taken out ten thousand and the survivors lacked water, electricity, gas, and medicine.

I knew the names of the key politicians and the broad strokes of the latest international peace plans. But I didn't go much deeper than that because I really didn't give a fuck about the history of the place, and I hadn't come all this way just to learn more. I was here because I was trying to start my life. Maybe a genocidal conflict seems a strange place for this purpose. But I had waited so long and I was determined.

Our plane descended below the clouds, and Sarajevo started sliding by: smashed roofs, houses gutted by fire, patches of rubble, tank traps. A smoky steel blue haze hung over the city and, even though it was summer, the few trees were bare and skeletal.

We landed at Sarajevo International, then run by the French Foreign Legion, at 4:00 p.m. Concertina wire ringed the perimeter. Machine-gun emplacements were dug in between the runways. Snipers were positioned in the sandbagged control tower. Everywhere I looked there were Legionnaires with assault rifles. Except for a huge Russian jet crumpled at the end of the runway, we were the only plane.

Within minutes a crew of Frenchies in khaki hot pants had unloaded the aid and was ushering us outside. I grabbed my stuff and followed the others out to the tarmac, where I caught my first whiff of war—a strange amalgamation of burning plastic and wood smoke, mixed with a dash of horseshit. Not pleasant, but exotic enough to have a certain allure. In the distance I could hear gunfire.

From the plane, we were led down a sandbagged alley where my papers were processed by a UN press officer. Within three minutes I was in the pickup area, a parking lot surrounded on three sides by a ten-foot wall of dirt. Except for the black SWAT body armor and the helmet I wore, everything I had brought from Long Island was packed away in a medium L.L.Bean canvas duffel bag I dragged behind me.

It held: four pair of boxers and socks, three golf shirts from the Gap, two pair of stone-washed jeans, a ribbed-neck sweater from J. Crew, two cartons of Camel Lights, a year's supply of the antidepressant Zoloft stuffed in a tube sock, three hundred dollars American, a shortwave radio, pens and a notebook, recording equipment from Radio Shack, a 35mm camera and film, half a bar of Toblerone chocolate, five rolls of two-ply Scott toilet paper, a Serbo-Croatian phrase book, plus *The End of History and the Last Man* and a dogeared, underlined copy of *One Flew Over the Cuckoo's Nest.*

But my most valuable possession wasn't in my bag: in my pocket was a crumpled-up cocktail napkin with a crude map sketched on it, a "reward" for my agreeing to be a courier for a Macedonian I had met in Croatia. The plan called for me to deliver a bag of mail to a woman named Szezana in Sarajevo.

Back in Croatia, I was told that the most important thing I needed to make it in Sarajevo was an ally, someone who knew the city and would be willing to give me a safe place to crash. Szezana, I'd decided, was going to be my ally, but to rendezvous with her I had to get into the city. To do that, I was to hook up with an Egyptian armored personnel carrier (APC), which would take me to some building called the PTT. But the Egyptian APC was nowhere in sight.

An Australian reporter was hovering close by, so I showed him my mailbag, told him about the Macedonian and Szezana, and described the map.

"Let me see," he said, storing his cigarette in the corner of his mouth. After glancing down, he grinned. "No way, mate," he said, handing back the map. "You go there today, tomorrow you go home in a box."

"What the hell do you mean?" I asked, panicked.

"Someone doesn't like you much. That address is the worst in the world. It's in the middle of goddamn Sniper Alley."

But that napkin was the Jesus-bolt holding my whole plan together: "What should I do?"

"If I were you, I'd get out of here. It's not a place to fuck around, mate." Then he hopped into an armored Land Rover and drove away.

I was as scared as I had ever been and I hadn't even been on the ground for ten minutes. In seconds, I had gone from this sense of having a friend in Sarajevo to feeling completely alone in the most dangerous city on the planet. But no way was I going to turn back. So, though I didn't really want to, I approached Mort—the tall American reporter who bitched and moaned more than anyone on the plane. Maybe he would help me, but it would probably cost something.

"*Who gave you this piece of shit?*" he roared at the map.

"A Macedonian," I told him, holding out my napkin. "I'm supposed to deliver some mail for her at that address."

"Nice of you. Piece of advice, though? Next time don't take shit from no one. You don't know what you're carrying in. Military maps. Messages. If the Serbs find any of that shit, you're fucked."

"Listen. Normally I would never ask this. But could you please help me. Just one night."

"Why don't you just stay at the Holiday Inn?"

I had heard about the Holiday Inn. It was on a front line and half of it was history. Rooms in the other half were going for two hundred a night—more if you wanted soup.

"No money."

"Freelancer?"

"Yeah."

He looked away, then back, then did it again. Someplace not far off, a machine gun burped. "OK," he said. "You've come this far, so I guess someone owes you a day."

"Thanks, man," I told him. "Really."

"But remember, tomorrow morning, whatever happens, you're on your own." Then he put his right hand on my left shoulder and looked me in the eye. "If you fuck up my gig at the church, I mean at all, I'll kill ya."

I swore I wouldn't, but I had no idea what the hell he was talking about.

Five minutes later, the Egyptian APC arrived. Locked away in its steel belly, we couldn't see anything. The highlight of the trip was getting stopped by four Serb soldiers who opened the back hatch to make sure we weren't hauling Muslims. My first look at soldiers at war, they were well armed and surly, but still they didn't seem like the genocidal maniacs I had seen on TV back in America. A little on the pudgy side, they were dressed in purple-and-blue tiger-pattern fatigues that could only have been useful if they were fighting their way across Liberace's living room.

After the Egyptians dropped us off at the PTT building, a Spanish reporter drove us to a section of Sarajevo called Old Town. To get there, we drove down Aldo od Bosna, the city's main boulevard, now called simply Sniper Alley. We were the only car on the road, and most of the time he did about eighty in order to give the Serb snipers hunting the street a more difficult target. But as Mort and the Spaniard were casually chitchatting up front and didn't seem too worried, I relaxed. Pressing my face to the window, I tried to take in as much as I could. I noticed there was no glass remaining in any windows anywhere; most of the taller buildings had been blown apart; the streets were littered with burnt hulks of cars and trolleys; and the few people I did see were either pushing baby carriages full of plastic jerry cans or pulling sleds piled high with firewood. The strangest sight I saw was an old man dressed in a three-piece suit walking down the middle of the road holding two dead pigeons.

．　．　．

Mort's gig turned out to be a room he had scored inside a Roman Catholic church that stood at an intersection of three narrow cobblestone streets. As we pulled up, a pack of scruffy kids were kicking the hell out of a patched soccer ball while two uniformed men with machine guns stood watching from inside a sandbagged bunker.

As soon as Mort stepped out, the kids started screaming, running in circles, and chanting, "Mort, Mort, Mort." A small crowd, including a cop, gathered as Mort grabbed his luggage, then took out some candy. The kids went nuts.

While Mort was doing his thing with the kids, the cop caught my eye and gestured for a cigarette. I had quit the day before, but brought a few cartons because I heard they were better than gold for making allies. Reaching into my bag, I tossed a fresh pack of Camel Lights to the cop, who pumped my hand.

After we got inside, Mort and I put down our bags. The marbled-floored church, lit by a few candles, was real chilly. In the dim light I heard whispered conversations. Mort ushered me into an office just off the main entrance and gave explicit instructions: "Sit-the-fuck-down!"

Confused, I just stood there.

"Fine, stand up, I don't give a shit. You really fucked up out there. You know what the fuck you did?"

"No."

"No? Put a gun to your head, and more importantly, mine."

"How?"

"The whole fucking street saw you toss those butts to that cop, asshole. Now everyone knows that the rich fuck American is here—with *me.*"

Mort spun on his heels and went out the door. Ten seconds later he was back and pacing.

"This is Vietnam, dickhead. These people hate your guts," he told me through clenched teeth. "Don't be a fucking fool, especially when you're around me. They hate you because you can leave. They hate you because you have money. They hate you for being here. Don't trust these motherfuckers for one second, not once."

A knock on the door brought a teenage boy—short, skinny, and dark haired. Putting a hand around the kid's shoulder, Mort was suddenly all smiles. After he mumbled something in Bosnian, the kid left. Mort stood there with this beatific smile on his face. I was starting to wonder what was under Mort's hood.

"Do you know who Satso is?" he asked, suddenly pissed again.

"No."

"Well, he's God to these fucking idiots. The local warlord. Controls everything in Old Town. Hates Serbs. Hates the UN. But the thing he hates most is you. In fact, he digs kidnapping foreign journalists."

Then Mort suddenly changed gears again, calming down and taking a seat next to me on the couch. "You know *The Lawrence Welk Show?*"

"A little."

"The one with the cascading bubbles?"

"Yeah, yeah. On PBS. Bubbles. Sure."

"Well, Satso used to be lead guitarist on the Bosnian version," he said, leaning back into the couch as if he was fondly remembering every bubble. "He was good. I mean real good, for Bosnia anyway."

He lit himself a cigarette.

"But in the first days of the war, Satso lost his arm. He couldn't play his guitar anymore and snapped, went psychotic. He did some bad shit, but what's important is he's a warlord now. Commands five thousand men and when they're not fucking up Serbs, they come down here to Old Town and do two things: kill police and kidnap foreign reporters. The point is: Don't give anyone any thing. Fuck 'em, they probably deserve it."

To calm myself, I lit my first cigarette. I wasn't so much worried about this Satso as I was about Mort. I didn't think he'd really kick me out in the morning if I hadn't yet found a place, but I wasn't sure. As I smoked, the teenage boy walked back in, mumbling something in Bosnian.

"Great. Our room's ready, buddy," he told me, suddenly Mr. Sunshine. "The kid here set up a cot for you. Let's drop our shit in the room. Then you can come with me while I drop off a care package. It will be good for you."

Except for the occasional gunshot up in the hills, it was quiet, more so than I thought it should have been. I guessed it was around seven, still light, but the streets were mostly deserted. Zipped up in my body armor, I was soaked in sweat.

We were headed to the home of the Kukic family so Mort could drop off a big bag of food. They were friends of his, he said.

"The old man's a surgeon," he told me. "Really well respected. A great guy."

Dr. Kukic and his family lived in a still almost-charming wood-and-stucco two-story house, about a quarter mile from the church. The home looked like an antique, with carved wooden shutters, Tudorlike trim, and a cobblestone driveway, walled off from the street by a solid high metal gate. But the place hadn't escaped the war unscathed: the windows had been replaced by thick, milky-colored plastic sheeting; the detached garage was sliced in half; and there was a large jagged hole in the upper corner of the house, as if a giant rat had taken a bite out of it.

"Listen," Mort said, as we headed up the driveway. "When we get inside, take off your shoes. It's custom. Also, they're going to offer you coffee. Take it because they're gonna give it to you anyway. But be a mensch. When they offer you food, don't take it. They barely have enough to feed themselves."

"Mort! Oh my God!" a middle-aged woman cried out as she hustled down a hallway toward us. It was the doctor's wife, Mrs.

Kukic. Mort unzipped his body armor, and she gave him a huge hug, held his head in her hands, and planted two big kisses on each of his cheeks. Then Mrs. Kukic's sister came down the stairs and repeated the hello frame by frame, only in Bosnian.

"We worry about you," said Mrs. Kukic quietly. "We did not hear for a long time."

"You know me. I'm fine," he told her, slipping off his shoes. "How are you is the question."

"Ah, good," Mrs. Kukic answered. "You know, not much shelling. But still, very difficult, of course."

Mort handed her the bag of food.

"Please, you do not need," she began. "Please, Mort. You are family. Welcome, gifts or not."

"I know. I just wanted to."

Mrs. Kukic and her sister were more carefully dressed and elegant than I would have imagined in these circumstances. Mrs. Kukic's hair was styled, her nails smooth and shaped, her blue house dress ironed and bordered with lace. The sister was basically the same.

We gathered in the living room, where there was a mahogany baby grand piano, china in a glass cabinet, a Persian rug on the floor, and expensive-looking artwork on the walls. Mort and I sat on the couch, Mrs. Kukic in an armchair facing us. Just like Mort said, the first thing she did was offer coffee. When we said yes, her sister excused herself.

Mort and Mrs. Kukic caught up on old times, dancing easily back and forth between Bosnian and English so it was difficult to follow. I did manage to glean that an elderly man close to Mrs. Kukic had been killed by a sniper recently, shot in his bedroom when a strong gust of wind parted the drapes, exposing him for a split second. The rest of the conversation seemed to concern water, candles, food, and the possibilities of American military intervention. After five minutes, I stopped trying to piece it together and looked out the window. I saw the sister on the patio, squatting over a small bonfire made of twigs and what looked like part of a chair. Motionless, she stared into an ornate metal pot she was holding over the flames, her hand wrapped in a floral dish towel. She was heating the water for our coffee.

Ten minutes later, she appeared with the drinks along with sugar in a china bowl. She handed us two tiny cups without handles from a silver tray. I watched Mort prepare his and followed his lead. It tasted like espresso. Mrs. Kukic reached over and tapped me on the knee.

"John, some cakes?"

I said no, as Mort had instructed, cleverly blaming a full stomach.

"How about you, Mort? Cakes?"

"What kind do you have?"

"War cakes. Even a little baklava."

"How about some of those war cakes, then. They sound good."

When she left the room, Mort and I sat there in silence. I was pissed and wanted to know why he fucked me out of the cakes. But he was silent until we heard the soft shuffle of Mrs. Kukic returning with the dessert tray. Then he leaned across the couch and whispered, "Pretty fucked up, huh?" I concluded then, for no particular reason, that come the next morning Mort was going to be true to his word: this prick was gonna kick me out into the street. No matter what bombs were falling.

Ten minutes later Mort told the ladies we had to leave. There were a few entreaties about staying, having dinner, and waiting for Dr. Kukic, but Mort insisted.

"I understand," said Mrs. Kukic. "Work comes first. But please, if you ever need a place to stay, you come to us first. I have a room upstairs anytime you want."

It was one of those moments when you know you shouldn't, but you have to. I really had to. I knew that. "I need a room," I told her.

She looked at Mort and smiled. Only then did she look at me.

"When?" she asked, obviously hoping I would say in a year or two.

"Tomorrow."

"For how long?"

"I don't know."

"OK. Be here in the morning."

With that, Mort and I strapped on our body armor, put on our shoes, and left. I knew I had crossed some kind of line. Way down the street, far enough from the Kukics' for some good screaming, Mort stopped and put his right hand on my left shoulder. I was ready to eat whatever abuse he was about to throw at me. But I wasn't prepared for what he said.

"You just might have what it takes to make it. I didn't think you had it in ya, so I'm gonna do you a big favor. I'm gonna show you a secret."

It was darker than anyplace I had ever been. We were taking shortcuts through the rubble of destroyed apartments and the beam of Mort's flashlight swept back and forth, giving me little flashes of lives as they had been before the artillery shells crashed through the wall: light blue wallpaper, the outline of a diamond-shaped sconce, the brass stub of a chandelier.

"Listen," Mort whispered. "Hear that?"

Standing in what I now took to be the living room of a gutted apartment, all I heard were the rat-tat-tat of machine guns in the hills.

"No," I said.

"The gunfire, stupid. Hear it?"

"Yeah?"

"What do you hear?"

"What am I supposed to hear?"

"The Rolling Stones," he said. "Listen."

Sure enough, when I concentrated, I could make out the

opening riff of the Stones' *Satisfaction* being played on an AK-47 assault rifle.

"Fucking weird."

"Yeah, they're doing a heroin deal up there," he told me. "Or exchanging prisoners. Or giving orders to someone." Almost imperceptibly, unconsciously, he rocked his head back and forth, keeping time. "You picked the right place, buddy. This really is a fucked-up war."

I still hadn't been shown the secret and moments later, we exited onto Tito Street, the prewar Fifth Avenue of Sarajevo. Mort still wouldn't tell me where we were going, but when we hit Tito I thought we had arrived. Actually, I smelled it before I saw it, an overwhelming blast of that powerful odor I snorted when I first got off the German C-130 six hours earlier.

Looking down Tito that night was like stumbling upon your first sight of the Apocalypse. The street was literally on fire and, except for Mort and myself, empty of life. It was lit up by bonfires jumping out of silvery metal Dumpsters. Each fire fed a column of black smoke, which melded together about forty feet above the street in a swirling, blackish roof. The light from the bonfires cast eerie down-up shadows on the buildings. As I was taking this all in, a pickup truck materialized out of the smoke at the far end and raced down the street. The headlights were out, but the light from the flames bounced off the tinted front window as it blew past. I saw a clean-cut blond boy standing bolt straight in the bay manning a giant machine gun. Moments later, a grainy fist of dirt and ash smacked us in the face. If the Devil had a driveway, I imagined it would look a lot like this.

"Holy fucking shit," I let out, lightly punching Mort on the shoulder. "Is it always like this?"

"Ah, Jesus Christ, man, you think this is something? They're burning garbage, that's all. Come on," he said, checking his watch. "We gotta move if we're gonna make it."

Fifteen minutes later we finally arrived: Mort's secret gift turned out to be a small stone building topped by a twenty-foot minaret. "Wait here," he told me. "I wanna make sure everything's OK first."

Mort walked across the street and lightly knocked on a green double door, but no one answered so he stepped back into the street and looked up at a window on the second floor. *Nothing.* He tapped the door again, waited, and then knocked one more time. In the distance I heard a series of loud explosions. After a few minutes he gave up. I expected his secret had to do with some kind of nightlife, an underground club or whorehouse.

"Fuckers are probably sleeping," he said. "It's amazing anything gets done around here." He put his right hand on my left shoulder, a sure sign something important was about to happen. "None of the other hacks knows about this, so keep your mouth shut. This is the morgue for Old Town. The others go to Kosovo looking for body counts. But this is the place to get the numbers. Trust me, when something goes down in Old Town and you wanna count bodies, come here. Just tell 'em I sent you."

We made it back to the church with five minutes to spare before the nightly curfew began. Mort used his flashlight to lead us to his room. It was small and without frills, like a monk's chamber with a bed against one wall and a cot set up against the other. There was a metal bowl full of water, two hand towels neatly folded, and a low wooden table. Mort lit a few candles, ate a Snickers, splashed his face with water, brushed his teeth, and then stripped down to a pair of multicolored, high-end jockey shorts.

"Stay up. Read, whatever," he said, getting into bed. "But don't forget to blow out the candles. You don't wanna be the one to burn this fucking church down."

Playing it safe, I blew out the candles right away and for hours I stretched out on my cot with my hands clasped behind my head listening to Mort snore and remembering the day that had begun in such a different place. For a while it was pretty quiet as I lay there, real keyed up, but around midnight something in the city woke. Gun battles broke out all over. Then came the shelling. At first it was far away, but then the explosions became sharper, louder, stronger. I opened the window and leaned out for a better look as the sound of war poured in.

The only thing I could see out my window was the stucco façade of the apartment house twenty feet away. But I could actually feel the explosions thumping closer, as if Godzilla himself was crashing his way through the city. I leaned farther out the window but couldn't see anything, though the tremors kept coming, stronger with each detonation. The explosions were incredible, concentrations of pure power. After a while I saw a light flash against the wall across the street, and then the detonations started moving farther and farther away.

Within minutes they were just rumbles again and I returned to my cot, sat on the edge, and eyed Mort who was still out cold.

I was glad because I had forgotten something. Reaching into my duffel bag, I pulled out a tube sock, shook out my prescribed 200 mg of Zoloft, and washed them down with a handful of water from the metal bowl. I rechecked Mort again to make sure he didn't see anything, but he was still sleeping.

Wiping the last drops of water from my mouth, it was hard for me to believe I was actually there. Seven months ago, a day like this would have been just been a fantasy, the kind of totally out-on-the-edge experience I daydreamed about to get me through the nights. And now, thanks to four little blue pills once a day, here I was, twenty-five and finally free to go out and discover those things I felt I had missed out on.

There had been a point when my biggest ambition was simply to make it to the next minute. I was that severely depressed. I wasn't sad, blue, anxious, upset, or any of those things. I would have welcomed those things. Rather, I was completely empty, devoid of emotions, living—if you could call it that—with no connection to anything other than the circular thoughts in my brain. It was life in a glass jar.

Things had come to a head late one night about two years before. I had hit bottom and was living in my childhood bedroom in my parents' attic, although it had been over a year since I had graduated from college. I had cut myself off from everyone I knew. I slept all day and spent my nights watching late night *Oprah* reruns. Life had become meaningless, pointless, an unnecessary ordeal.

I cannot say exactly how it was that I came to find myself rummaging through the crawl space that night looking for that old shotgun. But when I found it, it didn't disappoint. It felt solid, powerful, almost magical. I looked down the barrel into the steel-blue sheen. *What if?* I thought. *Just, you know, what if?* The idea that I would just cease to exist made my stomach muscles ease suddenly and my heart slow down. I didn't feel like a trapped rat anymore. Here, in my hands, was a way out. But I still had enough fight that night to put it away. Its day was in the future, though. I had entered the endgame.

That night I lay on our roof, looking up at the stars. At some point, the tears started coming, not for me because I didn't give a damn anymore, but for my family, especially my mother, who always made me promise that I would hang on, no matter what. "Trust me," she would say. "Just trust me. It will work out." But it wouldn't work out; that was impossible, and at some point I was simply going to have to break my promise.

At dawn, I finally crawled back inside my bedroom. Sometime later I realized I couldn't quit before I gave her a chance. I went downstairs and at the kitchen table I asked my mother the simplest and most difficult of favors: *Please help me.* This was the first time I had ever really reached out. I had never believed anyone could help me but myself.

The next day my mother drove me into Manhattan to see a

prominent psychiatrist. I remember thinking, *How the hell did it come to this?* I had always been a happy kid, always took for granted that I belonged. Then one day when I was twelve I awoke and, *poof,* just like that I was on the outside of life looking in. No warning. No whistle. Nothing. Just nothing. One minute I was in the world, the next I was watching it. Over time I believed that I had succeeded in making a kind of peace with my disconnection, which I couldn't get rid of. But gradually, as the years passed, it had worn me down. At twenty-three I was defeated, helpless, and on my way to a shrink, which, to me, was a kind of giving up.

In the office I went down a checklist of symptoms for clinical depression. *Prolonged and severe bouts of sadness, guilt, joylessness, hopelessness, and fatigue. Ideations of suicide. Difficulties in concentrating. Withdrawing from friends and family. Overwhelmed with feelings of isolation and worthlessness.* I had it all in spades, a check for each box. The doctor, whose name was Atchley, diagnosed me as a unipolar depressive, someone he described as having a long-term, low-grade fever of the spirit brought about by faulty brain chemistry. Traditional psychoanalysis wasn't going to help in my case.

Through the years I had put a lot of goddamn work into trying to figure out why I felt the way I did. I had believed I was miserable and lost in the world because I didn't know something about life that others did: there was some fundamental lesson or experience I had missed out on. Until I found what I had missed, or went through some transformative experience, my life was going to suck. I felt taking an antidepressant was cheating, but the doctor told me my head was full of jive. My only job was to relax, take the medicine he gave me, and wait to get better. After that first visit, I was put on Prozac.

Six weeks later, I crawled back into his office, worse, not better. But he told me I had to hang in there. New antidepressants were already in trial runs, and he was confident one would work for me. A year later, I was a grad student at the University of Virginia where I didn't attend many classes or do much else. I lived in the library of an old house and for company I had hundreds of my books, mounds of cigarette ash piled in makeshift ashtrays, and the endless cycle of my own thoughts. *What if* thoughts of suicide were never far away.

Then in late 1993 the doctor called and told me a new antidepressant called Zoloft had hit the market. I went on it the next day, and six weeks later I was walking across a bridge when suddenly, *poof,* I was back in the world. My twelve-year ordeal was over.

Over the course of the next month and a half, though, even with a bloodstream full of Zoloft, the world I had been trying so desperately to reconnect to didn't feel like the same world I had been snatched out of twelve years before. I had been missing and I was a stranger, completely out of tune with the rhythms of the everyday world around me. Even with Zoloft, there was still something missing.

To keep myself going when I had been really depressed, completely isolated both physically and emotionally, I had read books about extraordinary lives where people were able to have the kinds of experiences I could only fantasize about. My favorites had been war correspondents, people who went out alone to the edge of history and learned things out there that just weren't possible to understand back in the safe, structured world. I decided that maybe with Zoloft I could do something. I could have an adventure that would bring me back to life and return me to the world. Once I had learned whatever it was I had to learn, I would be able to kick away the crutch of Zoloft. Deep down, it still felt like cheating, like I wasn't normal.

That's how I got to Sarajevo. As I had no journalism experience or training of any kind, it had appeared impossible at first. But never underestimate the ingenuity of a man on a mission. This was my dream, and I wasn't going to let anyone's crazy little rules or worries get in my way. I essentially accredited myself, declaring John Falk the Bosnian correspondent for NBC Radio. Then I started worrying about the meds. I figured I needed a year's supply of Zoloft. Who knew how long I'd be over there? Unfortunately, my original psychiatrist had moved to Massachusetts and was semi-retired.

So I went down to a local clinic to meet with a shrink who could dose me up. But the doctor who had been recommended—dressed in expensive peasant wear and speaking in this unnaturally soft tone—told me that if I wanted the Zoloft I would have to place myself in her hands *for a long time.* "John," she said, in that voice of hers. "To truly get over depression, *yes* antidepressants are important, but just as important is understanding what you have just been through. You need time to heal, to learn life coping skills."

What she was essentially saying was that rather than diving back into life like I wanted to, I should tiptoe into the shallow end wearing water wings while holding her hand. No fucking way. I found Zoloft from a friend of a friend who happened to be a doctor.

A few weeks later it was time to go, but it was bittersweet. I was leaving my parents, who had stood by me through all my troubles, and they were very concerned about my going. We had been through it over and over. But I was leaving. I had lived in a cage and I had to break out before I fell too far behind in life to ever catch up.

As I lay on that cot the first night in Sarajevo, I assumed my life was starting over, a clean slate. I had been depressed, took some pills, and now I was better. What I didn't know then was that the shrink at the clinic had been right. It wasn't going to be so easy to leave my illness behind, even with the medication. My depression had changed me, made me who I was. I just didn't understand how far I still had to go.

two

Kind of a Secret

When I was a little kid, too young even to know where the hell I was, I remember there was one constant in my life: people. They were everywhere, and not just any old people, but people who knew me and loved me. They called me nicknames (Carrot, Roundy, Tunes), often slipped me candy, and seemed to get a special pleasure from rolling me around and roughhousing or tossing me up in the air. There were so many of them I could never get their names straight, but it didn't seem to matter. Whatever I called them, they just laughed.

I was born in 1968 in Queens, New York, the third of what would soon be four kids. My parents were childhood sweethearts, married ten years. At the time of my appearance, my brother, Quentin, was six and my sister Christine was eight. In 1969, when my little sister, Sara, was born, we moved out to the leafy Long Island suburb of Garden City, my father's hometown.

Dad commuted each day into Manhattan where he worked in advertising while my mom stayed home with the kids. Quentin, the quintessential older brother, was either joking around or torturing me. He was all seventies—flared jeans, flared hair, alienation, acne, and Aerosmith. My older sister, Christine, had a big unruly mane of red hair but none of Quentin's angst. She grooved to ABBA and Captain & Tennille, was earnest, hardworking, did well at school, and was almost like a second mom, helping to cook dinner and tucking us younger ones in. Sara was the baby, cute but always anxious, practically from birth. As for me, I was the golden child, or at least that's the way I felt for a long time. When I walked into a room it lit up because I was so full of life.

And I was good at things, at least all the important stuff: I was very fast, could throw a ball well, and knew how to flip baseball cards. But the thing I remember most about my childhood isn't baseball cards. It's the sense of home. My father always left for work in the morning and came back in the early evening with all the other dads. My mom was always there if I needed anything. There were no booze, no drugs, no infidelities, no big fights. For a little kid, I had it all: love, approval, stability.

As I got older, the feelings of home and safety only grew more intense. Those large, Irish-looking people who were always around when I was little—laughing and talking loud, and telling jokes that made my mom put her hands over my ears—were family, too. My father's family, his parents, brothers, and sisters, their wives, husbands, and kids, all lived in Garden City as well. Instead of having just one home in town, I had seven places to call my own. It was like being in a powerful tribe, like I was part of something special. But there was another tribe out there, one I would never meet, that would ultimately try to claim me for its own.

In 1976, when I was eight, my father was doing so well we moved across Garden City into a bigger house. A year later, I was racing a friend down the hill on our new street, Cedar Place. Doing a stunt, I caught my foot in the front wheel of my Schwinn and was ripped off the banana seat. I hit the pavement hard. When the dust cleared, my right ankle was swollen and bloody. I couldn't walk, so my father had to carry me home. All our neighbors came outside to see what the commotion was about. I was in physical pain, but the real hurt came from the embarrassment of being carried home by my old man in front of all my friends and their parents.

That afternoon the doctor told my parents I might have torn some ligaments. Until he was certain, I was housebound. The new kid on the block, I had carved out a place for myself through pickup football games. But as the youngest boy around, I lacked the pull to attract anyone to hang with me indoors on a summer day, playing Risk or Battleship. Until my ankle came around, I had to make do on my own.

Back then, my room was filled with the usual kid stuff from the seventies: a tabletop pinball machine, model rockets, green plastic soldiers, *Mad* magazines. I also had a small black-and-white TV balanced on an empty fish tank between the room's only two windows. At some point, I got sick of watching Betty White on *Password Plus* and throwing my brother's Bowie knife against the dresser. There was this crawl space just down the hallway from my attic bedroom, so I decided for a change of pace to hop down and scavenge around.

Most of the cardboard boxes I crawled over contained books, extra dishes, Christmas decorations, fishing gear, and my mother's winter clothes. There was a case that held my father's shotgun and two swords an uncle brought back from Vietnam. But it wasn't until I worked my way into the rear area of loose insulation and missing floorboards that I spotted a long red box bulging at the sides, held together with heavy twine. Across the top, written in black magic marker, was JOANNE, my mom's name.

After dragging the box into my room, I cut the cord with my brother's knife, and bunches of black-and-white photographs spilled out. To get a better look, I spread them around on my bed. Half the pictures were of my mother—a beaming little girl standing in the sea grass; the teenaged winner of something called the Miss Breezy Point Beauty Pageant; graduating from the Fontbonne Hall Academy for girls in Brooklyn; standing next to another young woman in a sequin Vegas-type getup.

In a lot of the other photos there were these three other people, none of whom I recognized: a beautiful, dark-haired gal standing next to an old-time roadster, or sitting in a deck chair at the beach, book in hand, squinting into the camera. There was also a man, thin and slightly bald, dressed as a cop in one photo or, in another, squatting in a garden with a cigarette in his mouth and holding a baby. The third mysterious person was a small boy, blond and serious, dressed as a cowboy in one photo, wearing a little white communion suit in another. *Who were they?* It didn't take me long to figure out that the adults were my mother's parents. From the inscription, I learned that the boy's name was Robert, but that's all that was written. I thought he might be my mother's brother but I wasn't sure. No one ever talked about him.

My mother's family had always been a sort of mystery to me. No one ever said anything, but I had the sense there was something about them that no one wanted to bring up. Actually, it was as if my mother didn't even have a family. She was all on her own. My father's family were so omnipresent and my mom just seemed part of their lives. Until I found the pictures. That day was the first time it struck me that my mom had this whole past that we really didn't talk about. But I kept this insight to myself. I knew somehow that bringing up something she had been so silent about would cause her pain.

Two of my father's brothers, Phillip and James, owned a popular pub in Garden City called Leo's Midway Bar and Grill, located at the intersection of the town's main shopping and business streets. Its simple brick façade was wedged in between a travel agency and a boutique called Things & Stuff. Inside was a lot of stained wood, brass plating, and stadium shelves filled with high-end booze. It was relatively small and the tight squeeze gave nights with even small crowds a kind of beehive buzz.

I went there a lot with my parents when my mom didn't feel

like cooking or my dad was taking me out after a Little League game. Sometimes our visits coincided with happy hour, where the commuters returning from Wall Street blew off steam. Sometimes I could overhear some bits of conversation from the bar: *"Federal Paper's a dog," "Take fifty for yourself, Danny," "Hardy, har, har, fat boy."* I remember my aunt Mary, whom I called Tante Marie, sticking it to a beer salesman: "Fine, have it your way, but I'm still gonna rip *your* tits off."

I didn't know many of those guys at the bar, but my father explained that they worked on Wall Street or were trying to get there. And to me, sitting off in the booth with my parents, sipping my Roy Rogers with extra cherries, their lives looked like fun. Those guys obviously had money, friends, laughs. There were always nice-smelling women around them, too.

My favorite part of Leo's, though, were the framed caricatures that ringed the place. They were done by a customer, a guy nicknamed Uncle Frank, who would do sketches of the other regulars when he wasn't losing money at the track: There was the Mayor, floating in a martini with a fedora on his head; the Rat, obviously wealthy and with a rodent's tail; or Bubba, another one of my father's brothers, lifting a load of weights above his head. There were others, too—the Prince of Darkness, Mongo, Hollywood, Chef Al, and Chubby. And I imagined that someday a sketch of me by Uncle Frank would be added. About six four, I'd weigh in at a trim three hundred and would be known by my current nickname, the Rooster. I would have a briefcase in one hand, a Dewar's and soda with a swizzle stick in the other, and it would all be topped off by a well-trimmed red Afro. I believe I picked this last part up from *Starsky & Hutch.*

So you see, as a kid growing up in a tight-knit town where people still knew one another, and as a member of a large family in that town, I always felt like I belonged. And it wasn't just my family, either. I had all the basic prerequisites of a no-complaints kind of childhood as I was athletic, sociable, good at school, and a bit of a wiseass, though not completely unbearable. Like most kids, I got up early and had to be forced into bed at night. Feeling part of the world was never an issue for me.

But even so there was, occasionally, a hint that not everyone had it as good as I did. There were people, I gradually noticed, who lived lonelier kinds of lives, who got swept away from the mainstream. I didn't linger on this realization, but I felt for them and I guess you could say they scared me a little. I really didn't want to be like them. But my mother seemed to collect them. It was like she had a special connection to those on the planet who never quite felt like they belonged. My mother's way with these types was part of our lives. It was a special kind of bond.

Maybe a year after I found those pictures in the attic, I was rooting around in the fridge. When I turned around this guy in town named Craty (whom people referred to—in their more polite moments—as nuts) was standing at our kitchen window, straight as a two-by-four, his dead eyes two inches from the screen. "Where is your mother?" he asked, as if he had been practicing. Startled, I didn't answer.

"Where is your mother?" he asked again, loosening up a bit.

"Don't know."

"When will she be back?"

"She moved."

He stared down into the recessed windowsill where the houseflies went to die, then—as if a switch flipped— did a sharp half turn and vanished.

Not long after, I came home from a baseball game to find a man on our couch with his head in his hands. Hearing me, he looked up, smiled, said hello. His name was James and his teeth looked like slivers of licorice. He was my mom's friend, he said, but he didn't really have to explain. I had figured as much. "I'm in trouble," he told me. "The priest around the corner wouldn't help. Then your mother came up to me while I was sitting on the front steps of the church and asked me what was wrong. I never saw her before in my life. She came to my rescue."

At that moment, Mom was off in the kitchen making him a turkey sandwich. Later, she got him a place to stay and a job and he succeeded at chucking drugs and alcohol. Eventually he moved to Buffalo and out of our lives.

And then there was our neighbor, Mr. Oliver Cooley—Cedar Place's own Boo Radley—who lived alone in an old colonial. Tall and skinny with gray hair, he had sallow, cornflake-colored skin and avoided eye contact the way cats do water. Mr. Cooley was not normal, that was clear. He wasn't fond of shaving, and he had a gardener, but no car. There was never a light on in his lonely-looking house, and he used blankets for drapes. Every now and then, he liked to drag an armchair onto his lawn and sit in it, although he never said a word to anyone as far as I knew. He had only one regular visitor, an elderly woman who came by every now and then with bags of food.

For a year or two after we moved onto Cedar Place, Mr. Cooley and my mother didn't have much contact. She was running after her kids all day. But sometime, somehow, a connection was made and Mr. Cooley gradually stopped averting his eyes when my mom looked his way. He even began raising a fingertip or two when she waved hello. Then, gradually, Cooley developed a routine that would go on for years: It started early, at about six a.m., with him picking up the *New York Times* from our stoop, and then stepping through my father's bed of pachysandra into our backyard. Lighting a cigarette, he'd recline on our chaise lounge and read, handling the pages with extreme care. When he was finished, he would neatly refold the paper and return it to our stoop. As usual, my father bore the brunt of my mother's good works. It was only when Mr. Cooley was finished with the paper that my mother would allow him to read it.

Sometimes the sight of Mr. Cooley sliding by our sunporch window in the morning fog freaked me out. "Gooey said Mr. Cooley might have killed a guy, you know," I told my father once.

"That's bullshit," my dad said. "He wouldn't harm a fly. Anyway, if I told your mother to stop she wouldn't listen to me. Trust me, this isn't new. I've been married to your mother for twenty years. Knew her since she was twelve. Leave her alone for ten minutes, some nut's spilling his guts to her. She's like a magnet that way. Most of the world is salt, but she manages to draw out the pepper. I'm telling you, kid, if she charged by the hour, I could have retired years ago."

Finally, my curiosity about Cooley overcame my fear of him. I wanted to see inside his house, how he lived, what made him tick. It wasn't for the adventure. It was that for me Cooley represented a dark undercurrent, that part of the world my mother seemed to have a connection with. So I simply picked a night midweek and walked across the street. My plan was to go straight through his front door, behind which I envisioned thick velvet curtains, spiderwebs in ceiling corners, heavy metal candelabras covered in mounds of bloodred candle wax.

My heart was pounding. My fingers were tingling and I was bouncing on the balls of my feet. The door was red and the knob glass, and after I turned it I peeked inside. No lights on, but it was still possible to see, though barely. No furniture except for a lone reading chair, newspapers stacked everywhere, and by the fireplace mounds of books next to a dirty mattress. There wasn't a sound. It was lonesome here and so quiet. Even though I was just a kid, I realized Mr. Cooley lived in some version of hell and I felt sorry for him.

I didn't make it farther than a yard or two inside the room before I heard something that made me jump and I took off, running back across the street as if Mr. Cooley was chasing me down with an ax. Bolting right through our front door, I ran up into my parents' bedroom. Only then did my heart slow down.

I told them what I had done more out of the adrenaline rush than any need to confess and my father was seriously ticked. "It doesn't matter if someone is not right in the head," he said. "It is still the man's home, for Christ's sake. You know better than that."

My mother just looked at me. She didn't say a word. But I somehow knew she would.

There was a restaurant in town called The Tivoli—in Bloomingdale's, just off the bed-and-bath department. It was always full of well-dressed women talking, usually two to a table, and every so often one of them would lean over her salad bowl and touch the other woman's arm. The room was always filled with whispers. I hated the place, but my mother used it when business needed to be done. A few days after I broke into Mr. Coolcy's, she invited me there to lunch. I was expecting a lecture on respect for other people's privacy. But that's not what happened.

As usual we took a table by the window overlooking the parking lot. We had more privacy that way. My mother had her usual Omelet Provençal. When the waitress brought our drinks, Mom stirred her Tab and looked out the window.

"Did you know I had a brother?" she asked.

"I think so," I said.

"He was your uncle Robert. He visited when you were very young so you probably don't remember him, but that's OK. Well, he was a sweet boy. I loved him very much, and several years ago they found him in California. Some priest he knew found him one morning, alone and dead on a towel on some stupid beach in Eureka."

"What happened?" I asked.

"They said he died of a heart attack. He was only thirty-four, but Robert really died because he had nobody. Your father and I tried over and over to help him, but the damage had already been done. He was a very sad young man."

"I'm sorry, Ma."

"My father died when Robert was just starting college. And my mother, well . . . Let's just say there are two distinct chapters in my family's life. Until the early fifties, when I was in high school and Robert was in grammar school, things were nice. Sunday dinners. Always lots of cousins around, much like you have now. My mother's sisters would come over, there would be card games at night, and my uncles would sit outside and listen to the Dodgers on the radio. The summers we spent every day out on Breezy Point. We shared a cabana at the Breezy Point Surf Club with my aunt Josephine."

"Weren't you Miss Breezy Point?"

"How did you know that?"

"I saw a photo," I told her.

"Well, that picture was from the first part of our lives. There are no pictures from the second. The change happened very quickly. My mother just turned against everyone, especially me and Robert. She resented me and blamed Robert. When he was a teenager Robert found it difficult to fit in. He was very self-conscious, so he was an easy target for her. He was vulnerable to someone like that. Over the years she destroyed him."

She squeezed a lemon slice in her Tab.

"When your brother Quentin was three I left him with her for an afternoon. I was headed into the city but had to turn around because I forgot something. The door to the apartment wasn't locked and when I came in I heard her. 'You miserable little monkey. You miserable little wretch. You think you're something. You're nothing.' Quentin tried to answer, 'But Grandma.' And she said, 'Don't you but me, you stinking little fool.' The voice was so foul, so full of venom and hatred. I realized I had heard it before. That's how she did it. That's how she broke Robert. And that's the reason she wasn't in our lives."

"Where's she now?" I asked.

"She died a few years ago, a few years after Robert. I didn't even know. She had made arrangements for herself at the funeral home years earlier that there was to be no wake, no formal funeral. She told the people there not to tell anyone and just bury her at their convenience. The tragedy is, she did the same to Robert. He was dead and buried for three weeks before anyone knew he was gone. She left a message that it was too much trouble to be bothered with the fuss of arranging a funeral and informing people."

"I'm sorry, Ma," I said again.

"It's OK," she told me. "It's why I try very hard with you kids to let you know you are loved. You have family all around who love you and are here to protect you. But remember, you're lucky. Things come easy to you, and sometimes people don't have people in their lives who can help. Robert never had anybody, so he was never able to find his place in the world. He was always very sad, always living on the edge of other people's lives. Eventually, he was so bad off I thought he would hurt himself. I had to have him committed to a hospital. So, when you see Mr. Cooley or the Craty boy next time, wave and say hello, even if they scare you or look away."

"I feel weird around them, Ma," I said. "Cooley probably doesn't even know I'm there."

"John, the most important thing you're going to have in your life is your character. The decisions you make are what shape you. People with character care about other people. Mr. Cooley is in there someplace and you're old enough now to know he knows that he's different. That's all I wanted to say."

three

Looking for a Story

I showed up at the Kukics' at 8:00 a.m. sharp and saw Mrs. Kukic walking toward me down the hallway. She just arched an eyebrow when I smiled.

"You made it," she said, mustering all the enthusiasm of a woman who had just found a mutt at her door, the same fleabag she had ditched outside Kmart a week earlier.

She let me in, led me up a short flight of stairs, and ushered me into a small bedroom decorated with celebrity posters and sectional furniture, the pressed wood and Formica variety found in the bedrooms of Long Island teenagers when I was growing up. In fact, except for the blown-out windows and a quarter-inch-wide floor-to-ceiling crack in the wall, it was all familiar enough to blunt the sense of danger. It was hard to envision being blown to pieces while sleeping beneath an autographed headshot of Luke Perry.

"This will be your room," Mrs. Kukic told me. "It belongs to my daughter, Aida. She is in America now, working with our embassy in Washington. Anyhow, follow me. I need to show you something important before breakfast."

Across the hall, she steeled herself and grabbed the handle on a blue door. I got the feeling she was embarrassed about whatever was on the other side of that door. She was. The door revealed a bathroom, a nice one with tiled walls and porcelain sink, but the stench was sharp and putrid.

"Sarajevo has no running water," she said, as if still she couldn't quite believe it. "Not for a year. So, if you go, you need to pour water into the toilet when you are done. We store the water in the bath." She pulled back a lime green shower curtain to reveal a pool of about six inches in the tub. "Take the pitcher, scoop up some, and pour it in the toilet. Just one though, as water is very hard to get. We must walk a kilometer to get it, and the Serbs bomb us when we do. And if you brush your teeth or shave, use just what you need, but no more. OK?"

I was trying to hold my breath, so I just nodded, as she pushed me back out into the hall and closed the door.

"Will you be working today?" she asked.

"Absolutely."

"Well, if you want, before you leave, you can have breakfast and coffee with us downstairs. About thirty minutes, and you can meet Dr. Kulsic."

"I'll be there."

My plan for the day was to hike up to the front lines and try to make contact with someone, a soldier or civilian, anyone that could lead to my first story. Once back in the bedroom, I laid out the gear I would be taking with me: green helmet; two half-inch ceramic inserts for my body armor to protect my heart from gunfire; a pen and notebook; my camera; a shortwave radio; a Serbo-Croatian phrase book; and two packs of Camel Lights. I had decided to postpone quitting cigarettes for a few days until I got my sea legs under me. Finally, as I had no idea when I'd be back, I rolled out my tube sock of Zoloft and shook out 400 mg, 200 mg for right then and 200 mg in reserve if I was gone for longer than a day. Not wanting to subject myself to the stench of the bathroom, I popped that first 200 mg in and swallowed them dry. As usual there was no discernable effect. I didn't feel energized, happy, high, or better. But I knew that without them the world would be a very different place, someplace I wasn't ready to risk going back to yet.

As I walked downstairs for breakfast, my plan was to accept just coffee but pass on the food and find myself something later. I still had Mort's injunction ringing in my ear: *"When they offer you food, don't take it. They barely have enough to feed themselves."* But when I walked in the kitchen, I was relieved because I was going to be able to feed myself with a clear conscience. On the table before me was an oblong serving plate laid out like a party platter with cuts of different cheeses and disks of pepperoni and wurst, with slices of freshly baked white bread in the middle. There was also a yellow bottle of mustard, a bowl of sugar, some butter, and three small coffee cups on saucers.

"Sit down," Mrs. Kukic said. "More coffee is coming, but, please, eat what you like."

I told Mrs. Kukic that in return for the room I would bring food back with me from Croatia like Mort had done. Politely she said I could if I wanted. As a down payment, I handed her my remaining carton and a half of Camel Lights. She thanked me and put them under the table.

With that out of the way, I made a pepperoni sandwich, smearing mustard on one piece of bread and a hunk of butter on the other. Mrs. Kukic and her sister, who had just drifted in, watched with great interest, which made me very self-conscious.

"So, who do you work for, John?" Mrs. Kukic finally asked.

"NBC Radio."

"Why do you have a camera then?" The question had obviously been hanging in her mind for a while.

"Pictures," I told her. "You never know, you know?"

"Yes. True. You never know."

When Dr. Kukic walked in, the cross-examination stopped and he introduced himself as he plucked cheese and pepperoni off the serving plate. Dressed in an ironed oxford shirt and slacks, he was wearing a little cologne.

"So what do you have planned for your first day in our Sarajevo?" he wanted to know.

"I'm looking for a story. Going up the hill to the front lines." As I spoke, Mrs. Kukic covered her mouth with her hands, but the old man smiled. "Good idea," he said. Mrs. Kukic then translated for her sister.

"Not clever, John," Mrs. Kukic said. "Satso's up there. He defends us from the Serbs, as you know, but he's a very dangerous man. He doesn't like foreigners."

"Mort told me."

The three started speaking in Bosnian. The women became upset. Dr. Kukic sounded like he was teasing them. "Come with me, John," he said, getting up from the table. "I'll show you the lines." Dr. Kukic walked out onto the patio out back as the women stood in the safety of the back doorway, warning me not to follow.

"He's crazy," Mrs. Kukic said. "All the snipers can see him, and they will see you, too."

Ignoring them, I walked out and the doctor put his arm around my shoulder. The patio was elevated, and from there you could see the high ground surrounding the city. "OK," he whispered, pointing over to a rocky ridge line to our left as I felt his breath in my ear. "Over there are the Serbs." He went on for five minutes, pointing out every trench line in sight. This guy knew everything, and when he was done I came away thinking the people of Sarajevo were in more trouble than I thought. The Serbs were everywhere.

"Well, good luck today," said Dr. K. "I will see you tonight, or in the hospital this afternoon perhaps, should things not go well up there."

All morning there had been sporadic rifle shots, but as the doctor left, the valley began to fill with the sound of gunfire. Running up to my room, I threw on all my gear, and hustled back downstairs to put on my boots outside the back door. When Mrs. Kukic saw me with my helmet on and body armor zipped up, she shook her head.

"You cannot go out like that. It is not clever to walk around Old Town like that."

"I'm going up the hill to the front line."

"Still, you are in more danger wearing that. Someone will rob you."

"Mort told me always to wear it."

"Mort doesn't know anything," she whispered, circling her finger against her temple. "Don't listen to Mort."

At that early stage, I couldn't for the life of me see how I was safer *not* wearing body armor and a helmet. Despite her warning, I then heard Mort's voice in my head. *"Don't trust these fuckers. It's Vietnam. They hate you."*

"No. For now I'm gonna wear it," I told her. "I'll play it by ear and see what happens."

I walked all day, up narrow cobblestone streets, past medieval-looking stone houses and mosques with their minarets blown off, through parks filled with scores of freshly dug graves. Every time I neared what I took to be a front line, I ran into a checkpoint. I would present my press pass, only to be turned away. All day there were sounds of shooting and explosions, just never around where I was. When I hiked over to where the action seemed to be, it inevitably seemed to move back to where I had just been. It was frustrating. I was a war reporter in the middle of a war and for the life of me I couldn't find it. What's worse, every time I tried to strike up a conversation with a local it never went anywhere. A little boy even threw a rock at me.

But the day wasn't a total loss as I saw things I never expected to see. There was this pack of dogs, mostly purebreds, poodles, spaniels, hounds, only they had become feral. They had all been people's pets once, but here they were ganged up together, filthy and vicious. As I was taking a break in the old Muslim quarter of the city, a gaggle of twenty-something girls snaked up the street toward me, some wearing knee-high leather boots, others dressed in colored tights. One chick even wore a spiked dog collar around her neck. They looked as if they were some long-lost tribe of Pat Benatar wannabes, and completely out of place. And there was this old man, a beekeeper, who waved me into his backyard and fed me bread and honey. He spoke only maybe six words of English, but I stayed with him for almost hour. By then I was human flypaper, rogue honey stuck all over my hands and face. An ancient lady, whom I took to be the beekeeper's mother, thrust a damp towel into my hand. I scrubbed myself clean and topped the snack off with two shots of coffee and a cigarette. When I was with that bee-keeper it was hard to believe I was sitting only a half mile or so below an active front line.

At about seven that night I found myself on a road high above the city. From that vantage point, I could see a good chunk of Sara-jevo. Old Town was low and lighter in color; Midtown with its Austro-Hungarian buildings and office towers was taller and darker; and the rest, something called New City, stretched westward in an endless sprawl of depressing apartment complexes, wide thorough-fares, and industrial parks. The whole valley echoed with gunfire. At some point, I picked out what I thought was the Kukics' neigh-borhood and decided to call it a day.

As I turned up the Kukics' driveway that night I heard some-one playing a piano. If I hadn't known that there was no electricity in the city, I would have assumed someone in the house was taking in a recital on the radio. I found Mrs. Kukic in the living room playing the baby grand while two Bosnian guys around my age lis-tened. The only light came from five red candles burning in crystal candlesticks and two cigarettes resting in an ashtray. Outside the window, I could see red tracers floating across a nearby ridgeline and beyond that a billion or so stars.

"John, why don't you wash up and then come down and join us for coffee," Mrs. Kukic suggested, without breaking her stride on the keys.

I went upstairs and tried to delouse. Dunking a hand towel in the standing pool in the tub, I scrubbed my vitals, changed shirts, and painted myself with German deodorant. I smelled like a crazy blend of used jockstrap and exchange student, but it was the best I could do.

The two guys in the living room turned out to be friends of Mrs. Kukic's daughter. They were dressed in tailored shirts, more Savile Row than war zone. The tall one wore Lenin specs, and they both smoked Gauloises cigarettes. It was only when Mrs. Kukic finished the piece I had walked in on that they addressed me.

"So, who do you work for?" the tall one asked, as Mrs. Kukic started up on a new piece.

"NBC Radio."

"Why the camera?" the short one wanted to know.

"Take pictures."

"Of course," the tall one said. "We're not trying to be clever. Just curious, a radioman carries a camera, wouldn't you say?"

It was odd. Although they were Bosnian, both of them spoke better English than I did and with upper-crust British accents. They addressed me with just a hint of contempt, as if they were a pair of Oxford dons chatting up a hooker.

"I'm a freelancer," I said. It seemed simultaneously owning a camera and a microphone was some kind of big faux pas in these parts and I wanted to clear my name. "I work for NBC Radio, but also I'm free to sell photos if I can."

"Oh," the tall one said. "That's brilliant." Then he turned to the short one and said, "A jack-of-all-trades."

"I hear you are from New York," the short one said. "It's funny, you don't seem to be from New York."

"I was born in Queens, but I'm from Long Island, which is outside."

"Yes," the tall one said. "Of course, Long Island. Posh. The Hamptons. Fire Island. I hear it's quite lovely."

"Not really."

"Then why do you live there?" the short one asked.

"I don't. I'm here."

"Then please excuse the inference," the tall one said. "But you must be some kind of bloody crazy." The short one loved that.

I eventually turned the questions their way. I found out the two were promising scholars in one field or another, but they got snagged in the siege of Sarajevo like everyone else. "A terrible miscalculation," as the tall one put it. They were exempted from the military because they worked as counselors in a mental ward, listening to the shell-shocked. The two were pretty open about the fact they didn't know what the hell they were doing, and only took the positions so they didn't have to fight. When not stuck at the mental ward, they were scheming together to sneak through the siege lines and make it to London.

"God," the short one said to me. "Will you look at that. It's almost pretty in a way, isn't it?" He was pointing out the window with his Gauloises at the tracer fire I had noticed earlier, only now there were green tracers as well as red arcing across the sky.

"I believe the green are ours," the tall one said.

"Doesn't much matter," the short one answered. "They're all crazy if you ask me. Bloody fools really. Not one of them could explain what they're fighting for."

It was only my first day in the city, so I didn't exactly have the standing to criticize them, but I felt they were wrong. Without those people behind the green tracers, I thought it likely the Serbs would come down off those hills and the first thing they would do is bayonet these two. It was strange, but I didn't expect to meet people like these two in a war zone. They had an intellectual arrogance and emotional distance I assumed could never survive under such hardship. I don't know where I got the idea, but I thought war wore down that type of thing. But here they were, one year into living under siege, still Leopold and Loeb, albeit without the murder.

After an hour, I excused myself, shook their hands, and waved good night to Mrs. Kukic behind the piano. As I was slipping into bed the piano playing finally stopped. For a few moments afterward, I heard some urgent whispering.

I woke up next morning around nine-thirty with sore legs and puffy white blisters on the soles of my feet. The night before I had every intention of hiking around the city again the next day looking for a story. But as I made my way downstairs for breakfast, my plans changed. I was walking on the sides of my feet, and my inner thighs burned so bad it felt as if I'd just dismounted a Brillo pad. Distance was now a factor, and the night before Leopold had told me about this gangster café off Tito Street. I decided to plant myself there for the day. At worst I would be giving my feet a rest, and at best maybe I could make some valuable contacts.

So I went to Tito Street. If it had looked like the gates to hell that first night in town, at eleven in the morning it was just grim. Even the eternal flame, a memorial to Yugoslav partisans from World War II, was snuffed out. There were people on the sidewalks, but their clothes were three sizes too big, many had heavy black circles under their eyes, and more than a few plodded along like the living dead. There were no cars, of course, and the lampposts were either twisted or shot up. Trolley cables were rusted and snapped, and the buildings that lined the street were dark and oozed the stink of urine. A chalky dust of masonry and stone pulverized by artillery coated everything, including my throat.

At the café there were round tables, large umbrellas with beer and soda sponsors' insignias, and waitresses in black miniskirts and see-through blouses. You could buy beer, Snickers bars and M&Ms, Marlboro Reds and cappuccinos. There was even music, a never-ending loop of an east European techno-disco kind of a thing. The Oz behind the whole operation was a gas-driven generator that kept the place literally humming. It was a little Eden of normal life in a city well into the later stages of rigor mortis.

It seemed that to drink in this bar you had to be a soldier, a thug, the Sarajevo equivalent of a mafia girlfriend, or someone with a few bucks in their pocket such as a foreigner like myself. The only person that didn't fit neatly into the scene was a skinny guy with bowlegs and long dark hair. His face, almost inverted, reminded me of a pie pan, and he stood at the bar reading a newspaper. Taking a seat near the entrance, I put my tape recorder and camera on the table, sat back, and waited to see what I could reel in.

An hour and three cappuccinos later, four Japanese reporters walked in. They were the first people I had seen except for myself in body armor and helmets. In their salad bowl–sized headgear, top-of-the-line flak jackets with raised neck protectors, and big boots, they looked like deep-sea divers poking around a shipwreck. I realized how alien I must have looked myself, and was suddenly thankful they dropped by. It was like being the biggest nerd in school, then showing up one day to find four new kids covered in acne and wearing tube socks over their knees sitting in the front row. They absolutely oozed fear.

All day I sat there like a wallflower. There was constant shooting up in the hills, and every now and then some detonations in the city, but from where I was I might as well have spent the day in Prague. It was completely normal, but for one little incident. At some point in the afternoon, two big dudes in fatigues with loaded AK-47s walked in and beelined straight for the Japanese. It was junior high gym class with assault rifles. The Japanese were robbed of their flak jackets and helmets, all four sets. They even handed over the stuff with a slight bow, as if relieved to have gotten it over with. I hid behind my cappuccino and the goons paid me no mind.

Then, just as I was getting up to leave, Pan Face, who was the only other person to stay in the café all day, folded his paper and walked straight over to my table and asked if I was a reporter. When I said yes, he told me that he had a story for me. If I wanted to, he said, he could arrange an interview with Satso. I asked him if that was a safe thing to do, and he said yes, that they were friends. He quickly sketched out a map on a napkin. I was to meet at seven-thirty the next night in a park near where I had met the beekeeper. From there he would lead me the rest of the way. He told me to bring plenty of cassettes for my recorder and film for my camera. I was also to tell whomever I was staying with that I wouldn't be back for a day, maybe more.

"And bring at least one hundred fifty deutsche mark," Pan Face told me. "We're going to need to pay our way through some of those checkpoints."

I agreed, but inside I wasn't so sure. It was all too easy and Pan Face was a shady-looking guy. His unsolicited interest in me was suspect. And Mort's warning to keep my distance from the locals was still very much in my head. But I had to get started somehow. I felt like I should investigate what could be a lead. It wasn't like I was doing anything else.

Late the next afternoon, after a short but intense artillery barrage in the Kukics' neighborhood, I left my room and hiked my way up to the park. I was early, so I lay down on the grass and smoked a butt. It was quiet there, though the occasional bird fluttering about broke the silence. I almost fell asleep. By eight o'clock, Pan Face still hadn't showed. I was starting to get pissed, and flicked on my shortwave radio to cool down. It received the BBC World Service perfectly.

"Bong. Bong. Bong. Bong. Bong. Bong. Bong. This is London. It's nineteen hundred hours Greenwich Mean Time. The news, read by Cabot Owen Jones. In Sri Lanka today . . ." Even if the news was about Madonna screwing her new yoga instructor, the style of the BBC News Service had this Graham Greene feel to it; it was like you were listening to a wartime broadcast during the Battle of Britain. I loved the vibe of the broadcast so much that it took me a moment to realize I was listening to news about Sarajevo, more specifically a Serb mortar attack on Old Town. There was some controversy about how many were killed, but it sounded gruesome. The key fact was that it had happened about six that afternoon, local Bosnian time, right around when I heard that barrage.

That's when I remembered Mort and his morgue down the street from the Kukics'. Suddenly, I was tossing the radio into my backpack before I even knew what I was doing. Fuck Pan Face and Satso. The war had nearly fallen on my head and I almost missed it. From the morgue, I would work the story.

Because I was actually getting to know the neighborhood, I found my way back to the morgue with no problem. Before I knocked on the double green door, I took out a pen and notepad and checked my camera for film. When everything was set, I knocked. After a couple of seconds, I heard someone calling. I couldn't make out what he was saying. Moments later, I heard him again. Assuming he was saying "Come in" in Bosnian, I opened the door.

Inside, it was very cool, dimly lit, and smelled like my high-school chemistry class. The floors were polished stone, the walls covered in patterns of white and green tile. About ten feet in front of me, at the top of a small flight of stairs, stood a man in a clean white gown with a salty brown beard. He looked exhausted, like everyone did in Sarajevo. But more so. So much more so. He was clutching a thick book with silver inlay on the cover. When I pointed to my UN press pass, he asked me something in Bosnian.

"Mort," I said. "Mort. Mort send me."

He waved me in and I followed. As we were headed to a flight of wooden stairs, he pointed out something in a room to his left. I glanced at it. There was a beautiful sky blue sheet, fine and without a wrinkle, like silk or satin. It was nailed to the top of what appeared to be a large orange crate, the kind I used to use to build go-carts as a kid. There were no sides to it, however, and I could peer inside because one corner of the sheet had yet to be nailed down. There was a leg, the bottom half of an older woman's leg. The foot was angled out but not severely; it was as if she was sleeping on her back. The leg was clean-shaven with no nicks or cuts. There were several large calluses on the sole and side of the foot, but the toenails were short and round as if a few days removed from a pedicure. The calf was thick, sturdy, but it really tapered around the ankle. It was a delicate ankle. I imagined she had been a catch back in her day.

The bearded man had already gone down the steps and come halfway back up. He said something and pointed down the stairs. I shook my head no and started to back up. He came up the stairs and spoke some more, words I couldn't understand. I just kept backing up until I got to the door.

"Thank you," I said. "Thank you. But I gotta go do something. I forgot something, but thank you." Looking totally confused, he uttered something, but I was already halfway out the door.

When I got outside I fumbled for a cigarette, something to take the edge off. It wasn't the prospect of looking at death, smelling something awful, or staring at dead eyes that got to me. I just couldn't go down there and count bodies. Take pictures. Take notes. Ask questions I had no right to ask. It was only part of the job, everyone did it, but still it felt wrong somehow. It felt too fucked up, or too fucked up for me to do it, anyway. I felt like a ghoul. I was very confused, and all I knew for sure was that I just had to get out of there and regroup.

four

Through the Looking Glass

I have no recollection of how I spent the Tuesday before that day in 1981. It was winter, so assume I went to junior high, hit wrestling practice, took a shower after I got home, and watched TV after I got into bed. Maybe I played a little stickball or shot my BB gun at my neighbor's roof with Tony Piccolo. I know what I didn't do. I didn't do my homework. I always did that in homeroom, and my grades were high enough that no one asked questions.

I probably did a million other things that Tuesday, but they were just little everyday matters that didn't require much thought. I most likely snapped my jacket shut when the winter air hit me, joked with Matt Bodden about his compulsion to wear tie-dye, tried to do as many push-ups as I could in gym. Maybe I picked up my pace a little as I walked home that night if I smelled wood smoke in the air and realized that it was making its way skyward from the chimney of our fireplace at home.

The first memory I have of that Wednesday was hearing my mom opening the window in the hall downstairs. She did it every winter morning, and as usual a minute or two later I felt a chill as the cold air rolled down the hallway leading into my room and worked its way up under my covers. It was her version of an alarm clock and it meant it was 6:15. I still had a few minutes before I absolutely had to get ready, so as I always did I put the covers over my head and prayed, *Please forget about me up here. Just let me sleep.*

But I couldn't go back under. I don't know how long I lay there—five, maybe ten minutes—but when I finally gave in to the morning and opened my eyes, I locked right in on my fingernails. They were *dirty, ugly dirty.* I focused in harder. I couldn't help it. It was *important.* I closed in like a telephoto lens on the specks of dirt lodged underneath the nails and wondered, *How could I have missed them during my shower last night? What was wrong with me that I didn't see that much dirt?*

I focused in close, down to the very granular texture of the dirt itself, and saw how my own body grease conspired with the dirt, enabling it to stay lodged in place between my nails and skin. I felt filthy now, complicit even, inside and out. I stopped exploring my fingernails only after I caught wind of my breath. It stank like my nails looked, the stench obviously coming from deep inside me. "Snap out of it," I told myself. "Just wake up." Kicking my blankets off, I flung my legs over the side of the bed, but touched down in a very different place than I had hoped.

The Pele poster over my bed was ripped. I had worked hard to get that poster. It had taken some effort to talk my dad into driving me to Hermann's Sporting Goods to pick it up. Now I saw a small tear in the bottom right corner that almost cut through the famous athlete's signature. That rip made me lose all faith in myself. It was a condemnation of me. The poster was clearly a piece of shit, not only worthless but stupid, which made me an idiot for having hung it over my bed. Someplace inside my head a part of me was trying to hold out, arguing the contrary, *It's just a dumb poster. John, it means nothing.* But I couldn't hold those calming thoughts in my brain; each time I let go, even for a millisecond, they were getting twisted up and turned against me. *That's right. It is dumb. It means nothing. And that's the whole point, shit for brains.* I closed my eyes, hard like I was cracking walnuts in my sockets, but I couldn't will myself back to the way I had been just last night. I suddenly felt alone, like I was stranded on an iceberg all on my own, and whatever I looked at only made it worse.

I recognized everything in my room, but at the same time it was foreign to me. The Daisy air rifle. Pong. Baseball mitt. My fish. Even Underdog, my friendly cockatoo, was now just another bird. I knew he was mine. Intellectually I knew I *owned* him and that we had a history, but I no longer *felt* connected to him. Or any of the other crap in my room, living or otherwise. It was all somehow outside me. The intimate familiarity I had with everything the night before, the warm-blooded sense of belonging here, was gone. Feelings so ordinary that I never realized they could change were missing. I had become a stranger in my own room, like I had been banished into some nether land outside and was now looking back in on my life through a very thick window.

As I was going through my Twilight Zone of a morning upstairs, the rest of the house was waking up as usual: I heard the news-radio jingle *"Give us twenty-two minutes and we'll give you the world"* as my father shaved in the bathroom. I heard Sara stomping down the hall, demanding something. Doors opened and closed. The dog barked, and the smell of coffee curled up the stairs.

It must have been about six-forty-five a.m. before my mom called up to my room, telling me that it was time to get going. But I couldn't answer. I knew every second counted, and I was trying so hard, hoping so much to snap back before anyone saw me. But I couldn't. I was under my covers, desperately trying to outthink myself and come up with some magic insight that would get things back to normal. My main weapon was the obvious, that nothing had changed in my life between last night and this morning. The thoughts in my head were just thoughts. They weren't real. Nothing was really wrong. Underdog hadn't changed and neither had I. Fuck Pele. I hated soccer anyway.

Come on, motherfucker, I thought. *Snap out of it! Stop thinking! Fuck, just stop thinking and it will all be all right!*

It only got worse when my mother walked in to jostle me awake. She felt far away, too. Not like usual. She was just feet away, but I was still alone. The tears started pouring out because for the first time that morning I realized how *real* this all was, how much trouble I might really be in, how something I couldn't even touch, let alone describe, was taking over my mind.

My mother heard me under the pillow, but I heard no footsteps, not a peep. I was praying she would go away, but she didn't. Instead, she pulled the pillow carefully from my face, so tentatively I felt guilty. I didn't fight it.

I remember her looking at me and saying one word, "Oh." Not, *What's the matter?* Not, *My God, what happened?* Nothing like that. Just, "Oh."

She sat on the edge of my bed, but didn't say anything until my dad let out a huge "Jooooaaaannnnnne!" He needed his ride, but she didn't budge. Only after she heard my father coming did she get up, intercepting him in the hallway. After a hushed conversation, she came back in.

Only after ten minutes did she get around to asking me what was wrong. At that point I wanted to try to tell her, but I couldn't. I just didn't know what to say. All I managed to do was repeat, "Leave me alone," over and over again. I begged her to just go. I begged her to just let me be. She didn't press it and told me to go back to sleep. Going to school was never mentioned. Even though I had been awake for only an hour, I was completely exhausted.

• • •

I woke up about two hours later and saw a six-pack of Hawaiian Punch on my nightstand. It was my favorite drink, and my mom had obviously put it there. Hours earlier, I would have gladly drunk myself into a sugar coma. Now I didn't make a move for the cans. I just examined them in that way I had done to my fingernails: the colorful cans with the pineapple guy on them struck me as phony, no longer a sign of a treat. I envisioned some fat sweaty bastard in a wife beater tee pouring sugar water into little metal cans in some dirty factory somewhere. I pulled the covers back over my head and hid from the world.

"Do you want to talk?" my mother asked me, nudging me awake maybe an hour later.

"No."

"What's the matter?" she asked.

"I don't know," I answered. "Just please leave me alone."

"Did anything happen?"

"I told you, no."

"Well, what is it then?"

I tried to actually answer her for the first time, but I just couldn't find the right words and that frustrated me because it seemed that if I could articulate what was happening that somehow it would go away.

"Something is gone, Ma," I said. "Something's just gone, but I don't know."

She left, but returned five minutes later.

"I canceled everything," she said. "I'm going to stay with you all day."

"All right," I said.

"Do you want to come downstairs?" she asked.

"No."

"All right, I'll be downstairs and you can call me if you want anything," she said. "But I'll be back up anyway."

I didn't say anything else, but I was relieved she had said what she did. I felt so alone, walled off inside my own head. Knowing she was sticking around nearby gave me a little hope.

At noon, I couldn't sleep anymore. I tried, but I couldn't. I wanted to because it was the only off switch I knew, but now that I was fully awake things only got worse. Not only did I feel like the last man on earth, but I was also consumed with a never-ending chain of questions.

Why get out of bed at all?
What's the point?
Why go to school?
Why do anything?
Why live?

I didn't just ask these questions. I felt compelled to try and answer them as well. A few years earlier my dad and my brother Quentin and I went to see the Monty Python movie, *In Search of the Holy Grail.* I had loved it, but on that morning I saw it in a different way. Curled up under my blankets, I kept remembering that scene where the knights of the Round Table approach a rope bridge crossing the Pit of Doom. At the foot of the bridge stands a gatekeeper, a ghoulish troll who tells the knights that to cross they must answer a series of questions. Should they fail even one, they are immediately cast over a cliff into the Pit of Doom. If they answer them all correctly, however, they are free to go.

It felt as if that troll was now smack in the middle of my head, guarding my way back to how I had been. To end the nightmare, I felt obliged to try to find the right answers.

Why have tropical fish?
Because they are more interesting than goldfish.
Why more interesting?
They're more colorful.
Why is colorful more interesting?

It is. More to see.

Why is it more to see?

Because . . .

Because why?

Why? Why? Why? That had become the impenetrable wall at the end of the chain. *Why?* really meant *What's the point to all this? To life?* Before that morning I was too busy living to think too hard about anything. Now every fiber in my being demanded to know the answer, in irrefutable form, and now!

I must have looked to her like that statue, *The Thinker.* I was so busy arguing with myself in my own head that I never heard my mom come in the room. When she saw that I was up, without a pillow over my head, she probably hoped it was some kind of sign of progress, the fever breaking.

"Do you feel any better?" she asked, without even a little hope in her voice.

"Worse," I answered, reaching out a little.

"How?"

"I don't know," I said.

"Is it school?" she asked.

"No."

"Is it your friends? Are you afraid of something?"

"No," I said. "Just *please* leave me alone."

"Are you sure there's nothing I can do for you?"

"Yes," I told her. "Please, just leave me alone."

She left.

At about five-thirty, an hour before usual, my father came home. I heard him and my mom talking downstairs, and then they both headed up to see me.

"Had a rough day, kid?" he asked, sitting next to me on the bed. I was turned toward the wall. He had his hand on my head.

"Well, I can't help if you don't talk to me," he said. "Why don't you come down and we'll go to Umberto's for dinner."

"No," I said. "I just don't feel like anything."

"Well, roll over and let me see you then," he said. He tugged at me, so I did. My face was very puffy and red.

"Oh, kid," he told me. "It will be OK."

I broke down again. I clenched every muscle to hold it in, but the tears came anyway.

"Trust me," he said. "It will be OK. Try and give me a hug."

I did and it felt good, but I still wanted him to leave. Being alone was somehow just better than being around people, even my parents, and I begged them to go. After a while, they did.

That night passed like I was slogging through quicksand. I couldn't sleep at all and spent a good part of it holding my head, as if the right application of pressure would make it all stop. The deeper into the night, the worse it became. The loneliness became unbearable. For the first time in my life I thought of dying as a nice thing, a way out, a proposition that brought more relief than terror. When the sun finally came up the next morning it was as if a cop had kicked in the door just as I was being strangled to death. I really didn't know how much more I could take.

I missed school the rest of the week. My mother told anyone who asked that I had the flu, and she kept her vigil over me. She kept trying to make it better, bringing up food and reminding me again and again that she was just a floor away, if I needed to talk. I sometimes tried to tell her what was happening, but the best I could do was keep repeating what I felt, that something was just *gone.* I didn't know what else to say, and not knowing how to say it only made me more alienated.

By Saturday, when I still hadn't snapped out of it, things started to become more urgent. My mother's trips to my room became more frequent and soon this was no longer going to be our little secret.

The first person my mom roped into talking to me was my uncle Phillip. The year before I had picked weekend shifts on the cleanup crew at Leo's and was supposed to work there that weekend, but she obviously told him more than I would have liked.

"Hey, Rooster," Phillip said over the phone. "Your mother told me that you're not feeling so hot."

"Nah," I said. "My stomach hurts."

He didn't even pretend to play along. "You know," he said. "It's not easy."

"What's not?" I asked.

"Sorry you had to find out now," he said. "But life sucks."

"Really?" I asked, sincerely. For a moment I was actually relieved because it was something simple and straightforward enough that I could work with. *What's the point of life? I'll tell you what the point is. It sucks. Now get off my fucking back.*

"But just know it, then just get the fuck on with it," he said, letting it sink in for a second. "Trust me, just get up, get out, and don't even think about it."

I promised Phillip I would, but moments after he hung up the beautiful, brutal logic of what he had said was torn down in my head. It wasn't a good enough answer when I was alone. I was paralyzed again.

A few hours later, Mrs. Murphy, one of my mom's good friends, stopped by. Tall, blond, she carried herself like a lady but had, according to my mother, seen her share of troubles over the years. My mom liked to describe her as a "survivor."

"The secret is," Mrs. Murphy told me, "what I do, is I prepare for tomorrow today. Everything I need to get through tomorrow I complete by the time I go to bed the day before. The laundry. The bills. Try laying out your clothes for school before you go to bed. Get your homework done early. Trust me, it works."

After Mrs. Murphy, I listened to my grandmother, who told me to relax, that life works out, and that dark moods happen to everybody. After that, I ran into my aunt Dot on the first floor. Dot was nearly ninety at the time, and grew up as the oldest of thirteen kids next to a slaughterhouse in an Irish ghetto. She was still working full-time for a plumbing supply company, where a few years earlier she had foiled a robbery by untying herself from a radiator and sneaking a call to the cops.

"You wanna know what your problem is?" she asked, looking around to make sure we were alone. "Your problem is, you're a big sissy. You don't know how good you got it. When I was your age I didn't have enough to eat, and I had to work to support myself."

I knew Dot was right. I was a big sissy. I knew there was nothing wrong. I knew I had it good. But then again, that was the goddamn problem. How the hell was I gonna shake this thing if there was no reason for it to exist in the first place?

The answer was to just do it. I decided that the following Monday, no matter what, no matter how hard I had to try, no matter how alone I felt, no matter how many pesky questions remained unanswered, I would show up for school. If I didn't, I was scared that I would soon lose control, that I would be forced to get help, be marked for life as some kind of retard. But really, what I feared most was that I *was* some kind of retard and that somewhere out there was a rubber room with my name on it. I'd be tough, prepare for tomorrow today, all the while knowing the whole thing was supposed to suck anyway and only a big sissy would bitch about it.

That Sunday I performed what seemed to me to be nothing

less than the Twelve Labors of Hercules. I selected and hung up my shirt for Monday, laid out my socks and underwear, even using my thumb to rub the dirt off the white stripes on my Adidas sneakers. I misted Underdog with distilled water and cleaned out his cage. I drained my fish tank, scrubbed the undersea castle and diver statues, and changed the charcoal in the water filter. I dusted off the shelves in my room and then the books and trophies that went in them. I reordered my closets, made my bed so you could literally bounce a quarter off it, and even repaired the tiny tear on the Pele poster with Scotch tape. I topped it off with an hour of vacuuming.

By ten that night I had been at work for over nine hours and was dead tired. I got into bed, expecting to fall asleep in minutes. Instead, I was awake for hours. Another night without sleep. But at least this one passed a little easier, the burning alienation tempered somewhat with hope, that maybe, just maybe, I had willed myself back. I felt like a prisoner awaiting a verdict: Was I condemned, or did my good works save me?

The next morning it was clear nothing had changed. Almost immediately, I locked in on the ugliness of the dry scales on Underdog's claws. The plastic sea grass in the aquarium seemed cheap and dirty. The rusty hinges on my desk spoke of decay and aging and the futility of trying to fight it. My mind was behaving just as it had for the past week, maybe more so because of the letdown. Everything I looked at still had that sense of *otherness* to it. Nothing was right. Then came the questions.

Why bother getting up?

What's the point?

What's the fucking point of any of this?

I was more lonely, uncertain, and isolated than ever, but if I stumbled now it would be a sign to the rest of the world that I had a real problem. I literally fought myself for twenty minutes before I got that first foot on the carpet. It was crazy but it was as if my brain needed a definitive answer to *Why get up?* in order to give my leg the order to move. Only by reminding myself that this was it, that I had to make it work now or else I was going to lose control, was I able to get started.

Gritting my teeth, I got dressed. I was like a boxer just before the bell: all nerves, knees clapping. My job was to simply appear normal, which meant putting one foot in front of the other with a smile on my face. I even clapped my hands before leaving my room to pump myself up.

When my parents saw me walk into the kitchen they were stunned. I was up and ready, and Mr. Cooley wasn't even done with the morning papers.

"How ya feelin'?" my dad asked.

"Great," I shot back. "Really, I feel great."

I amazed myself with my acting ability, but my mom was another matter.

"Feel great?" she asked.

"Yeah," I said. "I don't know what it was. Maybe it was school or something, but I feel as good as new. Really."

"Well, if you feel bad at school today, I mean even a little bit, just call and I'll come get you."

I had no intention of calling her, but I told her I would if I needed to. I left the house early because I wanted to get to school before anyone else. My heart was racing, and I knew I needed time to get comfortable before I had to see anyone.

It took me about twice as long to walk to school as usual, primarily because each step was accompanied by a burning dread that I was making the worst mistake of my life. It takes a lot of emotional energy to keep putting one foot in front of the other when you think you're about to walk off a cliff.

By the time I arrived I had only about ten minutes alone to wander the halls. The light green tiled walls, the metal lockers, the huge brown windows with the brass locks, and the sparklingly smooth maroon-and-gray-tiled floors, stuff that I always passed by without a second thought, now sucked the life out of the air. It was so antiseptic and cold. *Could these be the same hallways where I flirted with girls, bet on football games, and joked around between classes?* Suddenly, I broke into a smile. In a way it was a brief concession to the power of this thing I was fighting. The gulf between how I saw this stuff the last time I was here and how I saw it now was so huge, so alien, that it brought home how fucking weird it all was. I couldn't help but laugh a little. Then the kids came.

Matt Bodden was always a few years ahead as far as I was concerned, although some thought him a decade behind. He grooved at Dead shows, smoked grass, and bar-hopped with high-school kids. He was also a good athlete and student, but still his retro hippy thing rubbed some people the wrong way. I liked his energy and was always proud that he was my buddy, so when I heard him come in that morning I went right for him. Here, I thought, was a safe harbor in which to shake down.

As Matt opened his mouth I knew I was in deep shit. Usually I joked with Matt easily, running on autopilot, trying to get under his skin or listening to him rant against some perceived slight. But that morning, as he rambled on about whatever, I felt like I was watching a movie of the two of us bullshitting; the real me was up in the balcony, alone, studying, critiquing my performance. I was hyperconscious of every word, every movement I made, like I was now a mere witness to my own miserable performance here in the world of the living. What had been involuntary and natural the week before was now an act of will, like getting out of bed, and every word and gesture required a tortuous vetting before it was allowed to proceed out of my brain.

OK, John, I would think. *He's about to finish his sentence. Jump in with something funny.*

Maybe I should have seen it coming, but I just wasn't ready to find that even joking around with my friends had become a form of torture. I was close to losing it. I patted Matt on the shoulder mid-sentence and told him I had to run. And that's just what I did, heading straight for the boy's locker room in the basement. I paced the floor down there, taking deep deliberate breaths, until the homeroom bell rang. I was just trying to get from one second to the next. I had to, but it wasn't easy.

The day only got worse. With all the people I talked to—friends, teachers, coaches—I had to think about every word that came out of my mouth. Ease and spontaneity were things of the past. Nothing happened without deliberate effort. And it was humiliating to watch myself blunder through each exchange. I was so consumed with myself and how I appeared that I rarely had any idea what the person before me was saying.

Actors sometimes speak of forgetting lines onstage and breaking the bond between themselves and the audience. I learned that to pull my performance off, to convince everyone that nothing had changed, I not only had to remember the lines but I also had to stay two steps ahead of the conversation, writing the script even with my best friends. It was grueling, exhausting work, so much so that by the time I made it home that afternoon I went right to sleep. And not just because it had become my drug of choice. I was genuinely that tired. I didn't wake up until the next morning, when I felt the cold air come down the hallway and forced myself out of bed, only to do it all again with that fucking smile on my face.

The amazing thing was I pulled it off. No one figured out what was going on. To everyone at school, I was the same guy I was before. No one picked up on the fact I was now acting the part of me. But by Thursday of that first week back, I had had it. I couldn't handle one more exchange where I was simultaneously trying to keep a conversation going and look like I cared. I had to stay home and refuel in the isolation of my room. I faked a stomachache, going so far as to pretend I was barfing in the bathroom.

My mother didn't buy any of it. This was the crack in the

façade she had been waiting for, and she got right to the point when she found me still in bed, holding my stomach like I had been gut shot.

"Listen to me," she said. "I can help you."

"I don't need it," I said, realizing in an instant what we were really talking about.

"I think I know how you must feel," she continued.

"Trust me, Ma. It's not that easy. I just need a little time."

"Why won't you let me help you?"

"Because I don't *fucking* need help," I yelled. Then I pleaded. "Please, just leave me alone. Why can't you do that? It will be all right, I swear."

I never used curse words around my mother, but she didn't even seem to have noticed.

"Tell me if you can't understand what I'm about to say. Do you feel like before you were in some kind of parade, and now you're there on the sidelines watching it go by?"

I didn't say anything, but I knew exactly what the hell she was talking about, the sense of watching my life go by from the sidelines, of being an outsider, unable to join in.

"John, I'm asking you to listen to me," she said, her voice now cracking. "John, if you won't let me help you there is nothing I can do."

"I don't need help, Ma. Please, I just need to be alone for a little while."

"There are doctors who can help, you know," she told me. "It's no big deal. A lot of people go. It's just like getting your knee checked or getting your teeth cleaned."

There was no way.

"John, dear. Please, you have to really talk to me. I won't leave until you do."

"I feel fine. Just tired."

"That's no reason not to go to school. I know it's something more. Please, talk to me."

She wasn't going to leave until I did. I had to make a good show of it to get her off my back.

"Ma, I'm OK," I insisted. "I would tell you if I wasn't."

Avoiding eye contact until then, I really took her in now for the first time: her mouth was turned down, her hands clasped in her lap. She looked smaller, hurt.

"Trust me," I said, sitting up to put a good show on. "It's school. Homework. I just need a little break. Today's it, though, I swear."

"I don't believe you," she said.

I put out a smile because I wanted her to feel better, but more than anything I wanted to be alone. It felt best when I was alone.

"I'll be fine, Ma," I told her. "Don't worry. I know what I'm doing. Please, you gotta trust me."

five

The New City Nonoviches

For a nearly week after my visit to the morgue I just didn't make any headway. Most mornings I would head outside in my body armor and helmet and stroll around the neighborhood looking for people to talk to, make contact with. But I never got anywhere. By 1:00 p.m. I'd give up and return to my room in the Kukics' where I'd take a nap, have a smoke, look out the window, and listen to gunfire. Mostly, though, I read, trying to relight that fire I had felt when I first arrived in the city.

One Flew Over the Cuckoo's Nest had been one of my bibles when I had been depressed. Back then I was living in a cuckoo's nest of my own, estranged from life, and miserable about not being able to figure out what was wrong with me. Sometimes I thought the problem was the safe, predictable, suburban world around me. It was boring, just dead—everything like the inmates rebelled against in the book. I felt that if I could just break out and live a less conventional, more authentic life, I'd be happy. It had seemed pretty straightforward at the time. But now here I was in Sarajevo, free and doing my own thing, living in a city that was anything but safe and predictable, my brain even recalibrated on 200 mg of Zoloft each day. And instead of feeling liberated and more myself, I was rudderless and miraculously bored. Tossing Ken Kesey's book aside, I remembered thinking, *What the fuck does a person have to do to feel alive in this world?*

Things started to change one Monday morning when Mrs. Kukic paid a visit to my room. After planting a cup of Turkish coffee next to me on the bed, she took a seat.

"Do you know who Peter Jennings is?" she asked. Just mentioning the man's name made her smile.

"Yeah. Of course."

"He did a story on us, you know? It was really bad here the first winter and many people were dying."

"Really?"

"Yes. Peter Jennings was great. He cared and really understood what was happening here. He stayed with us, you know."

"Really?"

"Yes. In *this* room."

"Wow," I told her. "That's big. He's really popular in America."

Something like a five-second pause followed, along with a look that suggested a kind of dazed amazement.

"You're not like Peter Jennings," she said.

"Oh, well, you know, that's . . ."

"In fact, you're not like any reporter I've ever met."

"That's because I'm a radio guy," I told her, covering myself as fast as possible. "Takes me longer to work my pieces."

"I mean, don't take this the wrong way, please," she continued. "But you don't even go to the press conference. Everyone goes to the press conference."

"What press conference?"

"Every morning? *The UN press conference?* Every reporter in the city goes, but you don't."

"I didn't know," I told her, eager to find out more. "Where is it? When?"

"Nine in the morning?" she said. "The PTT building? Your company never told you?"

"Well, they're a funny outfit that way. Kind of a sink-or-swim thing with them."

She pushed herself up and walked to the door. "Sink and swim?" she muttered to herself as she made her way down the hall.

Hearing about this press conference did the trick. Suddenly I was in action again. The next morning, I got to the PTT building at a quarter to nine, fifteen minutes to spare, thanks to two Austrian news guys who picked me up in their armored car as I was hitchhiking.

When I walked into the press conference room, I saw about thirty reporters, including Christiane Amanpour, Scott Simon, ABC News, the BBC, the Associated Press, and the tall guy from the *New York Times* I had seen on *Charlie Rose*. Many were smoking and nursing espressos in little plastic cups, the kind you use to rinse your mouth out at the dentist. I put my microphone on the speaker's dais as if I knew what I was doing, then took a seat in the back row and flipped open my reporter's notebook.

The press conference got off on time, led by a Belgian press officer, who read off a list of statistics: food aid delivered; number of shells that landed in Sarajevo the previous day; number of people killed; activities of UN monitors in so-and-so theater of operations. Then he opened the floor to questions. He might just as well have saved himself the trouble and simply slammed his face into the table. The reporters sank their fangs in right away, haranguing him about why the United Nations no longer referred to the siege of Sarajevo as a siege but instead insisted on calling it a military encirclement. Everyone in that room, including me, knew why the UN switched nomenclature—a siege required the UN to do something; a military encirclement didn't. They also knew the spokesman couldn't say that, but they tried to make him confess anyway. It was all going nowhere, but it made good theater. As this was going on, Pan Face slipped in through the door, like an eel.

The siege line of questioning ended abruptly when a Bosnian woman reporter working for *Oslobodjenje,* the only operating newspaper in the city, demanded to know why the French at the airport were aiding the Serb snipers. She claimed they were turning searchlights on people as they ran across the airport tarmac at night in search of food. It sounded like the French were pouring blood over swimmers in shark-infested waters, but the spokesman had little to say, aside from advising her to speak with the French garrison. She was pissed and demanded an answer, but the spokesman wouldn't budge.

After the press conference ended, most of the reporters got up and started making their way to the door. They were talking among themselves, comparing notes and making plans for later, while I stayed in my seat and watched. They all had someplace they were rushing off to, but I had nowhere to go. And I didn't know anyone. Or almost no one.

Pan Face slid into the seat next to me.

"Hey, I've been looking for you," he said.

"Yeah," I said, still wary of him.

"I want to apologize for the other day. Just crazy time. But I wanted to tell you I have a bigger story for you than Satso. Only if you be interested, of course, but I can bring you to Igman, no problem."

There was intense battle going on at the time for Mount Igman, which loomed over the western outskirts of the city. The Serbs had been attacking it all summer, and there were rumors they were using helicopter gunships and mustard gas up there. Obviously the battle for Igman was a big story, but one off-limits to foreign journalists. It would be a huge scoop if I could get up there.

"Fuck, yeah, I'm interested," I told Pan Face. "What do I gotta do?"

"Nothing. I will arrange, no problem. You just got to be here and ready. Two days, OK?"

We shook hands and he left. As I sat sucking on my cigarette, full of this feeling I was finally getting someplace, this human Pez dispenser came up to me. His name, it turned out, was Harald and he was about to change everything.

"Weren't you the Yank at Maslenica Bridge?" he asked. "Using your boot as an ashtray?"

"Probably."

"Was that guy you were talking with before a *friend* of yours?" he asked, referring to Pan Face.

"No. Just a contact. I'm trying to cover Igman and he . . ."

"With him?"

"Hopefully."

"He's a fucking scumbag, man!" Harald shouted. "A complete and total *fucking fascist,* man!"

"You sure?"

"A *fucking fascist,* man!"

Harald had the build of a fourteen-year-old boy, the head/neck configuration of a giraffe, and the nervous energy of Tom Arnold coming off fourteen espressos. But he was the real deal—a breed of nut grown only in certain parts of Europe, a fire-and-brimstone radical, a Marxist-Leninist-Socialist-Progressive-Anarchist-Anti-imperialist-Anti-colonial-Anti-corporate-Anti-anything-not-run-for-and-by-the-*People.* He carried a picture of Che Guevara in his wallet and cried when he heard that the people of Nicaragua voted out the Communists. He threw stones at the U.S. embassy as a kid in his native Holland, and covered lesbian high-jumpers for his Marxist newspaper in college. But when Communism fell in the early nineties, he was out of a cause at the ripe old age of twenty-three.

In the spring of 1992, to find a new one, he rented a Volkswagen from a Hertz office in Germany and drove it straight into

Sarajevo during the first days of the war. The car was blown to bits minutes after he parked it, and he had been working in the city ever since as a freelance reporter. By the time I met him, about a year later, Harald was de facto King of the Freelancers. That day he took me under his wing.

After warning me off Pan Face, Harald escorted me over to the TV building, a concrete-and-steel behemoth meant to withstand everything up to and including a nuclear blast. Once we got there, he took me upstairs to this room he called the SAT Room, the only phone links to the outside world in the city. In there he began to teach me the ins and outs of making it as a freelance reporter in Sarajevo. Essentially, it amounted to attending the press conference every morning, taking notes, coming to the SAT Room, writing up a thirty-second story, and then calling the ten or fifteen news radio outfits that were in the business of buying English-language news reports. Selling radio spots was a freelancer's bread and butter. The afternoon was dedicated to finding that big feature story, the story that could make a career.

After my lesson was through and Harald filed his stories, he led me down to a dingy hole of a café on the first floor. As soon as we sat down, he asked me where I was living at the moment. I told him Old Town.

"Old Town's for fucking softies, man," he shouted, banging the table for effect. "Are you here to cover the war or what, man?"

"What the fuck are you talking about?"

"There's *nothing* going on in Old Town. Novi Grad is where the action is, man. The passion. The stories."

"Really?"

"Fuck, of course, man. The Serbs are everywhere out here. Sniper Alley. Dobrinja. Fucking airport. Igman. But you also need to be near the PTT for the press conference. You need to, man. If you're in Old Town, you gotta hitchhike to the PTT, beg rides from those corporate fascist softies that stay at the Holiday Inn. Jesus Christos, man, I can't take the amateurism."

"What do you mean?"

"Nothing, man. Listen, seriously, you gotta move out here. Otherwise, you're going to spend your time going back and forth, getting shot at by Chetnik snipers."

"Yeah, I would, but my problem is, I don't have much money right now."

"Jesus Christos," he laughed. "No money. What kind of fucking Yank are you?"

I shrugged. It was a good point.

"I'll get you a place. My translator, her family's looking for someone. They have a room. The son is being drafted, the father's sick, they need the money. Can you afford ten deutsche mark a day?"

"Yeah."

"Perfect, man," he said. "Get your shit from Old Town and bring it here tomorrow. I'll introduce you to her. Her name's Dina, Dina Nonovich. She speaks perfect English. Better than you. She's great, man, really. It shouldn't be a problem."

After my day with Harald, I was on as big a high as when I arrived that first day in Sarajevo. I felt as if I had just been initiated into something special. That night I broke the news to the Kukics that I was leaving for Family Nonovich. I wasn't expecting a scene out of the Waltons and I didn't get one. Mrs. Kukic looked relieved, but she did wish me luck. I told her I still intended to bring her food and other supplies from the outside (including the carton and a half of Camel Lights I had ended up smoking myself). She told me that I needn't bother. But, despite what she said, I was still going to do it. I owed them at least that much, and as a down payment I left my last roll of two-ply Scott toilet paper on my pillow.

•　•　•

At nine the next morning I walked out of the Kukics', exactly two weeks after I moved in. The Nonoviches lived across the street from the PTT, in a part of Sarajevo called Novi Grad or New City, and it was a good five-mile walk. I was to meet Dina and Harald at noon at the TV building. I still wasn't familiar enough with Sarajevo to chart my own course, so I attached myself to groups of people headed westward. Weighted down with my flak jacket, equipment, and L.L.Bean duffel bag, which weighed about forty pounds, I was sucking wind almost immediately, and it only got worse as I moved on.

The middle part of Sarajevo not held by the Serbs was a narrow strip with plenty of wide-open spaces and tall buildings. It was called Midtown and was a favorite hunting ground for Serb snipers. Every day some poor soul got shot, often many more. To get to New City that morning, I had to cross three of the worst sniper traps in town.

A Sarajevan sniper trap was communal Russian roulette, a dark lottery run by the Serbs. Hundreds of Sarajevans a day would cross an open space in search of food, water, wood, work, or family, and nothing would happen. Then, without warning, a jet of pink mist would shoot out of someone's temple and he or she would flop down dead. Soon the dead body would be dragged away by the UN or some don't-give-a-damn-anymore family member, and the whole game would start over again. It didn't matter—man, woman, or child—no one was exempt.

Everyone had their own theory on the best way to approach the sniper crossings: run, jog, zigzag, stutter step, or the surprisingly popular simple stroll. How you did it depended on a lot of things: your religious convictions, frequency of trips, peer pressure, pride, emotional exhaustion, and, perhaps most determinative of all, your belief in the immutable laws of fate. In the beginning of the war most people sprinted. But as everyone realized there was nothing that guaranteed safety, people slowed down. By the time I showed up at that first sniper trap that morning, most Sarajevans had converted to walking. Why give the Serbs the satisfaction of seeing you scurry like a rabbit?

I was a committed runner, but that morning I had stacked the deck against myself. To impress my new hosts, I wanted to look properly reportorial. I didn't want another Peter Jennings lecture so I dressed in my last set of clean clothes: chinos and a white oxford shirt combined with my black body armor vest and up-market brown duffel bag with heather green piping. I figured that to the snipers I would look like some crazed Yuppie as I streaked across their rifle scopes. The novelty was probably going to make me an irresistible target.

So I took off across that first trap running and never slowed down. When I got that eerie sensation that crosshairs had just landed on my head, I would change course just a little, zigzagging, keeping 'em on their toes. I passed maybe four walkers on my way to the other side and when I reached safety I collapsed onto my duffel bag. There I recouped, sharing a smoke with a gypsy kid, and then went on to the next one.

By the time I made it through the traps, I had four miles to go and already I was exhausted. Almost immediately shells started to fall—randomly, one moment a mile to the east, the next a few hundred yards to the north. The closer ones shook the ground. When it got intense, I took shelter in apartment buildings, hopscotching my way westward when there was a short break. By the time I got to the TV building it was two o'clock, two hours late.

"Jesus Christos, man," Harald said when he saw me blanketed in sweat with the seat of my pants black from soot.

"It was brutal."

"Forget it. Come on, Yank," he said, grabbing my duffel bag. "Dina's almost given up on you. She's upstairs. Gotta run."

Upstairs, Harald pointed out Dina Nonovich perched on a radiator in the hallway outside the SAT Room. She looked to be about twenty and was good-looking: tall, with dark eyes and hair, rail thin like everyone in this city, it seemed. But her head was perfectly

round and fine-boned, like a delicate bird's. When Harald introduced me, she smiled politely and firmly shook my hand. Then she
got right to the point. "You're late," she declared. "My mother is
waiting, and now we must hurry."

The Nonoviches lived in a huge complex of apartment buildings on a plot of land known as Ali Pashno Polje. It was built just
before the 1984 Olympics, and now housed mostly young working-
class families. If I had been living in Manhattan with the Kukics, I
was now moving to Queens.

As we walked, she explained that I would be living in her old
room, as she had moved to Old Town. Her younger brother, however, was still staying at the apartment and he was due to be drafted
into the army any day. "Why they would want him, I don't know,"
she commented, almost to herself.

I was looking forward to meeting the future warrior, as he
could probably help me get up to the front lines. But what she said
was strange.

"Why wouldn't they want him?" I asked her.

"My brother, Omar?" she said. "I don't know. He's . . . I don't
know. It's not worth talking about. You'll see."

At the Nonoviches', only the mother, Ella, was home. She,
too, had dark hair and amazingly intense gray eyes, and she was
big-boned but very fit. Unlike most of the people I encountered,
she didn't speak a word of English, but she showed me around the
apartment anyway. The master bedroom was more than half taken
up by an ultra-king-size bed, but in the two smaller bedrooms for
the kids the beds were tiny, less than an American single. There was
only a sliver of a kitchen, the kind you'd find in a Manhattan stu-
dio. The centerpiece of the place was the living room. It was almost
a third of the entire apartment, and like any decent living room,
was centered around a television. There was a big comfy couch, two
chairs, and a Persian rug on the floor. I noticed plastic sheeting

instead of glass in the windows, of course, but what stood out for me was the homemade potbelly stove now used to heat the place and a large painting of a stream in a rain forest. After my tour, Dina deposited me in her room and told me to wait there for an hour or two until her father, Nino, got home from work.

"Before you move in, he needs to speak with you," she said.

When she shut the door, I peeled off my clothes and fell onto the bed for a quick catnap.

What I didn't know at this time was that my life was actually hanging in the balance, depending on how I performed when I met old man Nonovich. Later I learned that word had been racing around Old Town, rumors of a spy who was making a terribly poor attempt at passing himself off as a reporter. He had apparently been trying to penetrate Satso's front line. I was that spy, of course, and earlier that day the Nonoviches had been warned about what might be coming their way. Their patriotic duty was simple: sniff out the truth, then notify Ali Pashno's warlord, Juka, should the rumors prove accurate.

"John," Dina said, nudging me awake. *"John!"*

"Ah-huh," I answered, clasping the pillow over my head.

"John, you have to get up. We all wait for you inside."

"Oh, Jesus," I uttered, rubbing my eyes. "I'm sorry. What time is it?"

"Three."

"Feels later than that."

"Three o'clock, *Thursday.* You've been asleep for a day. I wouldn't wake you now, but I must leave."

"Oh, Christ. I'm sorry."

"No sorry. Get dressed and come inside."

In the living room I found Mr. and Mrs. Nonovich and Omar on the couch. Mr. Nonovich was dark-skinned, short but powerfully built, and had dark eyes which were housed behind a large pair of metal-rimmed eyeglasses. Omar sat in a chair near the window. The seat of honor, a La-Z-Boy knockoff facing all of them, was left for me.

"Welcome, my friend," Mr. Nonovich said when I walked in. "Welcome to my home, friend. Please, please sit down."

He offered me coffee, cigarettes, and scotch. I declined them all so as not to impose any further.

"How sleep?" he asked.

"Pretty good," I told him. "Usually, though, I try to keep it to just twenty hours."

They looked around at one another, then back at me.

"Sorry, just a stupid joke."

Omar leveled his eyes at me from across the coffee table, giving me an absolutely blank stare. I smiled at him. He muttered the word *primitive,* smirked, and slowly started shaking his head. Dina reached over to smack him but he leaned his skinny frame out of the way. She then yelled something at him in Bosnian, which was apparently his cue to turn his head toward the wall and let out a deep, exasperated sigh.

"Sorry, my friend," Mr. Nonovich said. "*Family.* You understand. Never mind. Listen, I have, I have to, some important . . . I mean, *please,* ah, understand, no, I have a few questions."

It took a while and Dina translated a lot, but what he wanted to know was where I lived, where I was from, whom I knew in town, what I planned to do in Sarajevo, when I would leave, and so on. While he grilled me, there was a serious firefight raging on the front lines nearby. The machine-gun bursts and grenade blasts were loud enough that I had to speak up sometimes to make myself heard. Someplace along the way I finally accepted a cigarette from Mr. Nonovich.

"Please, friend, now tell me about *Arbeit,* ah, what's the, your, what you do?" he asked.

"Ah, yeah. I mostly do radio. You know, newsy pieces on the situation here."

"Yes?"

"Yeah," I said, pointing to a convenient trail of tracer fire that happened to be floating by outside. "You know."

"Yes, the war," he uttered, losing himself in the tracers for a second.

"Yeah. Of course, I'm looking to do bigger stories on the people here. Tell their, you know, stories. But that takes time, more work."

"Of course, of course. Too much work, bad. Need time to live. Man needs to live, not only work. Good." He slapped me on the knee.

"Absolutely."

"Yes, yes," Mr. Nonovich went on. "But what I would like to know, John, is . . . *Kak so Kaze?* How do you Dina, say, um, what I . . ."

"Who do you work for, John?" Dina blurted out.

"Oh, NBC Radio," I said, taking out my UN press card. As I did so, a large ash from the cigarette seemed to fall onto the chair. I jumped up to brush it off, but Mr. Nonovich grabbed my arm.

"No, friend," he said. "No worry. No. About this radio, as you say."

I started to bullshit, parroting back things I had heard, mostly from Harald. They were hanging onto my every word, so no one saw the fire spreading until Omar casually pointed at the smoke rising from the chair under me.

"Oh, fuck," I shouted, jumping up. I must have fanned the flames as I rose because the smoke got thicker. Mr. Nonovich leaped on the chair with his pillow, trying to tamp them out. He couldn't locate the fire, and the smoke grew even thicker. Then Omar snorted something in Bosnian, pointing at my crotch. There were tiny blue flames spreading across it.

"Fuck!" I yelled, hitting the flames with my hand. My pants were actually on fire. Pushing me into the chair, Mr. Nonovich finally got the fire out with his pillow. When he was done, the crotch of my jeans was gone and my paisley boxers were now clearly visible behind the remaining wisps of smoke.

"Oh my God," I said. "I'm so sorry."

"Pleeeeeease!" Omar blurted out, holding up his hand for me to stop talking. "Look at you. So very primitive."

Then everyone started laughing, including me. There were no more questions. Instead, Mrs. Nonovich made me take off what was left of my jeans and handed me a pair of her husband's trousers. Two sizes too small, they made me look like an aging rock star.

"Welcome to family," Mr. Nonovich shouted. He clapped his hands and put his arm over my shoulder. "Stay long as you need, friend. We, your family, here, in Sarajevo. You come to us. Any time, you understand? Welcome to my home."

The Nonoviches had been told to expect a cunning, wily master of espionage. Like most people, when the Nonoviches heard "spy," they thought James Bond. My act of self-immolation, however, laid all their fears to rest. There would be no call to Juka that day, or any day. And Mr. Nonovich was true to his word. He would treat me as family, but it would take me some time before I could feel that way, too. It had been a while since I'd really connected to anyone.

six

Birds of a Feather

"I'll be fine, Ma," I told her. "Don't worry. I know what I'm doing. Please, you gotta trust me."

That's what I had told my mom back in 1981 when she was standing over my bed and insisting I go see a psychiatrist. Even as a kid I wasn't the shrink type. I wasn't about to admit I needed help. I didn't want to associate myself with those people, the Craty types and the Cooleys who couldn't make their way among normal people. I didn't want to be marked forever as weak or somehow different. I didn't want to be on the outside. The only way forward was straight ahead, on my own. It seemed logical to me that if I kept fighting, sooner or later everything would go back to normal and I would feel the way I had.

For about another month after the depression hit, it was brutal. I forced myself out of bed every morning, making myself put one foot in front of the other, marching myself out the door to confront the day. And all the while, I was trying to keep up the front, attempting to joke around with my friends, sitting in class and pretending to take notes as I obsessed over living in a world that was suddenly pointless, meaningless, and sad. Sometimes I felt like an old man forced to hang out with teenagers.

When I got home after school I had to do it all over again for my family, pretending everything was cool, normal, no problem. At the end of each day I was exhausted from the act and I collapsed into bed, craving a break from being hyperconscious.

But after about six weeks of this, I was seemingly rewarded for my effort to keep on. What had started out nearly impossible—getting out of bed and heading out into the world—became easier and easier as the days passed. The intensity of the isolation I felt gradually waned. Either I wasn't quite so morbidly self-aware as I had been or I was getting used to my new way of being. But, little by little, my thoughts no longer crowded out everything else in life; the ruminations about the meaning of it all and the Big Why became a little less incessant. I even found myself concentrating better, not having to act the part of me so intensely, not having to think through each conversation. What never returned, though, was that childhood sense of belonging that I had treasured. That was history. It was just gone.

By high school, outwardly, I appeared to be the person who I considered myself to really be: well adjusted, reasonably popular, reasonably athletic, reasonably happy. In ways I was the kind of guy many high school kids would resent. Not that I was a prick or a bully, but maybe it seemed like I had it a little bit too easy. Anyway, as far as any alienation I did feel, for God's sake, I was a teenager and supposed to feel that way.

There was one thing, though, that definitely made me different and it was my big secret. It was my treatment, something I needed to do virtually every day. I called it Rocking. After a typical day of school and sports, I would get home around six-thirty, eat dinner, and then go up to my attic bedroom. There I would turn off all the lights and pull the drapes closed, put on massive headphones, crank up the volume on the stereo as far as it would go, and lie down my bed in complete darkness. There I would rock my head back and forth to the music, any of kind of fast music with a heavy beat. Soon I would enter into a trancelike state. In that other world, I would envision myself not so much being a star athlete, just living out and enjoying, participating in normal scenes. I envisioned myself at the beach with my friends, or with a group of buddies in a red Mustang cruising east down the Long Island Expressway. Or just walking down the hall at school with people whom I felt truly connected with. In all of these visions I would feel myself easily, effortlessly part of the world around me. I wasn't on the outside looking in, as I so often felt. I was on the inside looking out.

At the end of these nightly sessions, four, five, sometimes seven hours later, I would reemerge into the real world with a certain peace. Not the peace of what was, but the peace of what would be. Rocking gave me the one thing I desperately needed in order to get up for the following day: hope that the day ahead would be the day when it all changed back. The problem was that it never turned out to be that special day and I would burn through my optimistic energy like jet fuel. By the late afternoon I would always be back in a semi-isolated state, forced to play the part of me until I could get back up into my room and refuel.

I knew it was weird, and that's why I didn't tell anyone. But I didn't see it as necessarily a symptom of a problem. After all, I wasn't smoking dope, snorting coke, or drinking myself into a stupor every night. I was just doing what I had to do to keep my energies up and survive until a better day came along, which I was pretty sure would be soon. Then my parents and I took a trip—to Philadelphia.

And everything that was okay got turned upside down.

As long as I could remember, my little sister Sara had always been anxious, nervous about things, little things, everything. Every now and then she'd collapse in on herself—break out in crying fits, panic about stuff only she thought was serious. Then, when we were in junior high, she seemed to just snap out of it in a big way: she carried herself more confidently, got straight A-pluses, and was always perfectly dressed. But then in ninth grade she dropped out of the advanced-placement classes, stopped hanging out with her friends, and stopped eating. *Really* stopped eating. Finally, a month or so later, she detonated. She kept screaming, "I can't take it anymore."

Unlike me, Sara readily agreed to get help. My mother lassoed one of the best doctors in New York, Dr. John Atchley, a founding member and former head of the American Anorexic and Bulimic Association, whom she saw twice a month for the next year. At first talking seemed to help, but after a few months she was right back, eating little and doing less. In the late summer of 1984 things came to a head. Late one night, after my parents were asleep, Sara slipped a note under their door. It was on Little Kitty stationery and read: *Mom & Dad, Just a note to let you know that I'm going to have to kill myself. Just thought you would like to know. I love you both. Sara.*

The next morning my mother called Dr. Atchley and the decision was made to send Sara down to a first-class facility for young women with eating disorders outside Philadelphia called the Renfrew Center. Two weeks later, it was time for our first family session. As Christine and Quentin were away at college, that meant it was just me and my parents.

On the way down my mother explained a few things to me. According to Dr. Atchley, something called clinical depression lay at the root of Sara's anxieties and eating disorder. That, my mother said, had also been her brother Robert's problem. Or so she suspected. Late in his life, she had to have Robert committed. In the car, she told me he had suffered terrible bouts of depression before he died. What's more, my mother's mother had lived with depression for decades. It ran in the family, and poor Sara was the one who had been picked off this time around.

"Depression is something you probably can't understand, John," my mother said, prepping me for the family session to come. "But Sara's going to need all of our help and compassion, maybe for a long time. So don't try to understand. Just do as I ask and love your sister."

It was testimony to how completely I had fooled myself that, as we talked about Sara's depression, I never recalled that day back in 1981 when I awoke a foreigner in my own room and simply wanted to die. Depression, as I understood it, had nothing to do with me. I was normal, no way around it. My parents never made the connection, either.

The Renfrew Center is on a large estate just outside Philadelphia. The main house, a mansion in the style of a French château, sits about a hundred feet off the road at the end of a white pebble driveway. Walled off by a towering, manicured hedge, the sweeping lawn is fairway smooth, and the rose gardens are secluded behind stone walls. Except for tweeting birds, the place was still and quiet when I visited, despite being home to about seventy girls. It felt like we were driving onto the set of a murder mystery on *Masterpiece Theater.*

Inside, however, the mansion was pure dormitory with overhead lighting, dark high-traffic carpeting, and hallways lined with compressed wood doors painted pink. Many of those doors had cork boards with notes pinned on them, and taped below and above were bright flowers and smiling suns made of construction paper. One had the words GOOD LUCK, WITH LOVE carefully cut from colored paper and stapled right to it.

Sara's room was right off the commons, where the girls watched TV and chatted. As we approached, I heard the familiar sounds of girls talking and giggling around the corner. I didn't know what to expect, but when I walked into the area, I tried with all I had not to let my shock show on my face. I didn't want to make the girls feel bad. There were maybe seven of them in the commons, some just skinny but three just this side of skeletal. Sara was downright plump compared to them.

One of them, a girl with beautiful blue eyes and brown hair held back with a madras headband, looked close to death, although she seemed the leader of the pack. Her cheeks were so sunken in that I thought I saw her teeth rubbing against the skin. She was wearing Bermuda shorts, penny loafers, and a yellow Lacoste golf shirt. It looked as if a concentration camp inmate had been forced to model for the *Preppie Handbook.* Whatever was wrong with her, it was a cruel thing. "Hello," the girl said, with surprising vigor, flashing implausibly white teeth. The other girls followed in a disjointed chorus of hellos. We waved and said hello back.

"Are you the Falks?" she asked, playing perfect hostess.

"Yes," my father answered, smiling.

"Sara should be back in a minute. I think she's with her roommate, Brenda. Sara's told us all about you."

My parents politely went back and forth with this girl, my dad even going out of his way to make her and the other girls chuckle. It was weird because everyone in that room knew where we were, yet we all were pretending that we had just run into one another in the lobby of a country club. For my part, I kept quiet and just nodded along with what was being said because I was trying to maintain my distance. I didn't want to get any closer to them than I already felt.

There was something way too familiar about these girls. Not that I was starving myself. What struck me was the way they imitated normalcy. They were impersonating people who weren't suffering, but because of their emaciation, their act was obvious. But I knew. I knew they were living every second of every day in a void. Starving themselves was their way of reaching out, trying to reconnect, to belong. Somehow I understood this because that's what I was trying to do—reconnect. But no one could see I was acting. I was getting away with it. At that moment I realized I was closer to who they were than to the kid I thought and hoped I had succeeded at becoming. That's what freaked me out. Standing in that room, watching that horror with that stupid smile plastered on my face, I was scared shitless.

A few hours later our family session was over. Sara had spent most of the time screaming at me. I couldn't get out of there fast enough, but just as we were going to our car, my parents were summoned back inside. An hour later they reemerged from behind an ivy-covered wall with Sara in tow, my dad carrying her bags.

At the last minute, Sara had asked them to come back because she realized something. "I'm not like these girls," she whispered. "I'd rather be home, with you." My parents tried to talk her out of it, then triple-checked that she was sure, spoke with the counselors, and only then agreed to take her home.

"What happened?" I asked when they got in the car.

"Sara wants to come home," my mom answered.

"Really?"

"Yup," Sara answered, sounding almost peppy. "But only if you don't say a word for the whole trip."

"No problem," I told her. Then I reached across the backseat and put her into a soft headlock. "I'm proud of you, tiger. I told you, you don't need that crap."

She pushed my arm away.

"Well, it's not that. I just realized," she said. "You're the one that needs help, not me."

We all laughed.

seven

Nino's Secret

After Nino Nonovich welcomed me into his home that night, I was elated. I had felt dead in the water at the Kukics', but here was a fresh start in an even more active part of the city. What's more, I suddenly had Harald, King of the Freelancers, on my side, and he had promised that he would finish teaching me all I needed to know about filing radio from Sarajevo.

The first thing I spotted that morning when I awoke were my blue jeans, folded on a footstool next to the bed. They hadn't been there when I went to sleep and, obviously, had been cleaned. When I picked them up I noticed someone had not only washed but repaired them as well. A patch of denim had been sewn in expertly over the missing crotch. I thought it was the mother's handiwork, but then I saw a note on the floor.

> *Dear John,*
> *I fixed your trousers. I hope that is OK. I see you don't have many clothes. My mother is waiting inside for you with breakfast. Say hello to Harald for me.*
>
> *Good luck today.*
> *Dina*

I put on the jeans and walked out into the apartment, feeling great. Dina wasn't there to thank, but Mrs. Nonovich was, sitting at the table before a place setting for one. Through a cloud of cigarette smoke, she smiled at me.

"*Priscu babba moya dobya dubnik!*" she roared, laughing at my jeans. "*Googa schenk.*" She pointed to a chair as she spoke. Her words were pure gibberish to me, like listening to Latka Gravas on *Taxi,* but I figured she was asking me to join her. When I sat down, she disappeared into the kitchen. As her metal pots clanked, a machine gun belted out a few rounds nearby. A door not far off opened and slammed. Someone cried out. A shell exploded somewhere. All the morning sounds of Sarajevo came at me, one by one. Finally, Mrs. Nonovich reappeared, holding a cream-colored ceramic bowl. Steam rose from the top.

"*Grah,*" she declared before handing it over. "*Gr-ah.*"

"*Gr-ah,*" I repeated, thinking oatmeal, hoping oatmeal.

Smiling, she placed the bowl in front of me. It was gruel: darkish brown, lumpy, and dominated by beans, possibly the same beans I flew in with weeks earlier. *Fucking brutal,* I thought. Swallowing a spoonful, I forced a smile to be polite, but fucking-A. "Delicious," I said, putting down my spoon. "Excellent, but now . . ."

She shook her head. "*Babbo hungo dropnik,*" she told me, sternly. She picked up my spoon and handed it back to me.

It went on like this for maybe twenty minutes. Every time I made a move to go, she'd yell at me. Only when I started eating would she stop. By the time I managed to fight my way free, I had finished three bowls of *grah,* two cups of Turkish coffee, and three local cigarettes. I was late for the press conference.

After I got my gear and was about to set off, she grabbed my face and asked, "*Grabbo pistcu matte?*"

I shook my head, no, fifty-fifty.

"*Grabbo pistcu matte!*" she yelled.

I nodded, yes, but she shook her head again. *Yes and No, both the wrong answers?* She was still holding my face, waiting. Hers seemed to be an impossible riddle, so I threw my own right back at her.

"Those blue pills I take?"

"*Grabbo pistcu matte?*" she came again, sounding almost intrigued.

"True, they're for my head. It's embarrassing, but nothing to worry about, lady." Although she couldn't understand a word of what I had just said, it still felt good to let someone in on my secret.

She laughed, then squished my face even tighter and pecked me on each cheek. "*Dobro, dobro jevnik,*" she said. "*Pola luna, da, ali dobro jevnik.*" Then she pushed me out the front door in my body armor and helmet like I was late for school.

I did miss the press conference, but I caught Harald as he was coming out of the PTT. He was moving like a drunk on a pogo stick, bounding from one reporter to another, comparing notes. He blew right past me.

"Harald!"

He turned and looked. "Ah, Jesus Christos, Yanko! Not now, I'm too busy."

"OK."

He stepped away from me, but then spun around again. "Jesus Christos, fucking Yankee scumbag. Ah, fuck it, follow me."

After filing his stories in the SAT Room that morning, Harald taught me how to write a story; how to sound older than I was by lowering my voice; how to send "Boom, Boom," recordings of battle, over the satellite phone. Then he made the point that even if I screwed up all of the above it still didn't matter because the most important wasn't what I said, but where I was saying it from. All those stations really cared about was the last word of the tagline at the end of my piece, "For (fill-in-the-blank) News, John Falk, Sarajevo." Identifying my location let the audience know they were listening to the news firsthand, from a man actually in the field. On a busy news day, I could file four or five pieces, bringing in maybe a hundred dollars.

By noon, we had finished filing our pieces and were having coffee down in that dingy café. There Harald explained that, as freelancers, we had one unique advantage over the corporate news media when it came down to finding the great stories, the big feature story that could make a career. We were dirt poor, had to live off the land, and by doing so were closer to the reality of Sarajevo than anyone with an expense account, armored car, and room at the Holiday Inn. But to take advantage of this, I had to perform one critical task: ditch my body armor and helmet. "No one is going to talk with you when you're dressed like one of *those fucking police fascists who used to beat us outside . . .*"

"Harald!" I shouted, trying to get him back to earth.

"Sorry, Johnny Boy, do what you want, really. But dressed in a helmet and body armor, you can't get close to anyone in this city. You've got to live like everyone else here to find out what's really going on."

By the time Harald finished his mini-tutor session, I had an idea for a story. I knew it was a little out there, but it had been taking shape in my head for a while. I wanted to interview a sniper.

The word *sniper* is generally attributed to the British Raj in India and a small game bird called a snipe. Bored British soldiers on fort duty in the hinterlands of India used to take potshots from great distances at the agile little birds. If they hit the snipes consistently enough, their admiring buddies would dub them as snipers. It was probably the last time anyone, friend or foe, would use the term in a purely complimentary way.

By World War I, snipers were generally considered not soldiers but chartered murderers. In an age of mechanized, mass, impersonal warfare, they were the only intimate killers left on the battlefield, the only ones who personally selected, stalked, and then killed their victims one by one. For soldiers, being hunted by a sniper was a terrifying ordeal.

Knowing a sniper is loose is like knowing a cobra is at large somewhere in your house. It makes you paranoid. It freezes you. You stop walking by beds, couches; you open drawers. One is left with the eerie sensation that instant death is always just a moment away. People who live under the fear of snipers lose track of everything in the world but their fear; it's a very dark hold that these gunmen have on the regions they terrorize. That's why, if captured, snipers are almost always executed on the spot. It is also the reason why most armies disband their sniper units immediately after a war. Snipers are spooky even to the people they serve.

Sarajevo, during my time there, was a sniper's paradise, a five-mile narrow strip of city situated on the floor of a deep valley. Every house, window, building, and street was in view of at least one Serb-held ridgeline. The Serbs also controlled several neighborhoods entirely, giving them even more places for their snipers to nest. The gunmen took advantage of every vantage—upper floors of apartment buildings, office blocks, and hotels. The 450,000 people living in the city below had no choice but to venture outside daily for food, firewood, work, and water. It was the perfect mix of elements for a human shooting gallery.

In this atmosphere, rumors were inevitable. Whispers were routinely exchanged about snipers who had taken on almost mythical stature on both sides of the conflict. There was the Romanian Woman, a single mother and former sharpshooter for the Romanian Olympic team who hunted the streets of Sarajevo for child victims, collecting a five-hundred-deutsche-mark bounty for each Muslim kid killed. It was said she hunted in high heels and a red dress, and used the money to support her own kids back in Bucharest. Then there was the Hunter, a reclusive gray-bearded Bosnian Serb who lived deep in the pine forests of central Bosnia. Once a month, to avenge his son's death on the front lines a year earlier, he hiked to Sarajevo for a string of random killings. Perhaps the most widely told story, however, wasn't about an individual but rather a class of snipers called Safari Hunters. These were poets, businessmen, soccer fans, politicians, or any breed of psychopath from Serbia or other countries who made weekend hunting trips to Sarajevo to bag humans.

Snipers were the very tip of the spear in Sarajevo. It was a war of terror, and they were its main instruments. It was with them, up with the snipers in their perches, that I was certain I would find the greatest drama, the craziest shit, the razor's edge of the war. It was there that I would be certain to find my Big Story. Part of me, I suppose, was also attracted to the intensity of it. I had come all this way from Long Island to this war, crawling 99 percent of the way out onto the spear, and I saw no reason why I shouldn't take that final step into the darkest part of the war.

For the next six weeks, I followed Harald's plan to the letter, attending the morning press conference, filing my radio reports by eleven, and then setting out on foot—looking, learning, and listening. Pretty quickly, I had singled out one "rumor" to investigate. She was called the Raven, a cheerleader-type teenage girl from the suburbs who had morphed into a prolific, cold-blooded killer. The story went that she was dragged from her home with the rest of her family by Serb paramilitaries during the first days of the war, repeatedly raped, then shot and left for dead. She awoke days later in a ditch, only to find a molted black raven pecking at the eyes of her dead father lying beside her. Her vow from that moment on was to kill as many Serbs as possible. I was fascinated by this tale. I wanted to get a look at her if possible. Her story was something that even the least interested, most smugly suburban American wouldn't be able to turn away from.

I had found out that there were at least a couple of ways to go about looking for snipers. One was to sneak around the top floors of apartment buildings and abandoned office towers in the hope of catching one in action. But there were thousands of ideal sniper nests in Sarajevo and only a handful of snipers left alive and working them. The odds were against my just stumbling upon one, and if I did, then the chances were pretty good that they wouldn't react kindly.

The other method was simply to ask around for an introduction or information. Although less direct, it seemed the more effective, less lethal option. Every day I pounded the pavement, doing the grunt work of a reporter, striking up conversations anywhere I could, hoping to find that one person, that nugget of gold. I asked soldiers, UN personnel, politicians, drug smugglers, black marketeers, mercenaries, fixers, local and foreign reporters, kids, and even a random few old ladies on the street. I got nowhere with the Raven and generally I got stonewalled on the topic of snipers in general. Almost everyone denied they knew one, and those who did told me to forget about it.

As the weeks ticked by, however, I began to realize that my quest was almost certainly futile. Snipers weren't just loners on the battlefield. The society they had with one another was ultrasecret and mostly they kept their missions to themselves. They moved anonymously. Anyone I saw in the city could be a sniper: the widow next door, or the feeble old gent down the street. I literally would have had an easier time interviewing the Bosnian president than a bona fide sniper. That's not to say I didn't meet several people claiming to be snipers, but they were just hucksters, braggarts, or shady types floating "perfect story" bait to lure a naïve, cash-carrying reporter into the shadows. I turned to other story possibilities.

Mount Zuc was about half a mile across the valley from the Nonoviches'. I could see it perfectly from my bedroom window, and every night before bed I watched the tracer fire arcing back and forth over its front lines. By the end of September, it didn't take a military genius to figure out that the fighting was intensifying: More ambulances raced up and down the face of the mountain.

More flashes and thuds accompanied the nightly artillery barrages. More tracer rounds floated over the battlefield. The sounds of gunfire crested ever higher and for longer. It was the military equivalent of an approaching storm churning up an already shifting sea. But the battle was off-limits to reporters, at least those without the right connections. And that's how I finally got a break. I realized I had a connection.

I hadn't seen a lot of Omar during my first weeks at the Nonoviches. He spent most of his time in Old Town, trying to win admission to the University of Sarajevo's Art Academy. As most of the professors had already fled the city or were dead or penniless or without studios or offices, Omar's education was basically a pipe dream. Then in mid-September, as the fighting escalated in the hills, chewing up more and more soldiers, the word went out that Omar was due to be called up. He was only seventeen and had a medical exemption, but the local warlords no longer cared. They needed bodies.

He gave up on art school, returning home to prepare for the inevitable. My idea, if I could get him to agree, was to follow Omar through his brief training and then into battle. I would do a story on a green soldier's first days in combat.

At that point, I didn't really know Omar, so I wasn't sure how he would react. One morning, I found him working out in front of the hall mirror.

"Hey, when you get a second, can we talk?"

Pointing to the couch in the living room, he said, "*Sit.* I must now prepare for the militia. When I finish, we can talk."

I did as he directed and watched. With a towel folded under his collar the way a boxer does, he was dressed in an oversized purplish T-shirt and black shorts, and wasn't close to breaking a sweat. His workout was pre-aerobic: touching his toes, returning to a standing position, checking himself in the mirror, and then easing back down to touch the other foot. All he needed were the leg warmers, and he could have been just another housewife exercising to the old *Richard Simmons Show.* It was hard to envision him in anyone's army.

After about five minutes, he patted some phantom moisture off his forehead, then strode into the living room. Taking a seat in the easy chair, he crossed his legs and then folded his hands in his lap. "What?" he asked, a pure look of disdain on his face.

I made my pitch.

"Please, at least have the courage to just say it. You want to follow me and film my death."

"No, not film your death. Omar, I'm radio. And, two, I have no intention . . ."

"But you do know they want to kill me, don't you?"

"It's bad up there, I heard anyway, but . . ."

"No, you *primitive.* They, the militia, our side, *they* want to kill me."

"What do you mean, they wanna kill you?"

"They will not give me a gun. They will stick me in a hole up there to lure out the enemy. I am big fat worm for their fish."

"Come on. Why would they . . ."

"*Primitive!* Fat and hairy, ugly, like wild boar. No. Like mountain bear. Poor Johnny. I'm an artist, Johnny, they're primitive. And they must kill what they cannot have."

"I don't . . ."

"Understand? Of course you don't. So simple, no? Look at yourself."

He waited for me to look at myself somehow, but I didn't.

"Please, I mean it. For me, look at yourself. Come all this way to feed off our suffering, no, be interesting to whatever you come from . . . Please, I do not care anymore. OK? They can have me and so can you. Follow me, bear. I will try and make my death as interesting as I can for you."

I tried to speak, but he held up his hand. Then he rose and

strode toward his room, choking back tears. When he got to his bedroom door, he said, with his back still to me, "It's a war for the criminals, so they get rich. I try to tell my father, but he will not believe me. I do not care if you believe me. But now it must eat me and you want to watch."

Then he stepped in and slammed the door behind him.

"Jesus Christos, man!" Harald yelled. "Come on. Omar Nonovich? No way."

"NPR, man. Budding artist, sensitive soul in action kinda thing," I told him, trying to get my head around the right angle for an Omar story. "I think they would groove on something like that."

"Listen, man," Harald said. "First, he's right. He's gonna be bait. Of course, those guys hate him. Not their type, right? Man, no way are those guys going to let you go watch as they use little Omar as bait for the Chetniks. No fucking way."

"Goddamn it. One decent story, you know. I didn't think it would be so hard to find, something more than . . ."

"Yanko," Harald said. "You idiot. You're living with a story. Ask Nino. When he pedals off each morning to go to work? Where do you think he's going? You never asked?"

"No."

"He works on some secret project out there. Jesus, man. He likes you. If he will talk to you about what he does, that would be a great story."

Every weekday, Nino Nonovich rose at seven, shaved, brushed his teeth, had coffee, and then pushed his folding bike out the door. In heavy shelling, rain, or even if a sniper was on the loose nearby, it didn't matter. He always went off to work. At four o'clock in the afternoon he would return, park his bike in the hallway, grab a deck of red playing cards, and play solitaire in the living room until dinner. After dinner, he would play a few more hands, then go to bed, only to start it all again the next morning.

But he still loved to talk, and he had a lot to talk about. The man had a colorful past. For many years he had worked overseas as a mechanical engineer on large public projects in far-off places like North Africa and Southeast Asia. Malaysia was his favorite posting, and to remind himself of those days he had bought there that painting of that tropical scene. Sometimes, when the shelling was really intense, the building shaking, I half-expected to look up and see him frozen in that painting, having escaped back to his personal heaven.

Nino had also enjoyed some fame as a member of the Bosnian Rat Pack. He was Frank Sinatrovich, the lead tuxedoed crooner with a club act called Friends. He sang in Adriatic resorts for President Tito, holding court over lavish dinners after gigs, a rocks glass full of scotch in one hand and a Cuban cigar smoldering in the other. He had cut ten albums and even had groupies. But now that world was long gone. He lived in a perpetual shooting gallery and, worse, he had to watch his family endure that, too. Since the war began, he had four strokes.

So following Harald's advice, I went straight back to the Nonoviches' where I found him on the couch playing solitaire, as usual. After about twenty minutes of pure bullshit, I finally just jumped in and asked, "You work on some secret project?"

"I do."

"Can you tell me about it?"

"No. After war, maybe, but not now. Impossible. Sorry, my friend."

And that was it. Where else was I going to go with it? For the next ten minutes, I listened to him blow about his childhood, how idyllic it had been, all the different broads he had scored with when he was young. Then I noticed something over his shoulder. Two somethings to be exact. Two trophies, little gold men atop pedestals peering down what appeared to be pool sticks. As Nino droned on, I went over for a look. *Shooting trophies.*

"What's this?" I asked, holding one up.

"Ah," he said. "I was a champion shooter once. Steady nerves." He pounded his bicep.

"Really?"

"Yes," he said, now squinting down the barrel of an imaginary rifle. "I had very steady hands. Perfect nerves for . . ." He stopped dead, like he just caught himself saying too much.

"You were a champion shooter, huh?"

"Yes, long ago," he said. "But only so-so. There were many better."

"You must know snipers," I said.

He shook his head, then motioned for me to come over. "Sit," he said. I did.

"John, I know you are looking for story. Work very hard. Make me proud. But, please, not snipers."

"Why?"

"Because, you trust me. Because you will listen to me."

"But why?"

"Please, you are like my son. It's just not clever. Very danger-ous. And they not like talk, understand me?"

"You sure? Anything you could do?"

"No," he told me, wrapping his arm around my shoulder. "Please believe me. I am not liar. Sniper impossible, understand me? A sniper is different than all the rest."

eight

Are You Still Alive?

It was October 1986 and I was a freshman at the University of Vermont. Five weeks into that school year, I had yet to pick up my mail. It wasn't that I was disorganized. It wasn't that I had been too busy. It was intentional. I was avoiding that mailbox until I felt the time was right. I had my reasons.

Two years earlier, after we had returned from the Renfrew Center, I managed to push away that frighteningly vivid reflection I had seen in those anorexics. I got back on with my life, trying to hang in there, do well in school, play sports, and go to parties on weekends. By the fall of my senior year things were actually going great. My team won the county championships in football. I threw some decent keg parties, and after each one there was always some chick waiting around for me. Although gradewise there were no major victories, I applied for early admission to the University of Vermont. After scoring an interview with the dean of admissions, I stressed big-time, gradually honing a routine about my intense hunger to expand my intellectual horizons.

"It's unbelievable, but the town I come from is so homogenous," I told the dean during the actual interview. "More than anything, I mean *anything,* I want to meet people from all different places, backgrounds, religions." It was complete bullshit, but she bought it. Before I had even left her office, she penciled me on her admitted list. So, on paper, everything was squared away. The future beckoned. It appeared that I was actually going to have one.

But there was one big problem. Instead of my underlying sense of isolation diminishing, as I thought it would if I just kept trying, it started growing again late in my senior year. Every day I would walk around feeling more out of it, edging bit by bit farther out of the life going on around me. And then one day in the spring, a great sunny day when my friends and I had planned to go down to the beach, I awoke as that same panicked twelve-year-old—a complete and utter stranger in the world. It was just as intense as before, but this time I knew better than to even let out a peep. I kept it to myself, and no one, not even my mother, was any the wiser.

Before I had self-medicated with the idea that time was on my side. Eventually, I told myself I would feel part of the world again. This time, I used a new idea: if time couldn't do it, I told myself, a new place would. All I needed, I decided, was a change of scenery. So I lifted myself out of that second major depression by convincing myself that once I was around all new people, new situations, new challenges, I would be able to feel part of things again. In a twist of fate, I had actually morphed into a version of that hungry searcher I had channeled to sell myself to the dean.

So when I said good-bye to my parents in the parking lot behind the UVM freshman dorms that August, I really meant it. My good-bye was meant to be long-term. It wasn't anything they did; in fact, I felt horrible for having to do it. But to finally feel myself, find that place in the world where I could feel at home, I felt I had no other choice. I had to cut all strings with my past: Long Island, Garden City, my friends, my family, my parents. That was why my mailbox at school was so toxic. It was a big, throbbing string leading back to all that.

But college hadn't worked its magic like I thought it would. For the first month or so I didn't sleep much, went out every night, went to classes during the day, and even studied a little. I hooked up here and there, made a whole new group of friends, and we joined a jock frat together. But when the newness of everything wore off, I was right back at the beginning: absolutely overwhelmed with this sense of being alone in this meaningless universe. So when I actually did head to that mailbox, I went out of desperation. I was looking for any connection I could find—to anyone, even those from whom I had cut myself off.

When I got down to the student post office to pick up my mail, there was a ton of letters and pamphlets wrapped up with rubber bands. When the goody-goody kid inside the post office handed over the stuff, he asked, "You just getting here, dude?"

"Just give me my fuckin' mail, please."

I took the mail up to my dorm room and spread it out on my bed. Ninety percent of it was crap from the university or local businesses. The rest were letters, from family and friends, the very kryptonite I had been avoiding. Picking up the letter with the most recent postmark, I opened it and inside I found a tongue-in-cheek questionnaire from my father, the first page of which read:

**Please circle the best answer and mail back
to the Home Office in the
S.A.S.E. A.S.A.P.**

1) *Are you still alive? Yes or No.*
2) *Have you been kidnapped by gypsies? Yes or No.*
3) *Are you having fun? Yes or No.*
4) *Do you feel guilty for not calling? Yes, No, Don't Know What That Means.*
5) *New girlfriend? Yes or No.*
6) *Have you joined any variety of club, team, society or group, as your dear old pop suggested? Yes or No.*

7) *Classes are going: Great, Well, OK, Can't Say, or Haven't Been Yet.*

8) *You haven't called home because: too busy, forgot number, ran away with circus, or just lazy rat.*

I couldn't even turn to the second page, instead dropping it on the bed. It was my worst nightmare come to life. Here I was searching for any little connection. Instead I had just been cast off into cold space. I saw this questionnaire for what it really was: a love letter, from proud father to golden son, only the son my pop loved not only never existed, it was clear to me that he never would.

nine

Hare Krishna

It was now mid-October 1993, and I had spent nearly three months in Sarajevo, the past nine weeks with the Nonoviches, and unbelievably to me I felt no different. Yeah, I had come to Bosnia to begin a career as a war correspondent, and on that front I had made some real headway. Filing numerous radio spots each day for English-language radio outfits in America, Europe, and even Africa, I was getting good at boiling down the day's events into thirty-second bites. At one point, I even became the Balkan correspondent for a country I never heard of before, Bophuthatswana. I would sign off each broadcast with my best Walter Cronkite imitation, "For Radio Bop News, this is John Falk, Sarajevo." Not bad for a former shut-in who flew into a war zone with no employer, zero experience, and fake paperwork. Suddenly I was a voice heard 'Round the World.

But still, I didn't give a damn about any of that. If I had wanted just a journalism career, I would have stayed at home and cut my teeth at the local paper. I had really come all this way for another purpose—to change, to live, to find that certain something I had never been able to get at home. What that certain something would be I still didn't know, but I had believed that by now, after this long in Sarajevo, I would have ingested at least something transformative through simple osmosis. But here I was the same rudderless dickhead as always, dead in the water and still basically alone. In the mornings I would file radio, and in the afternoons I would loaf around the Nonoviches', doing little chores for Ella or smoking butts while listening to the BBC in bed. I became this hybrid of working journalist and the world's strangest couch potato. For two weeks I even upped my daily dosage of Zoloft to 300 mg, a hundred milligrams higher than the prescribed limit. I was trying to give myself a jolt, but it did nothing.

But then things at the Nonoviches' began to change, and then slowly so did I.

It had been a tough few weeks for everyone. While riding her bike to Old Town, Dina had almost been killed in a Serb mortar attack. Omar was certain to be called up into Juka's militia in two weeks. Winter was just around the corner, and with no windows or electricity, and with little left to burn, everyone was haunted by the vision of freezing to death. A sniper was also on the loose nearby, and a week earlier twelve kids from the neighborhood were killed, their teacher's head blown off, not sixty feet from the Nonoviches' apartment. With so much on their minds, the Nonoviches probably felt lucky that evening just to be together and all in one piece.

The night started off with Ella making coffee on the potbellied stove, while Dina and Omar sat on the floor, sharing a cigarette. As it was already past dusk, and there was, of course, no electricity, the only light in the apartment flickered off four candles. Outside it was unusually quiet, just a few random gunshots every now and then.

Any pretext of formality between Dina and Omar and myself had long since broken down. By then, both felt free to comment on my life and being at will. That night was no exception. After I filled everyone in on my day, kvetching liberally about how difficult it was to find a good story, Dina chimed in: "Maybe, John, you don't try hard enough. Harald finds stories all the time. He is a good reporter."

"Harald's a Commie."

"Maybe, but maybe you are too lazy," she added, nodding her head. "You should think of that."

"Well, I'm not gonna chase bullshit, Dina."

"Yes," Nino said. "John not lazy. Own rhythm, yes. But not lazy. He works smart."

"Thanks," I told him.

Then Omar added his two cents. "Works smart, Papa, yes, *like fat, sleeping bear!*"

"Whatever, dude," I said, blowing smoke his way. "And what's with you and these forest creatures, anyway? You're always calling me a furry bear, a wild boar, a mountain goat. And what the fuck is a *popok*?"

"A primitive," he declared. "A *popok* is a primitive, a simple villager. But do not worry, bear, you are too ugly to be a *popok*."

"Omar!" Dina shouted. "Please! Why must you be that way?"

"Don't worry, Dina," I said. "I don't take it personally."

"No, John, it's not that," she said. "It's true, you are fat and lazy, no? But my brother must learn not to be so rude."

She turned back to Omar, waved her finger, and worked him over in Bosnian. Before she could finish, there was a loud banging on the door. Nino held up his hand reflexively as if to say, "Be quiet," then got up to check it out.

After he opened the door, I heard him say something. Then some guy started talking. As usual, I couldn't follow exactly what was going on, but whatever was being said, it wasn't good. Dina looked worried, and Ella held her hand over her mouth. Moments later Nino returned to the living room with two soldiers in tow. They were about my age, mid-twenties: One was thin, scrappy-looking, like a sewer rat. The other one was a stocky, good-looking guy, a had-his-shit-together type. The front of his pants was soaked. There was a brief discussion before Nino asked Dina a question. She turned to me.

"John, what type is your blood?"

"O positive."

"Good," she said. "Their friend needs blood, John, a lot of blood. Can they have some of yours?"

"Of course."

Dina translated for the guys, and then after taking the Nonoviches' phone number, they left. It turned out that a young guy from the neighborhood was on the front lines that night, not four hundred yards from where we were sitting. It was quiet, so instead of taking a piss in his bunker, he sneaked out the back to relieve himself. As he was taking a leak, a Serb machine gunner fired a burst, severing the main arteries in both his legs. The stocky guy was his friend who had carried him off the line to a waiting ambulance—a VW Golf—soaking himself in blood in the process. When the ambulance returned, someone was going to call for me and then I'd be driven to the hospital to donate my blood as I was a universal donor.

Fifteen minutes later the phone magically rang, the first time that had happened since I moved in. Dina got it, nodding along with whatever was being said.

"They won't need you, John," she told me, after hanging up. "The soldier died on the way. But the guys say thank you anyway."

Omar paled, got up, and went to his room. Nino silently put his Bicycle playing cards in their box and went off to bed. Ella, wiping away a few tears with a baby blue hanky, helped Dina collect the coffee cups, empty the ashtrays, and puff the pillows. Then they went to bed as well, and so did I.

The next morning I got up late. If I hustled I could have made the press conference. But when I saw Ella, she didn't look so good. She held a photo in one hand and her ever-present baby blue hanky in the other. When she saw me, she blew her nose and sprang into action, fetching a bowl of *grah.* There was no use in saying, "Please, don't bother."

"*Nama pishnuk dabba,*" she said, sliding the bowl in front of me. I started eating, and a moment later she handed me the photo. It was a head shot of Omar.

"Good-looking kid," I said, giving it back.

"*Edin abba dabba. Moya Omar,*" she said, a few tears now dribbling out of her eyes. As I ate, she rubbed the photo between her thumb and index finger, just staring into it. Her nose was red, rubbed raw.

"He'll be OK, Ella," I told her.

Of course, she couldn't understand what I was attempting to communicate, but she seemed to get the idea that I was trying to offer comfort. Patting me on the shoulder, she walked into the living room, lit up a butt, and started flipping through a battered magazine. After I finished, I joined her. We sat in silence for a few minutes before she plopped the ancient periodical on my lap, pointing to a photo inside of a bowl of pasta, topped with marinara sauce, chunky style with liberal splashes of oregano and grated Parmesan cheese.

"*Pishcu matta, moya trobnik,*" she said, dreamingly.

"Yeah, looks *dobro?*"

"*Tribba, tribba,*" she said. "*Tribba i jank.*"

She tapped me on the shoulder, then got up and rummaged through a drawer underneath Nino's shooting trophies, muttering to herself. She stopped when she pulled out a big black photo album, the kind with gold trim. Taking a seat next to me, she opened it: all Nonovich family photos, happy Yugoslavs at play: skiing, on the beach, in a park. Then she got to the money shot. Sitting next to me there, she weighed maybe one forty, max. But here was a photo of her on the same sofa we were sitting on and she was easily a deuce sixty.

"Jesus," I said.

"Ahhh," she sighed. *"Chetnik barba dossonik."*

"Whoa, huh?" I said.

"Uh-huh," she answered, before turning to another photo of her as a slim teenager. She flicked her finger against it to make the point, *fuck that shit!* She laughed and then fell back into the couch, her eyes settling onto the ceiling. *"Moya pravo jesto blobnik: Lobdok. Trobdich. Novog. Puddich. Modock. Ah, criptich. Criptich, moya lubnik."*

I shrugged my shoulders, meaning, *I don't get it.* Whatever it was, it was important enough to break precedent. She took out an English/Serbo-Croatian dictionary.

For ten minutes she looked up words of food, sharing her pain by having me read the English translation: lobster, calamari, beef-steak, chicken, ravioli, pig's knuckle, leg of lamb. It went on and on. When she started to reminisce about pizza, she entered a sort of dream state. I swear to God the woman was not in that room, but off someplace in her past, feasting. It was contagious. I slipped away, too, returning to New York City and swooping down on an Original Ray's Pizza joint, before a bounty of melted cheese, pepperoni, mushroom, and crispy crusts. I'm drunk. My stomach's growling. The Mexican guy's about to take my order. I was almost drowning in my own saliva, and had to get out of there, fast.

"Shit. Sorry, Ella, but what time is it?" I asked, jumping up, pointing to my wrist.

"Devle, pole devle?"

"Fuck, I knew it. Sorry, but I gotta run," I told her, already making my way to the door. "Be back tonight. Early, though. *Pole shaest."*

"Pri machcu batta? Jesti?"

"Yeah, some bullshit interview. I gotta start writing this crap down, *nia dobro,* you know."

She nodded like she understood, but I was hoping this one time that she really didn't. At the door, she kissed me on both cheeks and then shoved me out into the hallway for another day in the field.

Once I got out of the building, I snapped into a brisk jog, making it to the PTT in a record five minutes. From there, I caught the Egyptian APC to the airport and hopped a return flight on a C-130 to the UN base in Italy. Once I was checked through security, I walked-ran up to the airport cafeteria, grabbed a plastic brown tray, and then hit the buffet. Before me lay trays of classic Italian meals: lasagna, chicken parm, eggplant, big meatballs, chunks of bread, bowls of soft butter, and chewy bowtie pasta.

I probably consumed close to eight thousand calories before I could take no more. It was a hideous display, biblical-size gluttony, complete with a giant sauce stain on my shirt. I waddled out of the cafeteria with my head down, with all the pride of a fallen junkie stumbling out of a crack house.

I caught the last aid flight back into Sarajevo that day, and by five-thirty I was back at the PTT. Fifteen minutes later, I tiptoed into the apartment. Thank God I didn't see Ella, but I wasn't alone.

"John," Nino called out from living room. "Is that you, my friend?"

"Yeah."

"Come in, sit, have coffee."

"Uh, can't right now, Nino. Got some work to do in my room. Freakin' headache."

"OK, but later you must," he said. "Work must come first, of course. See, I tell Dina, John not lazy boy. But please, later, come in, relax."

"Yeah, it's a bitch, Nino. But thanks."

I slunk into my room and rolled into bed, bloated in body and guilty in spirit. Never in my wildest fantasies when I was depressed did I think this was what I would be doing with myself in a war zone.

A week or so later, I returned from filing my radio spots and found a nice surprise waiting for me. In the living room was a handwritten note from Nino: Sabina Prevalack wanted to meet me at the Holiday Inn the next day at noon.

During my second week in Sarajevo, the Kukics had arranged for a "Lovely, Young Lady" to give me a tour of Old Town. Her name was Sabina and for her our outing was not just another day. Only a few weeks before, she had literally ventured into the city for the first time in a year. Like a lot of Sarajevans, she had been a shut-in, having spent the better part of thirteen months in her parents' basement trying to wait out the war, studying English and knitting sweaters.

I met Sabina at her parents' house in a part of Old Town called Balejesnica, high up in the hills just below Satso's front line. Our first stop on my tour back in August had been under a pine tree in their neighbor's backyard. "See that?" she had asked, pointing to a large mound of clay. The wooden tombstone gave it away.

"Whose is it?"

"Marcella's. My best friend from before war, since we were little girls. Everyone loved Marcella. Always got the best grades, the boys. I was jealous of her, you know."

She was staring into the mound as she spoke.

"It must have been tough," I said. "Losing a best friend like that. I really am sorry."

"Yes, it was terrible. She was killed by Serb grenade in first days of the war. She was so brave. But then tiny piece of metal go through her head. Small, like the tip of your finger. And, I think, how her? You know, she always had so much luck."

"Sorry."

"But then in war, suddenly she have bad luck, you know? And then, the day we bury her here, just after we finish, a big bomb fall on her grave. Again. Now she have the worst luck of anyone I know, Marcella."

"Mmmm."

"That day was my last day outside. If it could happen to Marcella, then I think, it could happen to anyone, no? Maybe me. But now, I see war not end. I must live. So let's go, I have many things I want to show you in my Sarajevo."

She wasn't kidding. We went everywhere that first day together, visiting sixteenth-century fountains, what was left of some famous mosques, good old Tito Street, the spot where Gavrilo Princip shot Archduke Ferdinand kicking off the First World War, the rubble of a boutique where she used to shop for shoes, and even Satso's café for a pop.

In the afternoon, she took me to a play in an old theater. With no electric lights, the stage was lit by candles and midway through the performance the Serbs starting shelling the area. When the actors continued on through the booming without a miscue, the packed house cheered. Soon after, Sabina took my hand. In the depths of my depression, if such a thing had happened I would have overanalyzed her gesture and ended up doing nothing. But with my brain now rebalanced on Zoloft, I squeezed her hand back.

After the play was over, we went for a stroll, Sabina pointing out this and that, soon ending up in a public square just down the street from Mort's morgue. As she was explaining why the tourists had loved the area, a bullet whizzed past our heads, smacking into the wall behind us. Before I knew it, I was hiding behind a kiosk in the middle of the square, but when I got my bearings I saw that I was alone out there. Everyone but me had bolted off the square, including Sabina, who was now standing in an alleyway, yelling, "Run, John, run. You must run." *Goddamn it,* I thought, feeling like rabbit on a rope. The wise thing would have been to hunker down for a few hours until the cover of dark, but that would have put a major strain on our date. After a minute or so, I took off. There was no second shot.

"*Ho!*" I let out when I got to her. "That was friggin' close, huh?"

"We have luck, you and me," she said, giving me a big hug. "Maybe sniper was drunk."

From there, we took the long way back to her place. Around seven-thirty we were nearing her neighborhood and we were both huffing and puffing pretty good, so we stopped in a tiny park that had an eagle's-nest view of the city. We sat under a tree at the edge for a long time, Sabina taking in the view, me pretending to. At some point, a firefight complete with tracers erupted on the slope of the mountain across the valley. Red, orange, and green pulses of light crisscrossed every which way, floating so slowly that it was hard for me to believe a person couldn't just jump out of the way. It was like watching a laser show at a planetarium. When it started to get chilly, Sabina snuggled up a little. Then I screwed it all up. I leaned over to smooch her but got a full cheek. If I had a rocket up my ass I would have lit it to get out of there.

"Oh, no," she said, flustered. "I thought . . ."

"No, no," I told her. "It's my fault. No. I'm a fuckin' idiot."

"No, I should have been clear," she said. "It is my fault. I like you, John, very much. You are simpatico."

"Thanks."

"But you and me, just friends. I would like that very much, if you want, of course, but only friends, you know?"

"Absolutely," I said, not meaning it. "That would be great."

"OK, so now let us just forget it."

But, of course, it doesn't work that way, in Bosnia or anywhere else. It became awkward, me trying to seem nonchalant while I knew she knew I had been scheming to take her clothes off. When we got back to her place, she taught me some Bosnian, gave me a chunk of bread, and put me to bed on a couch. The next morning I skipped the mandatory Bosnian coffee session and split. I thought for sure that was the last I was ever going to hear from Sabina. But now, almost two months later, here was Nino's note telling me to meet Sabina in the lobby of the Holiday Inn at noon that next day.

Arriving a little early, I parked myself in a red lounge chair with a good view of the back entrance. Around one o'clock, she finally walked in.

"I'm sorry, John," she said, giving me a big hug. "So difficult today to get here, all the guns."

I wanted to treat her to lunch in the hotel restaurant; it was a higher grade of gruel and usually it was even possible to obtain a slab or two of meat. We took a table in the front room, which was crowded with foreign reporters and other types: The boys and girls from the British newspapers were over there, along with some French reporters tasting wine. Susan Sontag, who was in town to direct the play *Waiting for Godot,* was lunching with a well-known British photographer. The air was thick with cigarette smoke and unregulated chatter at a decibel level well above what was typical anywhere else in the city.

"John, I wanted to see you because I have something important to show you," she told me, as we sat down. "I want you to meet some friends of mine, but you must have an open mind."

"Always," I said.

"But first, I must ask you a favor. Can we leave here, now?"

"Sure, but why?"

"I'm sorry. I know you want to help, be nice to me, but I feel very uncomfortable."

"Why?"

"Look at these people."

"What?"

"Look how they act. Treating waiters like servants. Look, they don't even look at them. It just makes me sad, that is all."

The waiters were gaunt, pale, even more so set against their green Holiday Inn uniforms. They looked like ghosts, serving foreigners lunch, careful to pour the wine over their left shoulders, forced to overhear their war stories.

"Let's go then," I told her.

We walked for an hour into the hills above Old Town, her arm linked in mine. Her friends' place didn't look like much: a one-story stone structure, it seemed more like a stable than a house. After knocking on a wooden door, a young woman, pretty and blue-eyed, perhaps a little older than me, opened it. She was dressed in a brown monk's robe, a saffron-colored rope tied around her waist. Obviously, she was happy to see Sabina. They hugged as I was introduced.

The woman led us through a small entryway and into a large room, which was neat and clean but had no furniture, only several multicolored pillows on the floor. She offered some tea and a snack, then disappeared through a back door as Sabina and I took a seat on the pillows. I could hear her talking to another woman through the door.

There were photos of old men in saffron robes on the wall, a headshot of George Harrison, as well as a painting of a young man on a mountaintop, arms wide open, looking up into a shaft of light. There was a large window along the outer wall. Like every other window in town, it was covered in plastic, but it was open, affording a great view of Sarajevo. Whatever the acoustics, the window seemingly sucked in the report of every gunshot in the valley.

"Here you go," the woman said when she returned, handing me a cup of tea and a ball of chocolate. As the woman sat down, two other young women came in and sat down as well. There were five of us now in the room, the focus squarely on me.

"My name is Shara, this is Bronka and Daniela. We are (she waved to the photos on the wall) followers of Hare Krishna, Our Lord."

"Really?"

"Oh, yes. Are you familiar with Hare Krishna?"

"I mean, a little, of course. Airports, Mr. George Harrison."

Shara laughed, then said, "Yes, but we are much more than that."

"I'm sure. I'm sorry, but I gotta ask something first."

"Of course," Shara answered.

"Where you from? You don't sound Bosnian."

"Oh, no. I'm German. Daniela is from Bulgaria, but Bronka is Sarajevan."

"How did you get caught in Sarajevo?" I asked.

"No. Not caught. We came to Sarajevo during the first months of the war. Back in 'ninety-two. Daniela and me, anyway. Of course, Bronka didn't have much of a choice."

"Are you nurses, or work with, you know . . ."

"No. It's more . . . You see, John, in our religion we believe in reincarnation. We also believe in higher states of consciousness. That is, the highest state a soul, as you might say, can achieve is Nirvana. It is sort of our heaven, when the soul achieves perfect freedom from the material world. That is what Our Lord, Hare Krishna, teaches us. We believe that you live your life over and over again until you gain enough wisdom to free yourself from the body, the physical world."

"Transcend?"

"Yes, John," she said. "Exactly."

"But why then did you come here?" I asked.

"In our religion, there are many steps to wisdom, to Nirvana. One of the most important is suffering, perhaps the most important. It can take many lifetimes to suffer enough. This war was just starting, and we realized if we can get to Sarajevo, the war, live here, then we can be through with the suffering in a year or two."

"Like a crash course," I said.

"Exactly."

Never a rubber truck when you really need one.

"Well, you picked the right place," I told her.

"We hope so," she said.

It took at least fifteen minutes, and me lying about having to get back to work, to get out of there. At the door, Shara gave me some literature and told me if ever, ever, I needed someone to talk to, "I'm always here for you."

"What did you think?" Sabina asked when we were out in the street.

"Don't take this the wrong way, Sabina, but I think your friends are nuts."

"Yes, some of it is strange but don't you find it interesting?"

"Honest? I mean, not really."

"You don't believe at all?" she asked, imploring me to find some strand of faith. "In the spirits, you know, powers you can't see? Religion? Astrology? Anything?"

"I don't know," I answered.

"What do you mean?"

"I mean, I don't know. It's kind of complicated."

"Of course, but you must believe in something?"

"Obviously," I said. Sabina's earnestness and her genuine concern for my well-being were touching. She was sweet, so I didn't want to tell her what I really believed: we're alone. She's alone. Nothing more, nothing less. There is no grand scheme. There is no master plan. Shit happens. The sooner you get that, the better off you are. But I didn't have the heart to say these things. "I guess, Sabina, I believe in life," was how I summed it up. Then, tired of all the heavyosity, I told her that I had things to do and needed to go. We hugged, promised to get together soon, but this time we parted company for good. A few months later, she slipped out of Bosnia. The last I heard she was a war refugee sharing a room with her brother in Bavaria and cutting hair.

It took a while to make it back to New City, but I finally arrived at the TV building around eight-thirty p.m. There, instead of heading straight home, I went up into the SAT Room where I was sure some of the American technicians working there were relaxing in front of the only working tube in the city. They were, and in search of a little levity and something familiar, I sat with them and watched episodes of *Mr. Bean, Cops,* and a *Seinfeld.* When I was done, it was past the citywide curfew but it was worth it because I felt better. Plus, I had been out after curfew before and nothing had happened.

The quickest route back to the Nonoviches' from the TV building was down a wide-open boulevard, a relatively safe stretch of Sniper Alley. There was little protection, but then again I wasn't crossing any front lines and there was little chance this way of stumbling on a nervous, trigger-happy neighborhood patrol. Except for a lone guard loitering in front of a bunker about a third of a mile down, I saw no one and heard nothing. Not even a distant gunshot, which was odd. Even the wild dog packs were nowhere to be seen.

I stopped in front of the TV building and lit a cigarette, seeing no need to rush things. As I smoked, I focused in on that lone guard down the road, using him as my canary. Three or four minutes later, he still looked as at ease as ever. I snuffed out my butt under my Timberlands and started out. I held my hands wide, palms up, trying to be as least threatening as possible. It was hard to tell in the dark if he was looking directly at me or just in my general direction, but when I got about halfway there I saw him look up the road to the north. And what he did next was unmistakable: he tucked his machine gun under his arm and bolted like a rabbit into his bunker. *One. Two. Three.* All at once, every assault rifle ever made started firing around me.

I hit the ground flat, trying to disappear into the pavement. *Oh my God. Oh Jesus Christ. Not now.* Jagged flashes of light were pulsating from the buildings. I peeked up but couldn't see anyone. Then I spotted a large metal pipe lying in the median. I began crawling to it, staying as low as I could. Then there was a whizzing and cracking over my head like supersonic killer bees hunting for prey. I froze, pressing the side of my face against the road, right eye staring at a square inch of pavement. Terrified, I envisioned chunks of my flesh being ripped off my back. I clung to that tiny patch of pavement for dear life. I became intimate with it. I talked to it, *Come on, man. Come on.* I tried to connect with it somehow, make it one with me.

I was alone and helpless, and that patch of macadam was my only friend in the world. Then I was suddenly blinded by light. I looked to the east and saw a car, its headlights lined up right on me, the perfect target. I had to move, so I scrambled hand over hand for the pipe. As I lay there, pushing myself up against it, I made all sorts of absurd promises to powers I didn't believe in. The gunfire hit a crescendo, then just as quickly it fizzled, one or two lone pops, then nothing.

For ten minutes, still lit up by the headlights, I didn't move a muscle. Only after the headlights died out did I work up the courage to stand up. I held my hands high above my head and started walking down the road toward that lone guard in his bunker, yelling, *"Don't shoot!"* When I finally got there and peeked inside, there was nobody.

It took a while to screw up my courage again, but I had to. Putting my hands over my head, I walked on to the Nonoviches', yelling, "Hello!" every twenty feet or so. By the time I got home, I hadn't seen a soul, living, wounded, or dead. As I clicked on my Maglite and headed up the stairwell, I felt myself come back into my body again.

When I got to the Nonoviches', I slipped the key into the lock as gently as I could, eased open the door, and tiptoed to my room. Taped to my door was a mock-up of a magazine cover, obviously the work of Omar. The faux magazine was entitled *The Fat American,* under which was a drawing of a fat, overly furry bear in a toga lounging on a couch, smoking. There was a column on the right featuring the title of this month's articles: "How to Stay Fat in a War Zone," "Big Bear Gives Big Interview," and at the bottom, "Bears Can Be Good People, Too." *Christ,* I thought, opening the bedroom door as quietly as possible.

"John, is that you, my friend?" I heard Nino call out from his room.

"Yes. Sorry, Nino."

"No, sorry," he said. "Too many guns tonight. Are you OK, my friend?"

"Yes, I'm sorry. I'm fine. Really. See you in the morning."

"Then good night, my friend," he told me.

"Laku noch," I said, closing the door behind me. Inside my

room I lit a candle by my bed, then lit a cigarette off it to calm down. My hands were shaking; I was still way too jumpy to sleep. Rolling into bed, I looked around for something to read myself to sleep with. On the floor, sticking out of the back pocket of my jeans, was the pamphlet that Shara had given me. It was a cartoon book, basically an Idiot's Guide . . . to Hare Krishna. There were a lot of drawings, one an exact replica of the painting I saw in the Krishna's crib earlier that day: a young man, alone on a mountaintop, gazing up into a shaft of light. I cracked a smile at their expense, the plain absurdity of it all. But then I thought, *Why are you laughing at them? Smug fuck. At least they're up-front about it.*

I tossed the pamphlet on the floor and curled up under the blankets. More than anything, I wanted to go unconscious, get to tomorrow, start over, but I couldn't because I was still far too soaked in adrenaline. Lying there, I tried to think of nothing, but a guilt took hold of me. My brain for the first time in a long time was not responding to directions. The Nonoviches were front and center in my thoughts. I believed Nino when he called me friend. He cared for me, and made me feel at home. They all did, even Omar. But what were they to me? *My friends?* Bullshit. They weren't my friends, they were part of my experience, "my amazing experience, man," just characters in my movie. I had a more intimate connection with that patch of pavement along Sniper Alley than with the Nonoviches or anyone for that matter. For the first time in nine months I could have checked off a few of those boxes for symptoms of depression.

ten

The SS *Dolphin*

The docks up ahead sounded dead. No hawkers hawking dope. No
dinking of metal drums. Even the drunken roar didn't reach this
far. I could only hear the water lapping against a seawall. It was
now just me and the night, the way I had grown to like it.

When I thought "docks," I pictured *On the Waterfront:* pea soup
fog, South American freighters, salty old bastards. But when I
arrived, I found the docks to be open, clean, well lit, all smooth
asphalt and modular warehouses topped with corrugated aluminum.
The place had the feeling of the loading dock behind Bloomingdale's.
But with nothing else left to explore in Nassau, I headed in, following the few shadows, peering through windows, jiggling knobs, generally working the place, searching for that certain something.

For forty minutes I cased the place before I found what I was
looking for: a behemoth of a cruise ship, the SS *Dolphin,* six stories
high, lit up like a city skyline and oozing adventure. I quietly slith-
ered into the shadows where the *Dolphin* rested against the pier.

I tried shimmying up the mooring line, but for the life of me
I couldn't get past the first rat collar. Finally, I dropped back down
onto the pier to catch my breath. I was stumped, but after watching

for a while, I noticed something about the lone officer manning the gangplank. He was standing well out onto the dock, leaving a ten-foot gap between himself and the entrance to the gangplank. If I could get in there while his back was turned, I would be home free.

I snuck in underneath the gangplank and squatted in the dark. A few minutes later, fate dealt me a royal flush in the form of two groups of tourists returning from a night out in port. They were all bombed, fumbling with their tickets and torturing the officer with liquored-up intimacy. When the officer cleared the first group to board and started working on the second, I came out from under the gangplank holding my wallet as if I had accidentally dropped it and slipped in behind the first group, following them up the gangplank. I waited for that bloodcurdling, "Hey, you!" but, mercy be, it never came.

When I reached the top of the gangplank, I was greeted by two officers, one I took to be the captain. "How was your night, sir?" he asked, politely.

"So far, so good," I said.

"Happy to hear it," he said, as I walked aboard. Twenty feet after entering the ship I slipped inside a disco.

Around six months before, after opening my father's questionnaire a black void had opened in my head and I became hyper-aware that I was somehow shut out from whatever it was that made other people tick. *What the fuck did I have do?* I had tons of friends, family that loved me, had accomplished things, but it meant nothing. *Why the hell did I feel so dead inside? I had tried so long and so hard to keep it together.*

It never occurred to me that I might be depressed because to me depression meant someone who had no fight left. To me, depression meant Mr. Cooley, that Craty kid, people swept away to a lonely place, people so far gone they just couldn't be saved. Yeah, I felt miserable. Yeah, I felt always alone, no matter what. Yeah, I felt empty inside. But I wasn't depressed. It was the dull-ass world around me that was the problem. I set out to find something more, somewhere, where I could feel alive and do something that felt good and right.

For weeks, I went out every night drinking, not exactly unusual for the fourth-biggest party school in the country according to *Playboy*. But, pretty quickly, I found that booze wasn't my thing. Getting loaded sure made me feel part of the world; it even stopped the compulsive ruminating in my head for a few hours. But it was too easy. For whatever reason, self-medicating with drugs and alcohol wasn't the answer for me. I was looking for a more liberating high.

By late October, I was slipping out of the college bars, walking the streets alone after midnight looking for that certain something. I strolled through the seedier parts of town looking for trouble but never finding it. One night, on one of my walks home, I came upon a mansion, one used for off-campus housing by upperclassmen. I sneaked inside and, as I made my way through the house, I was energized by the notion that if I got caught I would have to fight my way out of there. Two nights later, I went back and upped the ante by stealing a T-shirt. The next night I did the same, only at a different place. In a week, I had twenty or so T-shirts in my dorm room, which I handed out to anyone who wanted one.

Soon I branched out, taking more and more risks: chewing and screwing from every restaurant in town; stealing steaks from the local supermarket; breaking into a frat house, cadging a keg of beer that I rolled back to my dorm and shared with my suite mates. The funny thing was I had, by then, built up a notoriety on campus—and I liked it. When you're eighteen and male, being called a madman is kind of a compliment. Some guys even tried to copycat my little petty crime spree, but they never really pulled it off because they were doing it for kicks. I was doing it just to feel alive.

The problem was that, like with any drug, I built up a tolerance for danger, and this meant I had to up the ante every time out. I pinched a car, was arrested for fighting, and broke into the local post office and stole two mailmen's jackets. Only when I was busted that February with a ten-ounce sirloin shoved down my pants at the Stop & Shop did I slow down. It wasn't because I saw the error of my ways. It was because I decided to keep my powder dry until bigger things came along.

That spring break I took my game on the road. I was the only freshman who made the A-side rugby team, and the guys who ran it organized a trip to the Bahamas over spring break so we could go down there and get spanked by some of the local clubs. I had a few bucks left over from working construction over winter break, so I had the cash to go. It was the mid-eighties, the age of *Miami Vice,* drug lords, and Caribbean cocaine cartels. I was already bored shitless with Burlington, so there sounded like no better place in the world for me than the Bahamas.

That's how I found myself on the SS *Dolphin* that night. I was looking for action, big action. My immediate goal had only been to get on the ship and see what would happen. Come four o'clock that morning, I was still safely ensconced in the disco, no one aboard any the wiser. Pushing my luck a little further, I swung my legs up on the couch and caught some shut-eye.

The next morning I was awakened by the sound of a vacuum cleaner. It was the morning cleanup crew, who completely ignored me. After walking out on deck, I grabbed a complimentary cup of tea and a few crackers from a buffet table. Then there was an announcement, "Attention! All guests need to depart the ship as we will be leaving port in twenty minutes. All ashore who are going ashore!" And that's when I decided it wasn't going to be me.

Sipping my tea by the railing, I watched Nassau wake up. My fellow spring breakers, who were walking the streets in groups of five or six, stood out a mile. Even from up there on the ship, I could hear them hooting and hollering. That spring break world, the same one I had just been in, looked so small, dull, predictable. Watching those little shits run around down there, skimming by the upscale boutiques, all excited, hustling toward the next "amazing experience," I pitied them. Life could be so much more exciting if they just grabbed it by the balls.

Forty minutes later, the ship was pushed out to sea by two tugboats, and pretty quickly the Bahamas started fading in our wake. I had a hundred and twenty bucks in my pocket, the clothes on my back, and absolutely no clue where we were headed. Portugal? Brazil? Cuba? Who knew? But that was the great part, the key. As I stood out there on the bow, I had a peace in my chest I hadn't known since . . . since I had been a kid. I felt alive, part of the world again, because I had no idea where I was heading. Once again everything was possible.

eleven

Don't Be Cruel

In early November, Mort (the guy who had taken me in that first day) had his foot blown off in a mortar attack. Just before it happened, I had a chat with him in the Holiday Inn, where I had gone after delivering a food package to the Kukics'. By then I knew enough about the other freelancers to realize that most them were actually in Sarajevo for the same damn reasons I was. We couldn't make it in the everyday world and had come to the edge looking for something more. I knew this not because they told me—that would have broken the spell—but because nearly all of them were like me, middle-class, from a suburb of a major city. Nearly every one of them carried along books like mine; books such as *Dispatches, Homage to Catalonia, Seven Pillars of Wisdom, On the Road,* books that more than hinted that there was a better, more exciting world out there than the ones they had left behind.

I never saw Mort's book collection, but my guess was that he had one, too. We had hooked up again and saw each other occasionally for a drink. Once, in the Holiday Inn, I had started to bitch and moan to him about how lost I felt, how bored I was with Sarajevo. He told me he had just returned from a sojourn to Kabul,

Afghanistan, a place that was rocketed almost every day, and there was total chaos in the countryside. Sarajevo may have been labeled "The Most Dangerous City on Earth" but Kabul was the true titleholder. What's more, there were hardly any reporters working out of there. Or so we believed. It was wide-open. And before he left, he even gave me tips on how to get in there, set up shop, who to contact once on the ground. Before he had even stepped out the door, I was energized again. It was my old pattern reasserting itself, even though I was medicated: there was somewhere else to go, even farther out, and from what Mort had said, Afghanistan was what Sarajevo was meant to be.

Before I could do anything about Kabul, I had to first finish this gig I had scored with MTV News. I was to produce and direct a feature piece on Bosnia. My first story idea was to cover an underground rock scene in the Serb stronghold of Knin where bands took the stage in fatigues, playing punk rock stuff about massacres and gang rapes. They used AK-47s as percussion instruments, and I pitched it as sort of a CBGB scene, only with the bands heavily armed. *Irresistible.* But after a little research I got the sense that these guys didn't just sing about massacres; they had probably taken part in one or two. I just got a bad vibe about it, envisioning my head being kicked around a jackbooted mosh pit, so I went with Plan B instead: *A Day in the Life of Dina Nonovich.* Not so cutting-edge, but Dina was nineteen, pretty, smart, and spoke excellent English. She was someone MTV's target audience could relate to.

The morning of the shoot I didn't have a chance to talk to Dina before filming. When I got up she was already scrubbed down and putting on the final touches in front of the hall mirror. She had grown up watching MTV and intuitively knew what they were looking for. Dina didn't have a lot of funk; she was more class president than hip slacker, but she was trying her best to add a dash of groove to her look. Like many kids in Sarajevo, Dina always wore a bandana tied around her neck that could be used as a tourniquet in case she was wounded. When I saw her that morning, that was the fashion accessory she was working on.

I left the apartment at about seven-thirty as I had a lot to do: pick up the local crew I had hired; buy three gallons of gas on the black market for the crew's car; meet with a shady moneychanger to convert my dollars to the preferred deutsche marks so I could pay the crew; and finally affix the nifty little MTV News cubes to my microphone. By nine-thirty we were ready to shoot the first stand-up. The idea behind that first shot was for Dina to introduce herself and give the viewer a little background on the war. When I told her what to do, she balked.

"That's stupid," she said. "I'll feel stupid. John, this may not be important to you, but it's important to me. I'm out here, you're not. MTV has a certain style. They film their reportages differently, cut here and there. Me standing still will look stupid."

"Dina, I know it's MTV, but it's still MTV for God's sake. I mean, as long as you don't throw up on yourself . . ."

"See, you're the director and you think like that. I knew it. I knew you didn't know what you were doing."

"Mary and Joseph, why me? Can't you just . . ."

"OK, let's go," she said, nodding to the cameraman. "But remember, I gave you a chance, John."

It took a few minutes for her to get comfortable, but after four takes she nailed it. More than satisfied, I called it a wrap and we piled into the car and raced down Sniper Alley to the location of the next shot, a small intersection near Old Town where Dina was going to run through a fake sniper trap. As we were setting up, a guy about my age rolled up. His name was Ibra-something, but I knew enough of his story to know he was really a palace coup on a bicycle.

"John, this is my friend, Ibrahim al-Ibrahim," Dina said. "He will be our director from now on."

Ibrahim al-Ibrahim. Born into privilege in Tripoli, a diplomat's son, boarding school in Switzerland, university in France, film school in London, and he could converse on any topic in six languages. Unfortunately for Ibrahim, he had married a Bosnian and found himself trapped in Sarajevo, a holder of one of the world's most useless passports: Libya. He tried escaping once but was taken prisoner by the Serbs. In an ironic twist, he managed to escape them by dashing back across the front lines into Sarajevo.

My initial reaction was to agree. Ibrahim had some idea of what he was doing, and I didn't. To save a little pride, I didn't roll over right away. When I finally acquiesced, we agreed to share the director credit while Ibrahim did the actual work.

"John, I'm sorry," Dina said, obviously relieved. "But it's necessary that someone knows what they're doing."

Ibrahim's effect on the shoot was immediate. Dina was more comfortable, the crew was energized, the pace quickened, and I secretly was relieved. I was in good hands. But as the shoot wore on, and we moved from location to location, I became uneasy. It wasn't Ibrahim or Dina, or the crew, it was everyone else. The closer we got to the center of town the more the MTV News cube acted as sort of emotional flypaper, drawing an ever increasing amount of venom from the folks watching. When Dina would ask someone what they thought about the war, they would almost invariably say, "Fuck you and fuck MTV, too." Dina, ever earnest, pressed on, trying to get people to talk, but few would. It got hard to watch, Dina holding up the microphone, bracing herself for the invective sure to come. By the time we reached Obus, an underground art gallery, her attitude had changed: she had left behind the excited girl she had been in the morning and had taken on the cynicism of the crowd.

The last shoot of the day was a jam session Dina had organized with her guitarist boyfriend, Laylo, and some of his army buddies. No doubt the best shoot of the day, it included bombs falling in the streets outside, the stage lit by candles, the off-duty soldiers playing unplugged. Their music was heartfelt, young men facing death while playing in tune, perfect for MTV. But like the rest of the city, they knew they were being exploited. At some point during the session, the lead singer grabbed the microphone with two hands and screamed, "Fuck you America, wherever you are!" Like everyone else in the room but me, Dina hooted and clapped.

When I found out it was twenty minutes past the contractual end of my time with the crew, meaning I was now paying overtime, I stepped forward and called out, "That's a wrap. Thanks everybody."

The drummer yelled, "Fuck you!"

"Great job today," I replied. "Thanks everyone."

Half an hour later, we were all back in the car racing down Sniper Alley at ninety miles an hour. Up front in the passenger seat, Dina seemed no worse for wear but I knew this had not been a good day in the life of Dina Nonovich.

By then I had known Dina for almost three months. She was the straightest of arrows, now forced to live in a world where straight arrows got bent. It was almost impossible to remain good, decent, and innocent in an irrational, upside down, and inside-out place like Sarajevo, but she kept on trying: working two jobs without pay; studying old textbooks by candlelight to better herself; doing chores for her family; keeping up friendships and falling in love. Despite every reason not to, Dina kept living, never complained, and never lost faith. She kept planting seeds in a desert and for someone like me, who had walked out of paradise because it wasn't enough, being around Dina was uncomfortable. Dina was a constant reminder not only of what I left behind but my utter inability to make it work, before the Zoloft and even after. Dina made me feel like I wasn't running to something but rather running away. Although I never meant it, I tainted her with a bit of cynicism that day. Watching her stare out the windshield into nothing as we raced down Sniper Alley that evening, I wished I was a better person.

A few days later, New City received a few hours of electricity. You didn't need to see the lightbulbs flick on to know it had arrived. When it kicked in, a roar went up in the neighborhood, as loud as a soccer stadium. Suddenly people trapped in the Dark Ages could vacuum, iron, listen to music, and watch TV. Dina and Omar invited me over to a friend of theirs for a little TV.

As we sat on their friend's bed, she turned on the television: MTV Europe. No one said anything, but all of us, I think, were secretly hoping to see our footage. Instead a Nirvana video came on, *Teen Spirit,* Kurt Cobain dressed like Bobby from the Brady Bunch.

"Look how he dresses," Omar said, blowing smoke at the TV. "So ugly."

"It's grunge, stupid," I told him. "It's cool now."

"I don't care," he answered. "It's still ugly."

No matter how many times I went through this ritual, I always found it bizarre. Outside, people were shooting at one another as we watched TV. Only hundreds of yards away, genocidal maniacs were scheming to kill everyone in that room because they thought they weren't like them. The disconnect between the videos, the hipper-than-hip VJs, the Pepsi commercials, and the reality of Sarajevo always blew my mind.

"John, I must ask you something," Dina said.

"Sure."

"Do all American kids dress like that now?"

"I guess so."

"So strange. Like children. You Americans are so strange to us."

"And ugly," Omar added.

After the video, a good-looking German VJ came on, updated the audience on what was to come, and then broke for commercials: jeans, cars, that type of thing. Then Bono, the lead singer from U2, appeared, sitting on a wooden bar stool. "I know some of you out there in Sarajevo get electricity for a few hours and may be able to see me right now . . . (Cut to camera two) . . . I want to tell you that a lot of us out here haven't forgotten about you . . . (Cut to camera three) . . . You're not alone . . ."

"Fuck you," Dina spit, the first time I had ever seen her so angry.

"Bono, you're so cool," Omar sneered.

"Turn it off," Dina said, disgusted. "Just turn it off."

Their friend clicked off the TV.

"You want to help? Come here, come here like you promised," Dina said to the now blank screen. "Otherwise, shut up."

I thought Bono's heart was in the right place, but sitting where we were sitting, it did come across as slick and self-serving, just more cheap talk. As the others continued to cut into Bono, I watched them. I knew why they were doing it, they had every right to, but still it was ugly. The man was just trying to help. Then I thought of my mother and remembered for the first time something she had made me promise her before I left for Bosnia back in June, one of those crazy, not-tied-to-anything-practical favors only a mother could ask. A guilt had taken hold of me, and then these words started rising up out of me, like an air bubble racing up a water cooler.

"I'll help you," I heard myself say.

"What?" Dina asked, sharply.

"I said, I'll help you."

"What do you mean, help?"

"I'll get you out of here."

"Sarajevo? John, please. No one gets out of Sarajevo."

"I'll do it," I said.

"John, don't be cruel. Really. You shouldn't promise things you can't do."

"Dina, I swear. I'll get you out of here. Omar, too."

"And then what, John? Refugees?"

"No, I'll send you home to America, get you into university."

"Really?" Omar asked, suddenly wide-eyed.

"Absolutely, buddy."

"Don't listen to him, Omar. John, stop," Dina said. "Just stop."

"Trust me, Dina. I said I'll do it, and I will."

twelve

Cuckoo's Nest

Instead of Cuba, Portugal, or South America, the SS *Dolphin* pulled into the port of Miami. Although I had never been there, it was too familiar to work any magic. It seemed as dull, flat, and senseless to me as Burlington. With the extra money I had won at the blackjack table, I flew back to the Bahamas and hitched a ride from the airport into Nassau. I had been MIA for three and a half days.

Because of my reputation for wandering off from the crowd, I found when I reunited with my friends that no one had even suggested maybe going to the Bahamian police. Over some beers, I filled them in on what had happened, only I changed one key fact: I told them that after sneaking aboard the *Dolphin* I passed out and woke up at sea, in essence turning the trip into a drunken mishap, a frat prank. To tell the whole truth, to say that I was consciously searching for something way beyond the bounds of normalcy, was way too big a risk. I wanted to be thought of as crazy. Not *crazy*. No one, really, had a hint of who I was. Or how badly I was in need of something.

• • •

I barely got out of my freshman year a free man. I was feeling pretty terrible most of the time and the only way out was extreme action. After another fight, I had been arrested again, and in the spring I had the state police and the FBI all over my ass for a bomb scare that cleared out half the campus. It got to the point where I stopped going to class and smoked dope all day, spending my remaining hours reading up on the French Foreign Legion just in case I had to go on the lam.

But when I ultimately made it back home that summer and walked through our front door, I immediately snapped back into my old role—the guy who was alive and well and in love with life. It was like a scene out of a Campbell's Soup commercial: My parents hugged me, and my older brother, Quentin, helped me with my luggage. Everyone smelled of Dial soap. Two of my uncles, who lived on either side of us, came over. We gathered in the kitchen around the big butcher-block table, and over coffee and bagels I filled them in on my year, a complete fantasy right out of a Jimmy Stewart movie: late nights at the library; A-side rugby against Dartmouth; taking in foreign films and the changing of the leaves; the simple pleasure of real maple syrup; ski weekends with friends at Sugarbush.

But spouting those lies had a strange effect on me. On the one hand, I felt like a dirt bag. I had let myself down and, more important, I had let them down. I had spent the past year pissing on all the advantages I had been given. I had not gotten better. All the old problems were still running rampant. On the other hand, I found that just by painting that fantasy picture of this well-adjusted, positive-thinking Joe College kind of guy, and seeing everyone in that room just accept it as natural, I felt better. I experienced a moment of warmth, acceptance, even though I knew it was all bullshit.

There was only one hiccup that summer—when my grades arrived. I tried everything to get to them first, but my mom was quicker. I knew she found them just by looking at her when I got home from work. "What are they?" I asked, trying to appear upbeat.

"What do you think they are?" she asked back.

"I'm guessing B-pluses," I answered. "But econ was tougher than I thought."

"Well, you'll be happy to know that you have achieved a 2.2 GPA and have completely thrown away your future. Congratulations, John," she said. "There's no chance now of ever getting into Harvard Law School."

Harvard Law? I thought. *Holy shit, lady, at best I'm shooting for the French Foreign Legion here.*

"You had no right to open my mail, you know."

"Oh, really," she said, tearing up the grade sheet into confetti, tossing it on the floor, then stamping on it for good effect. "Well, there's your mail and that's where it belongs."

The self-loathing I felt that night fueled my major attempt to transform myself that summer. I was determined to become that guy they thought I was, once and for all.

I got a job in construction, gutting old houses in town and rebuilding them, inside and out. I went on a strict protein diet and worked out each night after work at the Excalibur Gym. I broke myself down through sweat and blood, and was exhausted at the end of each day. And no matter how tired I was, in order to get up the enthusiasm for the next day, I resorted to an old trick: Rocking. Every night I lost myself in that trance and pictured myself out there, somewhere in the near future, effortlessly part of the world again. I convinced myself that all I had to do to make it happen was stick to the straight and narrow.

That fall I made the dean's list. Then I made it again. Then again. And again. Later I won two prestigious internships with United States senators. Gone was the shoplifting, breaking and entering, and wandering off nights looking for that certain something. Of course, I still felt unnaturally isolated, unusually alienated, as if I was stuck watching life through thick glass instead of participating in it like everyone else, but as usual I kept that to myself. I just kept plugging along knowing that come graduation, if I kept my grades up and remained viable, I could finally start to live. I would feel better then, for sure. Finally, it would all be okay.

There were hard days along the way, usually sunny days, perfect afternoons when all my friends would be out playing softball or driving down to Lake Champlain to barbeque and get loaded. I went along usually because I had no choice. People sought out my company because I was funny—good, easygoing company—and sometimes I did actually have to accept the occasional invitation. To say no to a trip to the lake on a sunny Friday when there was nothing else to do was too weird and brought up too many questions. I didn't want anyone to get wise to me. But I had to counterbalance those social outings and get the alone time I needed to recharge. Rocking was pretty much impossible in a fraternity house full of guys with babes always coming in and out. Instead, I took up jogging. Strapping on a Walkman, cranking up the volume to full, usually at night, the worse the weather the better, I would run eight, eleven, sometimes fifteen miles out into the farm country that surrounded Burlington. By my senior year, I was doing it so often that I could cover thirteen miles of hilly terrain in an hour and twenty minutes. But I didn't care about my mile split. I wasn't doing it to get in shape. It was the only way I had to feel remotely alive until that magic point at graduation when I knew I just would. This time, really, had to be the change.

In the spring of 1990, I turned in my greatest performance. They should have given me the Oscar because the difference between who I was pretending to be (Mr. Normal) and who I really was (a desperately alone and hollowed-out shell of a human being) had never been so great. But as graduation neared, I did what everyone else did: I partied hard with my friends, tied up academic loose ends, handed out my résumé to the corporate recruiters, and booked hotel rooms for my family for graduation weekend. The whole time I was doing so, however, I knew it was a sham. I was just buying myself time until I was awarded my diploma and could skip out for good. Not just Burlington, college life, but the whole damn shebang, again: all my friends, my past, my family, everything. I was looking for a new world altogether.

But then came the ceremony, that magic juncture, and instead of feeling transformed, I felt more isolated, more alien, more empty inside than ever. And I realized that if I didn't do something drastic and soon, I just might be stuck on the outside of life forever. I was living a meat-locker-cold existence I couldn't bear very much longer. I was aware that other kids heading out into the real world also had certain trepidations and a sense that they didn't know who they were. I knew I had a big problem on my hands, but never once did I think even the word *depression*. To me, it was the life I was leading, a life in serious need of an overhaul. I wasn't sick. I wasn't different.

To this end, I toyed with several ideas of what to do after graduation to break away completely from my past. I could (1) work on a fishing trawler in the Bering Strait; (2) join the Forest Service and fight fires out west; (3) enlist in the French Foreign Legion. But the more I planned and fantasized, the less appealing each alternative became. Whatever I chose, you see, inevitably narrowed my range of possibilities. I finally settled on just going to Europe after graduation, not as a backpacker on the Grand Tour, but someone in search of a completely new identity, a new life I could call my own.

The day after I got my diploma I drove out of Burlington secure in the knowledge that soon I would be leaving behind all I had known and starting over from scratch in Europe. On July 15, 1990, with graduation gifts in hand and some money I had saved waiting tables, I flew to Germany to begin my new life.

I knew I was screwed as soon as I stepped off the plane in Düsseldorf. Just like back in high school when I looked to college to perform some miracle, I thought just by setting foot in Europe—this completely new place—I would feel different, at least more hopeful. But I was the same lost, miserable bastard who had gotten on the plane at JFK eight hours earlier. I thought I had no choice, so I kept going, disappearing into Europe to find my way.

My only genuine interaction with others on that European trip took place during the two weeks of Oktoberfest, when Munich shut down to get wasted along with thousands of foreigners in these gargantuan beer tents. On a typical day, I would arrive by noon, have my five or six quarts of beer, and then cruise the crowd looking for a fight. And as the tents were filled with mostly drunk young guys, there were usually several options available. The Australians pretty much got it; they understood that my anger was nothing personal. They were also the kind of guys you'd have a beer with afterward. The Irish were into it, too, but were more apt to fight to the death, a little more of a commitment than I was looking for. The Japanese were really bombed and looked promising, but were impossible to get to as they were locked away up in the VIP balconies. But the Turks were the ones. When I wanted that special rush, I would saunter over to the roasted chicken booth, openly start gnawing on a leg without paying, and wait while some pissed off Bavarian summoned the Turkish security guards. Often seven to a team, we would go at it hard, me trying to inflict as much damage as I could on one while absorbing the kicks and punches from the other six. Not exactly a recognized form of therapy, but at least during those melees, my mind was off my troubles.

Alas, getting wasted and gouging Turks with chicken bones was no way to go through life, but history threw me a bone when Saddam Hussein invaded Kuwait. I had seen *Platoon* many times back in college, and remembered that final scene, as the now wiser, turned-on, changed-forever, even hip-with-black-folk Charlie Sheen character flies off into the sun, weeping, and says, *"It is our duty now to teach others what we know."* If war could change Charlie Sheen, it sure as hell would change me. In October, when war looked certain, I flew back home to join the army. The day after I got home I drove down to the recruiting office in Hempstead.

"And none of that peacekeeping crap, either," I told the recruiter.

"But you understand, I can't guarantee you'll get to the Gulf in time for the war," he said.

"I know," I told him. "But if you had to put a number on it, percentagewise, what are we looking at? Fifty-fifty?"

It took me another five minutes or so to pin him down, but he finally put my chances of making the war at about 15 percent. A 15 percent shot at the possibility of a complete transformation? "Where do I sign?" I told him as he explained that it would take three weeks for my induction to become official.

Up to this point, I had been hiding from my family my desperate search for some other life. To them, I had gone to Europe on one last fling before hooking into some broker job down on Wall Street. But I couldn't just enlist in the army without telling them, so I broke the news to them late that night while they were in bed watching *The Honeymooners*.

"*What?*" my father yelled after I got to the good part.

"Yeah. Army. *Infantry*," I repeated.

"JOANNE!" he roared instinctively, although she was lying there right next to him.

"Why, John?" my mom asked, calmly.

"Because it's not fair," I said. "I've been blessed, and I can't sit back and let others do the dirty work. I would just feel too guilty."

"So you believe it's something you need to do?" she asked.

"Exactly," I answered.

"JOANNE!" my dad shouted once more, before taking a deep breath. "All right, hold on here. Let me say this. The military's all fine and good, John, but I don't get it. I mean, you never once . . . Do you have any idea? Jesus Christ, this is crazy."

"Well, wait, Art," my mom interrupted, patting him on his belly. "Let's just hear what he has to say first."

"Well, there's really no more to say. I got three weeks before basic."

"I'm sorry, but this is nuts," my dad said.

"Well, *I'm sorry,* but it is what it is," I said. "But please, don't tell anyone 'til I'm gone, all right? I just don't feel like explaining things."

For the first time I was stepping out from behind the mask I had been wearing for ten years. Suddenly enlisting was not something the guy I had been pretending to be would be desperate enough to do. No one in my family bought the idea that I was doing it for my country. They knew I was doing it for myself, and it was dawning on them, finally, that there was something big missing in me that I was looking to fill, something they were only now sensing wasn't there.

My parents were on the phone with my uncle James before I was halfway back to my room. One of the owners of Leo's and a Vietnam vet, he was one of those guys who had that golden touch when it came to living. His nickname had been Captain Creamy because he was so smooth. The next day I had to walk down to Leo's to have a chat with him.

"So, you want to go to the Gulf?" he asked as soon as I got there.

"Yeah."

"It's not going to happen, you know that?"

"What do you mean?"

"I mean, Kuwait is not Vietnam. No jungles. It's a desert there, nowhere for them to hide. Once it really starts, it's going to be over in a week."

"Really?"

"Yeah, really. And then you're going to find yourself digging ditches in Kansas for two years."

I stood there mute, embarrassed, and crushed. I believed my uncle.

"Look, if you want to help, do something," he said. "Aunt Sue and I are thinking of working with Habitat for Humanity. If you want, we can all do it together."

"Yeah, that would be great," I lied. *Habitat for Humanity?*

But that was it for the Gulf. My visions of combat were quickly eviscerated. Far worse was the fact that my secret, my instability, was out for all to see. Or so I imagined. Panicked, I scrambled back to my old mask as fast as I could. I tried to convince myself that everything would be fine once I landed a normal job and worked my way into a normal life. I simply had to accept things as they were. A week or so later I called the contacts I had made through my senate internships and arranged some job interviews. With zero sense at this point of who I really was, the following week I fingered a guy in a Brooks Brothers catalog—a totally together-looking young man-on-the-go type—and appropriated his dress and winning attitude. The next day, with my power rep tie around my neck, my wingtips polished to a perfect sheen, my résumés in my briefcase, I came down from my attic bedroom ready to drive to D.C. On the way out the front door, I ran into my mother.

"Wow! You look great," she said.

"Ma, I'm not a chick."

"Come on, now, don't be so touchy," she told me. "You know what I'm saying. Don't worry about a thing. You're going to do wonderfully today."

"I'm not worried."

"I know," she said, patting me on the shoulder. "It's only that I know you're going to do great. You're doing the right thing, John."

"I know."

Then I kissed her good-bye, walked out to the family Acura, dialed in the I-man on the radio, and took off. After picking up a coffee at Hoffman's Deli, I drove to the Southern State Parkway and soon was cruising along in the middle lane, just as planned. It was a little after nine a.m. . . .

It was almost five p.m. when I pulled into our driveway. I was home a good three hours early, but even so my mom was still out on the front stoop before I had switched off the engine. She was smiling, expectant. I found it hard to look at her, so I turned away and pretended to fumble with my briefcase. I could hear her through the window, calling out, "So how did it go?"

I had already decided to tell the truth, because I didn't have the fight left in me to lie anymore. I never made it to D.C. In fact, I never made it out of New York, and I wasn't sure how the hell it happened, either. It started when I got on the Interboro Parkway instead of the Belt, which fed me into the heart of Brooklyn. Once I was on those streets, I kept driving, looking for a way back to the parkway, only to find myself eventually in Queens. After that, it was the Bronx, then back to Queens, then Brooklyn again. Not only didn't I know where I was going, I couldn't remember how I got where I was. I was so fucking lost in my head that I couldn't concentrate for ten seconds on the world outside. Twice, I found myself even going the wrong way down a one-way street. Around one, I made one last push to get to D.C., but somehow I ended up in Manhattan, even cruising at one point straight past my dad's office. I knew somewhere in there he was going about his day, dictating to his secretary, butting heads with his partners, but on the inside he had his fingers tightly crossed for his kid, the one whom he had never had to worry about, who at that very moment was a zombie cruising by on the street below.

When I finally got out of the car and looked my smiling mother in the face, I was overcome with this guilt. I was about to open up a nightmare for her, one I had been certain she was never going to have to see.

"Sooooo? How did it go?" she asked.

"Ma, I never got there."

"What do you mean?" she said, checking the car for damage.

"No, I didn't hit anything. I got lost, Ma. I never made it out of New York."

"What do you mean, 'lost'?" she asked.

"Ma, I mean I think there's something wrong," I mumbled, staring at my feet. "I mean, really wrong."

thirteen

The King Cobra

Offering to help Dina and Omar was an incredible turning point for me. Looking back, I realize it was the first time since I started taking Zoloft—the first time since I was twelve years old, actually—that I was able to take my eyes off my own troubles and focus on someone else. This was a radical departure for me. The depression had buried me inside myself: the problems I'd been obsessed with were always my own. But here I was, actually coming up out of my head long enough to realize that there were other people in dire straits. I'd promised to save these kids and, what's more, give them a fresh start in America. Now I had to live up to my words.

My initial rescue plan for Dina and Omar was long on lofty goals and short on details: I'd get the kids out of Bosnia, find them a nice place to stay in Italy or Croatia, secure them scholarships in the United States, get them visas to America, and then send them off to their new lives. But the first step, getting Dina and Omar through the siege lines surrounding the city, would be the hardest. Or so I figured. The typical method of escaping Sarajevo at the time, for those frightened and desperate enough, was to simply make a break for it across the siege lines. Mort, who has been known to take a photograph, had actually managed to capture one of the war's truly iconic images just before I had first arrived in the city. It was of two lovers, a Muslim and a Serb, who had been shot dead on a bridge trying to flee Sarajevo. The photo was dubbed "Romeo and Juliet" by the international press, and was an indelible, heartbreaking reminder of the dangers of simply taking flight across the lines.

Some people had made it, but unfortunately, 99.9 percent of the city was surrounded by Serb troops, who were likely to rape, torture, imprison, enslave, or just murder those they caught making this attempt. There was no way I could subject Dina and Omar to this deadly lottery.

There was, however, one small gap in the siege lines—the airport, which was controlled by the French Foreign Legion, who had agreed with the United Nations not to let any Sarajevans use the place as a means of escape. But, after dark, when most of the French were asleep, Sarajevans at the end of their ropes would crawl out of the rubble and sneak under the barbed wire and over the minefields at the airport. When the time got right, they started sprinting across the tarmac toward a small Bosnian-controlled village on the other side. But the French, being the French, had the nasty habit of switching on giant searchlights when the runners were midway, silhouetting them like ducks in a shooting gallery for the Serb snipers lurking outside the perimeter of the airport. Come sunrise, the French would roll down the runway in APCs and harvest that night's human roadkill.

To be a Sarajevan at this time was to be a pawn in a game where only the Serbs were being up front. *(Brother, believe me, I only want you dead!)* The United Nations, which professed sympathy for the people of Sarajevo, was also, in the name of objectivity, conspiring with the Serbs to keep the siege going, the French at the airport being Exhibit A. And the Bosnian government, working the world stage to garner support, also had a vested interest in keeping their own citizens trapped: the more suffering inflicted for the media, the better the public relations war would go for them.

I concluded that to get the kids out, without getting them killed and breaking their parents' hearts, we needed to go the legit route, which started with actually obtaining passports for them. This wasn't a simple formality in a country that was not fond of issuing passports to their citizens. Getting a passport was barely possible *if* you made a tremendously convincing case.

Sarajevo didn't have gas, electricity, cars, public transportation, firewood, food, or even money. But the city still managed to find itself ass deep in bureaucrats. Like termites to wood, they collected in the gloomy, Kafkaesque, Habsburg-era office buildings, where they pased their time smoking and playing cards. Going in there with business to do was like entering a DMV from hell. These charmers were pretty up-front about the fact that they were there to bust balls.

In the two weeks following my offer to help Dina and Omar, I lived in a sea of passport paperwork: residency certificates, military records, birth certificates, school certificates, transcripts, attestations, medical records. Everything had to be translated and covered in stamps, each stamp requiring a hard currency fee. At first I tried to do the work on my own but it was impossible because I barely knew the language. So Dina and Omar took the lead in gathering the right documents and slugging it out with the bureaucrats.

It was strange watching this train I had actually set in motion begin the process of trying to chug out of the station. I had a lot of nervous moments but, for once in my life, I was blessed with a surprising faith that we were going to accomplish what was required. There was no rational reason to believe this, but I knew in my bones, as they say, that everything would work out in the end. Yet every time I looked at the world outside my window I was reminded that things didn't necessarily turn out the way we expect. At that time, things were heating up militarily in the Nonoviches' neighborhood.

The days were often quiet, but the nights were something else all together. Usually around midnight, the Serbs would start walking mortars all over Ali Pashno Polje, going up and down the streets, as if the shells themselves were out on the town looking for people to kill. When those shells walked across the courtyard below, the shock waves from the detonations were so strong that they would blow the plastic sheeting taped across my window into my room and all the open doors in the apartment would slam shut as if we were sleeping in a horror movie. One of these nights the Serbs concentrated their fire on only one building, a tall one, about two hundreds yards to the west, home to a reputed Bosnian sniper nest. As the fire was concentrated someplace other than where I was, I leaned out the window that night for a peek. There were these intense bursts of light on the roof followed by a boom that was strong enough to literally shake our building. Then came the tracers, thick rods of green and orange, that cut through the upper floors. Whomever they were after, I was glad it wasn't me.

As we began to try to negotiate our way through the Bosnian bureaucracy, Omar—who had basically been preparing himself to die—was fatalistic. He couldn't let himself believe that he was going to be saved, and I didn't blame him. But I did see that a little grain of hope had begun to blossom in him. He still called me a primitive and a wild boar, but it had none of the old vitriol.

Dina, actually, was tougher to melt. Maybe she didn't want Omar to get his hopes up. Maybe she didn't want her parents to get their hopes up. But, as our efforts progressed, Dina actually became more wary of me, afraid to put too much faith in some slob she regarded as, at best, a Pied Piper, and at worst, just another nut burger full of crazy dreams who had floated into her once orderly life on the tides of the war. As for Ella, it was all hugs and kisses.

Nino, however, was harder to read. He sort of watched from the sidelines for a while, going to his secret project during the day and playing cards at night as always. But he saw us working and one morning about a week into it he came to my room to have a chat.

"John, you are family here," he said. "You owe me, Ella, Dina, Omar, nothing. You owe us *nothing*. Understand?"

"No."

"John, please listen, for this is important. I cannot let you do what you said you want to do, what you *are* doing for us."

"Why?" I asked, truly confused.

"Because, it is too much. *Too much,* maybe more than you know now. Listen, John, this war is our fate, not yours."

"Nino, I want to help."

"I understand, yes, you want to help, but you do. You bring us food, are our friend. I tell you, it's OK."

"Nino, I wanna to do this. I wouldn't have said it if I didn't."

"John, then you must tell me. I must know, why?"

"Nino, if I'm off covering another war after this, smoking some stupid cigarette in some bush in Africa someplace, and I get a message that Dina has been killed back in Sarajevo, I would never forgive myself. Nino, I don't how to say it, really, but if I knew I had just sat on my ass here, laughed with you, ate your food, made money off this, and did nothing other than that, and Dina died . . . I mean, it would all be shit after that."

"Then this is what you feel you have to do? For you?"

"Yeah, I guess that's right. I mean, who the fuck knows. I don't know why I do anything, really, but yeah, for me, more than anything, I wanna do this."

"OK. I trust you now with my children. They are all I have, you understand? Of course, you do. But remember, please, you will always be in my heart whether you can help us or not. You are always to be a good man to me, no matter."

• • •

A few nights later, I came to understand, if I didn't already, how serious the stakes had become. I was lying in bed listening to the BBC, when this horrific argument broke out between Dina and her father in the living room. I couldn't understand a word, but it was serious enough that whatever was being said, Dina, who always deferred to her father, was yelling at him. Then I heard sobbing, deep sobs, and she kept saying over and over again, "Papa. Papa. Papa." After about twenty minutes and a very big knot in my stomach, there was silence. Then came a knock on my door. It was Nino.

"Listen, my friend," he said. "Dina is still girl. Young. My Dina younger than she know. She tell me, 'Papa, I cannot leave Bosnia without Laylo.' But I tell my Dina, 'Daughter, Laylo good boy, I mean good boy, but only boyfriend. Girl's love.' She not want to hear, understand what I say, that she must first think of herself, save herself, then maybe Laylo. And then I tell her, if it's real love, woman's love, then what will be will be. They will find each other some day."

"Oh shit," I moaned.

"No shit, my son. Dina will go. She will forget Laylo in time. I know this. But I wanted you to know this because you are now family, too."

As November drew to a close, I was so busy with the kids, my emotional energy so focused on them, I had stopped pursuing that big feature story. And I wasn't happy about it, despite my growing attachment to the Nonoviches. Then the door literally opened onto one of the best stories of the war, and more important for me, onto a secret world I had been trying to penetrate for a long, long time.

Nino came into my bedroom one morning and asked if he could speak with me about something important. I figured he wanted to talk about the kids, but then he pulled up a chair to my bed, slapped my knee, and said, "You remember that night when you play with my shooting trophies and ask me if I know snipers?"

"Yeah."

"Well, I didn't tell you everything that night. I was honest, yes, of course. I not lie to you. And truth be, I do not know any snipers. I did, of course, but they are all dead. But I know an antisniper."

"What the hell's an antisniper?"

"When war start, the enemy comes and puts snipers all around us. We cannot move, do anything because Serb snipers everywhere, killing people: mans, womans, childs. They do not care. Our side, we have no tanks, rockets, to blow up sniper positions. Only weapon our own snipers. An antisniper is a kind of sniper, true, but is one who only hunts and kills other snipers. One of these men is a friend, kind of, a former student from shooting club, long ago. And he was very good, world-class shooter, excellent."

"Really?"

"Yes. And he comes tonight, here, seven o'clock to meet you. I don't tell you before about him because I thought he would not talk with you. But I ask him, now, favor to me, and he say yes. But please be careful. Sniper war different kind of war than here. I do not want to call your father in America and tell him, because of me, his son, my boy too, is dead."

To say I was excited would have been the understatement of all time. My head was spinning I was so happy. I mean out of all the freelancers in the city, I had just been hooked up with the best possible subject matter for a story. What's more, this guy would take me to a place no Western reporter had ever been.

That night I sat in the living room with Nino and waited for our guest to arrive. While Nino played solitaire, I jotted down in my reporter's notebook a list of questions to ask: *Who was the most difficult sniper you ever had to kill? Have you been shot? Can I come with you while you hunt a sniper? What's the craziest antisniper story you know?* When I was done, I had about twenty questions written down, the last of which read, *Has the war changed you in any way?*

The antisniper arrived alone at 7:00 p.m. sharp and walked into Nino's living room. He was tall, about six two, very lean and angular, weather-worn, looking older than I thought he would be, like fifty, with gray hair and a chin line covered in coarse gray stubble. Although he was wearing fatigues, he looked to me like an old gunfighter out of central casting, the kind of wiry bad-ass who would push through the swinging doors into a saloon and the whole place would go quiet. He had that gravity. When he spoke with Nino out in the hall before being introduced to me, Nino talked to him with a deference and solemnity I hadn't heard in him. The antisniper had unusually large, fine-boned hands: in one he held a pack of local cigarettes and in the other a green cap. I wrote in my reporter's notebook, *Perfect.*

"John, this is Vlado," Nino said, finally introducing us. We shook hands, then sat down. Before I could start in with my questions, Vlado spoke. "Nino tell me you want to talk with sniper." His voice was cold and flat, like winter in Kansas, just right.

"Yes, very much," I answered.

"OK," he said. "But long time since I practice English, you understand. So, speak slowly, please, and I will try to answer your questions, if I can."

I was tempted to just jump right in and ask the meatier ones, but that wasn't the way these things were done. It is better to start slowly, build a rapport, so I started with some general questions: *What did he do exactly? For how long? For whom? Did he work alone? Did he only antisnipe, or did he do other things?*

He took a while to think through his answers; they were never long, and always specifically tailored to the question I had asked. If I didn't know any better, I would have thought Vlado was struggling to put his answers in English. But he wasn't. He was being careful for another reason. He was there as a favor to Nino, but all the same he wanted to tell me as little as possible. Normally I would have pressed, been persistent, kept asking, kept schmoozing, kept going down my list of questions because invariably people would say something of value. But this time I couldn't.

I had interviewed soldiers before in Sarajevo and civilians who had just lost their loved ones, and they always carried with them this aura of complete exhaustion, not so much physical as spiritual. They talked to me as if I was a piece of furniture, their minds clearly in another place. They were never quite there in the room with me. Vlado was different from those people in two ways. He answered my questions with that carefully crafted deliberation that was unusual, but he was also more distant-seeming than anyone I had ever met before, in Sarajevo or anywhere else. He looked at me as if I was nothing. Like I didn't exist. He took in everything but gave absolutely nothing back.

Vlado, I decided, was simply enduring me as a favor to Nino, and I had no right to exploit that. About fifteen minutes into it I just stopped asking questions. And then for thirty seconds, as I pretended to jot down notes, no one said a word. It was Nino who brought me back to earth by clearing his throat. He looked at me, as if to say, *Hey, talk up stupid, you know what I had to do to get this guy here.* I had to do something for Nino's sake, so I asked the first meaningless thing that popped into my head.

"How old are you?"

"What?" Vlado asked.

"You know, how old are you?"

He thought for a moment and then said, "Thirty-eight."

Before I could think better of it, I laughed because he looked a lot older than thirty-eight.

"Why you laugh?" Vlado asked.

"I'm sorry, but to me you just look a lot older than that."

He looked over at Nino, said something in Bosnian, and Nino chuckled, then turned back to me.

"It has been a tough year," he said, grinning.

I nodded as if I somehow understood, and then stopped talking again. I literally could not speak. This was my big interview. But I could not speak. This man was real. I was only posing.

"Is that all you want to know from me?" Vlado asked.

"Yeah. That was great, but I think that does it."

He twisted his head, as if he was confused, then leaned forward and asked, "You sure, you have no more questions for me?"

"Yeah, I'm sure. But thanks. It was great. I have all I need."

Vlado raised his eyebrows, as if to say to Nino, *I tried.* Then he snuffed out his butt, shook my hand, and said good-bye. Nino escorted him to the door, and that was that.

It couldn't have been but two minutes before there was another knock at the door. Three freelancers, two Belgians and Harald, whom I had told about my big scoop, had been downstairs, waiting for him to leave. When they saw him split, they came up to the Nonoviches', notebooks in hand, to share the wealth.

For a while I played ball, like I really knew something important. We were all sitting out in the living room, them peppering me with questions, me trying to answer them but not give away what really had happened. Finally Harald, sick of the generalities of what I was feeding them, asked, "What did you find out, man? Come on!"

That's when Nino spoke up.

"Johnny asked him how old he was."

"What?" Harald asked, not fully believing what he just heard. Nino confirmed that was about as deep as the conversation got. Then Harald exploded. "Jesus Christos! You Yanko-Fascist-Softie! You have an antisniper in here and you ask him how old he is?"

What was there to say? I choked. All of us were looking for great stories, something to make our names on but, more to the point, something extraordinary to experience, even by Sarajevo standards. I had my chance, and I blew it. There really was nothing more to say. I went to bed that night completely disgusted with myself.

• • •

The next morning I woke late, just Ella and me in the pad. I was hunkered in my bedroom, licking my wounds, when she knocked on my door and came in.

"Plava budd nutnik telefon," she said.

As usual, I didn't have a clue what she was talking about, but I heard the word *telefon.* I got up and walked into the living room, and sure enough the receiver was off the hook and laying on the table. I actually had a phone call. I picked it up and said, "Hello."

"John?" the caller asked in that voice.

"Vlado?"

"Yes, it is me. What I want to know is, tonight, after dark, would you come and see me? If you wish, of course. Nino will explain you how to find me. So, you come?"

"Absolutely."

I hung up the phone and locked eyes with Ella. I must have looked deliriously happy because her eyes lit up, too, and she smiled big. *"Habba lubnik!"* she shouted.

"Amen to that," I said.

Although it often made me edgy, I loved Sarajevo at night, shelling or not. In decent weather, and as there were no lights in the city, the sky was always carpeted in stars. There were rarely any people out and those who were usually hung in alcoves and in doorways, their faces lit for brief moments by the orange light of their cigarettes. There was a sense of mystery, too, walking around at night, a hint of film noir. This night was even more special because I felt like I was finally back in my own movie, although it was still a mystery to me why he had called after I let him off the hook as I did.

Like Nino's building, Vlado's didn't have any windows to let the moonlight into the stairwell, so I had to click on my Maglite to find my way up. I was to meet Vlado on the eighth floor, which was a real hike in my body armor. When I got up to the eighth-floor landing, I didn't see Vlado, or anyone. But there was a buzzer with his last name, Sarzinski, on it. Since a lot of these buzzers worked on batteries, I took a shot and rang it. Instead of letting out a *ding dong,* it sounded like a little bird fluttering away. Two seconds later, Vlado opened the door dressed in his fatigues.

I walked into a room full of shoes and jackets, a communal mudroom he shared with a neighbor.

"Take off shoes," he said, pleasantly.

Because of Ella force-feeding me gruel every day and my trips to Italy, I had put on at least twenty pounds over the past few months. When I had put the body armor on at the Nonoviches', I already had my shoes on. And now when I tried to take them off I couldn't reach them.

"Perhaps, take off armor first," he suggested.

"Good idea," I answered, but I couldn't undo the damn armor. The pressure on the zipper was too great. This wasn't even remotely close to how I wanted to kick things off with this guy.

"Here, let me help," he said. At first, he just tried to force the zipper down and, God bless him, he acted like nothing was askew. But the zipper wouldn't budge, so he had to push all his weight against my torso to give the zipper room to run. When it finally hit the last tooth in its track, and the front flaps of my body armor gave way, my stomach burst out.

"Ho!" he blurted as he reached out and patted my now liberated belly. "You *are* fat. Someone cares for you *very much.*"

Vlado's apartment looked and smelled just like every other apartment in Sarajevo; that is, it was impossibly clean but full of the stench of burned wood and other flammables. It was much smaller than Nino's, with only two bedrooms and a tiny eating area off the kitchen that doubled as a living room. There was a potbellied stove but, unlike Nino's, the only illumination came from an open flame shooting out of a pipe halfway up the wall. The apartment couldn't have been more than six hundred square feet. On top of a sideboard there was a pile of large bullets, a grenade, and a woman's purse.

"Sit," he told me, pointing to a small table. "My wife is not here, but she prepared coffee before she leave."

"You're married?" I asked as he was walking into the kitchen.

"Of course. Why not?"

While he was gone, I jotted into my reporter's notebook: *Married.*

"Ah, here," he said when he got back, reaching over my shoulder and placing a cup of Turkish coffee before me. "Sugar?"

"Sure."

He put a tiny sugar bowl down with a mini-spoon in it and then took a seat opposite me. As I prepared my coffee, a little blond-headed girl in pink pajamas, holding a stuffed yellow lion, slid open a door and walked into the room. I got up to say hello.

"This is my daughter, Diana," Vlado told me. "She is nine."

She hid her face behind her stuffed lion, then spun around and ran back to where she came from, sliding the door closed behind her.

As I sipped my coffee, Vlado started asking *me* questions. He was curious about my past: where I was from, what it was like, did I go to New York City often, did I have brothers or sisters, how long had I worked as a reporter, were my parents still alive? I answered as well as I could, but I left the depression part out, as always. In particular, Vlado was interested in my hometown, the fact that a lot of people knew one another, lived there for a long time, and my father's family was very close and lived near one another. He thought it was odd, not what he expected of Americans.

"I think here," he began, "we don't see Americans living that way. We see Americans moving, always moving, like leaves. Not so much neighborhood, community. Just interesting to me, but no matter."

He took a drag of his cigarette, yet kept those intense eyes of his locked on me.

"Nino tell me, you are helping his children escape Sarajevo."

"I'm trying my best, you know, but it ain't so easy."

"Yes, but you try. That's what's important, the rest, that is fate."

Another drag.

"So, what do you think of our war?"

"I think the Serbs are wrong. They want the land, the country."

"Yes, but you must understand, it isn't all Serbs. Not all Serbs are doing this, just the ones we call the Chetniks. Before war we live together, everyone, no problems. No one cares who is what, or who is who. It is rich city where many different people live in peace. Listen, my neighbor now, the apartment next door, she is Serb. But I fight for her, maybe more so, than I fight for anyone here, to live in this city. Her husband fight and die with me on front line. Killed by Chetnik sniper. His wife, I will die for her right to stay here. Chetniks want us to think that we can't live together, but no, never will I, my wife, bring up our daughter to think that. That would be a defeat alone."

"Sorry, I didn't mean all Serbs. Just, overall, it's more of a good versus evil thing, you know?"

"Yes, the Chetniks are wrong, but evil? Those are your words, not mine. We have saying here: 'That in war, real war, it's hard to keep your face.' You might say, maybe, 'In war, it's very hard to be a good man.' The point being, war is ugly, up close, and it's hard, very hard to remain good man. Perhaps impossible, I don't know. But let me ask you something. Why you interested in reportage on sniper?"

"I just think it's something people, maybe only me, I don't know, but the idea that snipers are alone, it's just something interesting to me."

"Yes, maybe you are right. I mean, you are wrong, of course. I don't go alone. I have partners, but yes, it is very lonely. Hard lonely. So, what is it you are looking for from me?"

"Let me shoot it straight here. I don't know if this is in the reporter's handbook or anything, but what I am looking for is a story. I need a story."

Leaning back, he blew the smoke at the ceiling. "Yes, but if you are really interested in sniper, or antisniper, then why don't you come with me. That would be better for you, no?"

I tried to appear nonchalant. "Sure, it would be better for me."

As he was leaving early the next morning, he invited me to stay over. By then it was around nine and Diana was fast asleep, but Vlado was taking me to her room, obviously where he intended me to spend the night.

"Wait, Vlado," I whispered when we were near the girl's door. "I can't kick your daughter out of bed."

"Do not worry," he said. "She sleeps like bear and enjoys waking in our room, like gift to her. Also, only other place for you to sleep is in my bed and that is not going to happen."

Vlado went in the room, scooped up Diana, who was sound asleep yet still clutching her stuffed lion, and carried her into his bedroom. Then he came back with some blankets, which he lay over Diana's bed, and then wished me good night.

"I'll be in early to wake you," he said, sliding the door closed.

I have no idea what I dreamed of that night, but I'll never forget how I woke up. Something started drawing me out of my sleep. When that happened, I remembered where I was, in Bosnia, in a little girl's room, and I realized something was wrong. Then I opened my eyes and I saw, about a foot away, Vlado, sitting on a stool, staring at me.

"Awake?" he whispered.

"Yeah."

"That's how we wake each other on the line when we cannot talk."

"What time is it?"

"Never mind the time," he said, still whispering. "What is important is, you were asleep, yet you knew I was here. You felt me watching you. Not with your eyes, but you felt my presence. With snipers, John, it's important to follow what you feel because what you feel is often more important than what you see. Now get up. We must go."

After I laced up my boots and Vlado helped me squeeze into my body armor, we headed downstairs to the street. On the way, he let me in on where we were going: to one of his "best positions," one of many secret nests in the neighborhood from which he stalked Chetnik snipers.

Ali Pashno Polje was a planned residential community, similar to an urban public housing development in America. Inside this vast complex, most apartment buildings were under four stories. But those on the outer perimeter were usually over ten, and in this war that came in useful because they acted almost like the outer walls of a castle, concealing the movement of the people inside from the enemy. Unfortunately for these residents, these "walls" weren't continuous, so Chetnik snipers had several openings through which they could hunt.

For an antisniper, though, the upper floors of these outer buildings were ideal, high ground from which they could look down on the enemy. The position Vlado was taking me to was located on the fourteenth floor of what was called Building Six, the middle apartment building in the western outer wall.

To get there, we only had to walk two hundred yards, so close was the front line. Once inside, we entered a sunlit stairwell and started hiking up. On the lower floors there were some people milling about and all of them smiled when they saw Vlado.

After we hit the eighth floor there were no more people and it became dark; the windows onto the stairwell were covered over with thick blankets. "So the Chetniks do not know we are coming," Vlado said, pointing to the blankets.

On the fourteenth floor, the stairs ended and we walked into a hall, its walls black with soot. It was also freezing cold because the winter wind was ripping through it. At the end of the hall, there were no walls, only sky. I followed Vlado, ducking under twisted pipes hanging from the ceiling and through instant dust devils of plaster and ash, until we came to the edge of a rubble pile. Hidden behind it was a man in fatigues and wearing a black headband looking through a huge pair of binoculars. He had an AK-47 leaning against his leg, its barrel wrapped in green cloth.

"*Habba i trika?*" Vlado whispered to the guy.

"*Neme nishta,*" the guy whispered back, not taking his eyes from the binoculars.

Vlado tapped me on the shoulder to follow him, and he pushed aside a Persian rug covering a door frame and walked into a room.

"Bathroom?" I asked.

"Yes, bathroom. Very good for me, because bathrooms are the strongest rooms," he said. "Much concrete, metal."

Instead of a toilet and tub, this bathroom held two small wooden tables. On one table there was a phone and a closed spiral notebook, and on the other an ashtray full of snuffed butts and an empty glass.

"See here," Vlado said, pointing to the notebook. "That is where we write down our notes. Whatever we see, we write down. No matter how unimportant it may be at the time: man walking here, tree cut down there, window open. Whatever, it doesn't matter."

"Why?"

"Information. Second only to position. When hunt sniper, sometimes not so easy. Like puzzle, never know what information may help."

"What's with the phone?"

"Phone? Connected to headquarters, in case trouble coming to us, or we see trouble coming for everyone. Eh, but first, come here, look."

Carved into one of the inner walls were three holes, about five inches in diameter, each one corked with a ball of foam tied to a string, the other end of which was tacked into the ceiling. Vlado plucked one of the foam balls out of the wall and held it up for me to see. Most of the foam ball was yellow, probably cut out of a sofa, but one side of the ball was charred black.

"This part must always face out," he said, meaning the black part. "The wall on the other side has been burned, so this way enemy cannot tell holes have been cut in wall."

He dropped the foam ball, letting it dangle, and then picked up a large metal spotting scope, maybe a foot long and three inches across.

"Here," he said, handing it to me. "Look out the hole, but do not let the end go through or else they may spot you."

I took the scope and peered out into the Chetnik-held area to the west. It was an amazing sight because from up there what seemed a confusing maze of trenches and buildings held by the different sides took some order, a twisted logic, even. Maybe a mile and a half away, I could see the airport. I turned a knob on the scope and zeroed in on the tarmac. I could see French soldiers patrolling.

"Shit, I could see the airport like it's in front of my face."

Vlado put his hand on my shoulder, so close I could feel his breath on the back of my neck when he spoke. "I have probably watched you arrive in Sarajevo many times."

"Really?"

"Of course. We must always know who comes and goes. Never know who is danger. Probably you are in that book over there, someone write down what you look like, what you carry, when you get off plane. You know, you come to Nino's for first time, every one knows you coming. Satso's men send word, maybe danger, maybe spy for Chetnik. You never noticed, of course, but you were being watched. But Nino do right by you, tell everyone: no danger, just reporter."

I tried to turn around, but he squeezed my shoulder just so.

"Keep looking," he said. "Tell me what else you see?"

"Trenches."

"Of course. What else?"

"Buildings."

"Yes. Anything else?"

Scanning across a village on the Chetnik side, I spotted an elderly man and a woman walking down a dirt road, maybe a hundred yards behind the lines.

"People."

"Yes, but what kind?"

"Serbs."

"Yes, but they not wear uniforms, no?"

"Yeah, they look like civilians, old people," I said.

"You know why?"

"No."

"Because, from here, we do not shoot their people, only soldiers. But their people are free to come and go as they wish."

I watched for a few more seconds before I heard three loud gunshots, one right after the other, *bang, bang, bang,* from directly in front of our position.

"Here, give me scope," he said, grabbing it back. He put it on the ground and then recorked the hole with the foam ball. "Best we move a little," he said.

We walked back down the hall, but instead of going down the stairs, he led me behind an elevator. "The strongest part of building, elevator," he said. "Here is safe, so we can talk."

"Great," I told him.

He gave me a cigarette, lit it, and then lit one for himself. After taking a puff, he asked, "So, are you frightened?"

"No," I told him.

"That's because you don't know any better," he said.

fourteen

Prozac's for Losers

"Something's wrong," I had told my mom when I returned from the aborted D.C. trip. "I mean, really wrong." I had spent that day driving around the boroughs of New York City, so lost in my head I couldn't remember how I got from one street to the next. It was a new low. I was sinking. I had to fess up, but all I could say was, "Something's wrong."

My mother wanted to talk, but I couldn't. Not then. I just had to be alone. All weekend I stayed in my room and thought: *What the fuck is wrong with me? I'm in deep shit here.* My skin started burning as if my nerve ends were popping. My heart raced as if I were running for my life. I was hyperventilating as I racked my brain for some way out of this invisible prison my life had become, but I couldn't even focus coherently. Thoughts flew through my brain like it was a wind tunnel.

There was no doubt in my mind now that I was depressed. I couldn't imagine my life hurting any more than it did. But I still didn't consider myself as suffering from depression; that is, some condition within me that was beyond my control. I still thought the answer lay somewhere outside myself. I still believed that if I made a series of right decisions, then everything would fall into place. By the end of that weekend, I had decided I would cure myself again.

"John, this isn't normal," my mother said when she finally forced her way up into my room that Monday. "You try one thing, then another. You can't work, and you lock yourself away up here. Won't take calls from friends. Won't talk to anyone."

"I know, but I just need a little time, that's all," I told her.

"John. I don't know if you want to hear this, but you are depressed," she said.

"I'm not depressed."

She smiled, and asked, "What do you call this then?"

"Look. Am I unhappy? Yeah. But so what?"

"John. You're miserable. There's a difference."

"All right, fine. Miserable. Look, I just need to figure things out, figure out what I want to do with my life. That's normal. Everyone has to. I just need a little time."

"John, you're depressed. There's nothing wrong with that. It runs in our family, but these days there's help."

"Mom, listen to me!" I exploded, red in the face. "I'm sorry, I didn't mean to yell, but it's . . . I got to figure out, you know, things."

"John, I'm not going to leave you alone."

A few hours later my sister Sara came up. For years, Sara was a mess, but my mother was always working with her, holding her when need be, pushing her when she felt that was needed. Eventually Dr. Atchley put her on Prozac and slowly she came into her own. She was finishing college, had a boyfriend and a ton of new friends. I was happy for her, but I wasn't ready to have her preach to me.

"John, I don't care what you say. I mean, look at yourself." I was swaddled in blankets, a three-day growth of beard. "John, you're depressed."

"Sara, listen to me. Whatever was wrong with you, I'm happy you're cool or whatever. But I'm not depressed. I just need to figure things out, that's all."

"Like why, why, why," she mocked. That pissed me off, because in many ways answering that Big Why was the key to getting on with life.

"Sara, listen to me: I'm not taking any fucking drug," I said. "I'm not gonna cheat." Then in the most obnoxious way I could, I whispered, *"Prozac's for losers."*

What followed was a fragile stalemate between me and the rest of the house. To everyone else I was a kid with serious problems who was in a state of denial, unwilling to listen to reason. At first, my parents simply tried to bully me into getting help, but I wouldn't budge. During many of these confrontations, I would get very angry, insisting until I was hoarse that I wasn't depressed. That to me meant it was all over. The talks went on for weeks, but then it all stopped. No one said anything; they believed sooner rather than later I would hit rock bottom. But I knew they were wrong. I was certain I could find my own way out.

When I was up there in my room, alone and looking for answers, books—just the look of them, the smell, the feel of the pages—had a mysterious allure. And my attic was full of hundreds of them, from the classics on. The first that had caught my eye was *Steppenwolf.* What drew me in was a drawing of a head on the cover: half man, half wolf. It was disturbing, but all the same it seemed familiar. I started thumbing through it. Then something remarkable happened: I recognized myself in the words:

> {He} *listens to the world beneath his window and the hum of human life from which he knows that he is excluded.*
> *He belongs to those whose fate it is to live the whole riddle of*

human destiny heightened to the pitch of a personal torture, a personal
hell.

> *But the worst of it is that it is just this contentment I cannot*
> *endure . . . In desperation I have to escape and throw myself on the*
> *road to pleasure, or, if that cannot be, on the road to pain . . . A wild*
> *longing for strong emotions and sensations seethes in me, a rage*
> *against this toneless, flat, normal and sterile life.*

Not exactly words you want to recognize yourself in, but at that moment in my life they were comforting. To date, I had never leveled with another person about these feelings. Now it was like someone finally knew what I was secretly fleeing. Over the course of the next months I went through Somerset Maugham, Hemingway, Faulkner, Steinbeck, F. Scott Fitzgerald, Conrad, Truman Capote, Shakespeare, and Tolstoy. In almost all of them, I found some kindred spirit and I would underline passages almost as little reminders to myself that, no matter how alone I felt, indeed there were others who felt the same. Passages I marked up in James Joyce's *A Portrait of an Artist as a Young Man* were typical of the lot:

> *His very brain was sick and powerless. He could scarcely inter-*
> *pret the letters of the signboards of the shops. By his monstrous way of*
> *life he seemed to have put himself beyond the limits of reality. Noth-*
> *ing moved him or spoke to him from the real world unless he heard in*
> *it an echo of the infuriated cries within him. He could respond to no*
> *earthly or human appeal, dumb and insensible to the call of summer*
> *and gladness and companionship . . .*
> *His childhood was dead or lost and with it his soul capable of*
> *simple joys, and he was drifting amid life like the barren shell of the*
> *moon.*

But after a while just knowing there are others down in hell with you isn't enough.

It's hard to describe accurately what complete hopelessness feels like because ultimately it's a perfect void, a state of nothing. There's nothing at stake. Reason doesn't apply, logic is useless, and faith is something for fools. It had been over seven months since I ascended the stairs to my attic bedroom once again resolute in my belief that I, and I alone, could figure a way out. Now it was July 1991, and the only conclusion I held dear was that I was screwed, a mutant, and there was nothing I could do about it.

More to the point, I despised myself for having to live this way, chained to esoteric, self-indulgent bullshit while decent folk were out in the real world, getting dirty, doing what needed to be done. For whatever reason, I couldn't lick a nanosecond of pleasure from living, and now even the pain was gone, too. There was no Alpha to strive for, and no longer an Omega to run from. From where I sat, sleeping my days away, navel-gazing my nights into oblivion, I didn't deserve to feel anything anyway. I was at a point where I considered myself a waste of resources.

It was a Tuesday afternoon, late July, perfect weather, the sun forcing its way through my tightly drawn drapes. It was the kind of day I would do my best to sleep through because it was the kind of day that I knew others loved, even lived for. For me it was hell on earth. But I couldn't sleep, so I went over and reworked the drapes to block out what sun was getting through.

Then the lawn mowers kicked in, and there was no way I could stop the sound waves from reaching me. I tried to hold a pillow over my head, but it didn't work. I hated the lawn mowers because Mexican immigrants were pushing them and they had every reason to bitch, working their asses off for below minimum wage, scrambling to make a life for themselves, but they were alive, doing something, taking part in the day. They even smiled, and here I was, a whining, spoiled-rotten white kid with nothing to complain about yet filled with only resentments and angst. For the rest of the day I just lay there, sweating in my underwear, hiding under a pillow, wishing life away but not having the guts to do anything about it.

About two the next morning, a calmness fell over me. I felt a certain peace, but to keep it going I had to follow through. I rolled out of bed, walked down the hall, and went into that crawl space off my bedroom. It was dark, so I couldn't see what I was doing, but I was sure I would know it when my hand touched it. I felt over crates, boxes, probably even my mother's old red boxes of photos, until I rubbed my hand against the hard plastic case. I knew it was here.

I dragged the case back to my room and flipped it open. Inside was my father's old shotgun. I picked it up and it felt heavy, real, not like my thoughts or stupid theories on how to get through life. I clicked it together, then looked down the barrel: hard, clean, perfectly round. There were no ifs, ands, or buts about it. That gun was what it was, a killing machine, and it felt good in my hands, good for the soul, soothing, the ultimate yet only surefire way out to freedom.

I had no intention of blowing my head off that night, but when I thought of the gun I knew I had to find it. Every other corner of my life I had already explored. I had looked in other directions for a way out of this prison I was in.

I folded up the gun, put it back in its case, and carefully placed it back in the crawl space so it would still be my secret, an option. About four a.m., I did something I occasionally did when my skin was on fire, my head bursting. I climbed out onto my roof and lay there, four in the morning, just me and the stars. It was weird, but the stars had a way of soothing me, like they were in on the joke, that life is a pointless parade of misery leading nowhere. And that night they were there for me as usual. But all the same, for the first time in a really long time, tears just started rolling down my face. I wasn't crying for me. I didn't give a flying fuck about my fate anymore, but I still mattered to my mother.

About three months earlier, during one of my up kicks when

I thought I was figuring this out, she had come up into my room to talk. It had been a bad year for my town, three suicides: one a man a block over, and two guys who went to my school, both a few years older than me. They were "promising young men," seemingly without any real problems, full of accomplishment and what have you. Then they killed themselves, and everyone shook their heads. What my mother said to me was, "No matter what you're feeling, ever, if you ever think of killing yourself you must come to me." By then, the thought of death was an old standby for me, a proven method of getting through really harsh and lonely days. But I didn't tell her that. I didn't have the heart, and I didn't want to worry her. The truth was, to me, then, it was more a tactic to boost my spirits than a real aspiration. But up on that roof, I realized I had crossed a line that night. Eventually, I would have to push the envelope farther and farther to find relief until . . .

My mother never gave up on me. She never wanted anything. She was always there. But she only asked one favor from me, ever. If I thought of killing myself, I had to come to her. I swore I would, but never thought I would really reach that point. My life was nothing now, but it still meant something to her. If I killed myself without giving her the opportunity to help, then I deserved an even more special place in hell. My jaw was quaking, tears dripping off my face, a twenty-three-year-old kid on a roof in a nice town under the stars.

Dawn was breaking by then, and I climbed in and headed downstairs to the kitchen. My mother, looking ten years older than when this year began, was already sitting at the table. I went around to the other side, put my head in my hands, and asked that most difficult of favors. "Please help me."

fifteen

The Plastic Man

When Vlado asked me if I was frightened that first time up in his nest, I had casually said no. His response? *"That's because you don't know any better."* When he said this, I had the sense that he really didn't mean the danger we were in at that very moment just by being up there. He was alluding to something else entirely, something he knew I didn't know, and for the first time I felt comfortable enough with Vlado to push him, so I asked him to explain what he meant by that. He answered with one word, "Impossible." For me, that was like a flame to a moth. Just as Serb snipers were his puzzle to solve, he became mine. I believed there was something I could learn from him.

A few minutes after that exchange, Vlado led me back to that bathroom stronghold, where I sat on the floor while he went to work, searching the Serb lines with his scope, trying to pinpoint Serb gunfire, fielding phone calls. It was a classic stakeout. And like most stakeouts it didn't go anywhere. Later that afternoon, Vlado walked me off the line and we parted ways with the promise that we'd get together again that night.

As soon as I stepped into the Nonoviches' that afternoon, I knew there was something wrong. Ella and Nino were at the kitchen table waiting for me.

"Johnny, come here," Nino said when I walked in. When I sat down, he put his hand on top of mine and told me that the militia had come the previous night for Omar. The only reason they didn't take him was Nino had told them about my scholarship promise, that I would get the kids full rides to American colleges. But the man told Nino that he would return in three days and Omar would have to go unless he had some official paperwork stating that he was the recipient of a full scholarship to an American university. The paperwork had to be officially translated in triplicate, and Omar also had to produce a waiver from a ministry I had never heard of before. Only with all that would he be immune.

"John, only if you want," Nino said, reminding me again it was my choice. "But if you can, Omar now needs those papers from America."

By that time, I had come to realize that no matter how many ancillary papers we filed on Dina and Omar's behalf, to get the Bosnian passports we were going to need proof that they had scholarships to an American college. I figured that would have been my last step, but it turned to be one of the first. But being in Sarajevo, it wasn't possible for me to do all that needed to be done on that front. So weeks earlier I had called the one person I knew who would understand and would help. I sent all the relevant documents ahead—birth certificates, transcripts, health certificates, letters of recommendation, both the originals and the translations. I thought we would have a few months to get everything wrapped up, but now, at least for Omar, we were now talking two days at best. Running out of the Nonoviches' that afternoon, I told Nino not to worry, although I didn't think we had a prayer.

I ran to the TV building and called home on the satellite phone. My father answered. "Is that you, kid?"

"Yeah."

"What's wrong? Are you all right?"

"Fine, just put Mom on. Love you, but don't have much time."

When my mother got on, I told her the story. "There's nothing I can do here," I ended. "Do you think you can do something?"

"How much time do I have exactly?"

"Two days," I said. "But more like thirty-six hours, really. These commie bastards need everything stamped and translated, triplicate out the gazoo, so I need extra time."

"I'll do my best," she said. "Thirty-six hours."

I gave her the number to the fax in the SAT Room, and then she hung up.

Thirty-six hours later, Nino, Omar, and I were standing in front of that fax machine in the SAT Room. As usual, it was spitting out letters from various news outfits to their correspondents in Sarajevo. For twenty minutes we stood there, me promising what I couldn't know, Nino assuring me that whatever happens, it will all be OK, and Omar pacing back and forth, so nervous he couldn't speak. Then the fax started churning out a cover sheet addressed to me, then the next page: a full scholarship offer on the official letterhead of The New York School of Visual Arts in the name of Omar Nonovich. There was no time to celebrate, and father and son ran out to take care of the rest.

I had no idea how she did it, and no one was home when I called to ask. About five, I got back to the Nonoviches', where Nino had on the kitchen table a bureaucrat's wet dream: sheets of stamped papers, all official and signed by someone important, stacked in threes and reeking of mimeograph ink. Right on cue, the Shanghai team arrived to haul off Omar, the guy from the night before and his two goons with sidearms. Omar met them at the door with the goods. The head guy, older and fat, looked over the paperwork carefully. Surprisingly, when he was done and satisfied that all was in place, he shook Omar's hand and seemed to wish him luck, like he was happy for him.

That night we celebrated a little at the kitchen table while the city crackled with gunfire. Ella took the fax my mother had sent and went alone into the living room. She put the paper on the coffee table, put on her reading glasses, and pulled a candle close so she could see it. Ella didn't speak English, let alone read it, but she studied that scholarship letter the best she could, rubbing it between her fingers, holding it close to her face, running her finger over what I imagine were the only words that she could understand on the page: *Omar Nonovich.* Tears were rolling down her face.

Omar's emergency meant I wasn't able to meet up with Vlado as planned. And once the dust settled with Omar and I was ready to go again, Vlado had disappeared. Nino told me he had taken a secret tunnel under the airport and gone into the forest deep in the mountains on the other side in search of food. He'd probably be back in a week.

If this had been a month or so earlier, I would have probably just gone back to my old routine: Zoloft and gruel, filing my radio gigs, and then by noon returning to the Nonoviches' to bemoan that Sarajevo turned out to be so dull while I did housework with Ella. But now I had a lot going on: Omar was saved and ready to go, Dina was in the chamber, and best of all Vlado. I couldn't wait until he returned. I had to move forward somehow, and that somehow was named Slobo.

Slobo was a Serb defector living in Sarajevo. Not a Serb nationalist, certainly not a Chetnik, Slobo nonetheless got caught up in the chaos of the early days of the war and was conscripted into the Serb army surrounding Sarajevo. Within months, he got assigned to the trenches across from Ali Pashno Polje, the same trenches that were right under Vlado's nests. If someone could give me good background detail on Vlado, it was someone with a perspective from the other side. I met him for coffee and cigarettes at that café in the TV building.

"Everyone out there knows of Vlado," he told me. "The Chetniks call him the Ustashe, and he is the devil to them. Anyone there long enough fears the Ustashe. The new guys come on the line, but they don't know. I would try to tell them: Be careful, the Ustashe is out there. This man will kill you if you are not careful. Young guys, stupid, don't believe."

"Why?"

"They think they are something, big men. The snipers were even worse. Seventy Chetnik snipers come and shoot on that line when I am there. Seventy! They stay in Hotel Ilidza nearby. Treated as heroes. Food, drink, women. They sit around table, fancy equipment, and talk big. And one by one they leave to hunt on Ali Pashno, and one by one they come back dead. Like I said, we try and tell them, but they not listen. After while, we even stop. They aren't worth it anyway."

"Really? Seventy?" I asked.

"Yes, and it get so bad," he continued, "that we lose many snipers, they have to call in a Chetnik hitman who kill many Bosnian snipers in Sarajevo. The best they have, he come and say, 'I kill the Ustashe.' And he is trained by army before war. Much experience. Very careful man. Perfect shot, too. He watches Vlado's position for weeks and then comes back with plan to lure Vlado out. He takes position in house and through small hole already in roof can see where he think Vlado will be. That day he orders an attack by us on bunker nearby. We lose no one, but don't get bunker. Hitman doesn't see Vlado. Orders attack again for next day. We lose two men in attack, both by sniper. Must be Vlado, but hitman can't find where he is. Next day we attack and when we return we find hitman dead on floor, shot in head. The Ustashe."

By mid-December, Omar had his passport and militia waiver, but I still had to figure out how I was going to get him safely through the Serb lines and out of the city. The only sure-fire method was a UN press card like mine, but since he was a local he couldn't be issued one. There was a special class of press pass that was for locals only, but the person had to be employed by a major news organization to get it. That press pass was one of the most valuable commodities in Sarajevo. It gave the holder the power to enter and exit the city at will via the UN humanitarian flights. But considering I wasn't officially employed, there was no way I could convince some news group to hire an eighteen-year-old Sarajevan. Then I started getting some breaks.

When I began filing radio spots, I always imagined my listeners to be American office grunts stuck in Fords in bumper-to-bumper traffic. But during my third month in Sarajevo, a freelancer got shot and I got the chance to reach a different crowd. I managed to land a few of the injured journalist's gigs—including that gig for that tiny African nation of Bophutswana.

Unfortunately, by December my new client went belly-up, exactly when I was looking for a way to get Omar out of the city. I wasn't the Edward R. Murrow of Africa or anything, but I had managed to build a rapport with an editor at the London agency that served as my connection to Africa. We spoke numerous times over the satellite phone in the TV building. After I heard the news that they were going under, I cold-called this editor and pitched Omar's case.

"Right now I'm trying to get Omar out, but it's almost impossible." I closed with, "But if you faxed a letter to the UN saying this little bastard now worked for you, then he could get that UN pass."

"Just tell me what to say and where to send it," he told me.

"We're out of business now, so it would be nice if some good came out of it. Yeah, I'd be glad to help the kid any way I can."

The next day the fax arrived at the UN offices in the PTT building, and the following day Omar Nonovich had his press pass and was now officially an employee of a small African nation. Just like that, everything was in place for him to go. After he got out, I was planning to stash him in Italy someplace until I got Dina out. But I hadn't really worked out the details yet. I thought I had time, but events started moving faster than I expected.

While we were scheming to get Omar's new press card, the UN was in the process of canceling the whole local press pass program. Some cards had gotten into the hands of smugglers, chief among them Mr. Pan Face. They were traveling out of the city on UN flights, buying goods wherever, and then flying back in to sell them on Sarajevo's black market. The Chetniks got wind of this and protested to the UN. To keep the peace, the decision was made to nix the cards. That meant Omar had to get out immediately, before the new regulations went into effect.

In early January, when I was out of Sarajevo and the day before the program was scheduled to end, Omar's parents escorted him to the PTT, where, with his UN card, he was able to get on the Egyptian APC, and from there was driven to the airport. Two hours later he landed in Ancona, Italy. Barely eighteen, he was now just another of the almost one million refugees who had fled their homeland.

It took me three more days to finally get to Ancona and meet up with Omar who was staying in a pension in a small seaside village close to the airport. In my mind, I had already checked off Omar from my to-do list. He was out, had his scholarship, and the only thing left to do in the short run, as money was very tight, was to find him a cheap, stable place to crash until Dina got out. I had no idea that the fun had only just begun.

"Johnny," Omar said when I walked into the lobby. "Johnny, Johnny, Johnny. You have no idea how good it is to see you here."

"Dude, seeing *you* here is the important part," I told him. "Omar, it's almost hard to believe you're actually out, in Italy. You look good, buddy."

After I checked in, Omar and I headed up to my room where I was going to drop off my stuff. Then I figured we could go out and celebrate a little. But once up in the room, Omar took his mask off.

"Johnny, I don't know if you can understand me," he said. "But I'm scared."

"Don't be, buddy. From here, we're good to go. Just hang tight and soon . . ."

"No. You do not understand me. I'm scared. I want to go back to Sarajevo."

"Omar, that ain't happening."

"You do not understand. I don't know this place; I don't know peace. I can't explain. Hard. I can't use money. I don't know how anymore. It is all strange for me, understand."

"Yeah, I do. But listen to me, all right," I told him. "You're going to hang tight, have some fun. Then you're going to America. You're going to be great, trust me."

"Oh, Johnny," he said. "I want to die. Don't you see? I am lonely. Alone. You can't understand, but I cannot stay here."

"You gotta, Omar. You have no choice."

"I can't. And you can't leave me. I'm scared!" he screamed, then whispered, "I'm scared, really."

He was starting to really freak out, and I couldn't talk any sense into him: his greatest wish in life was to go back to Sarajevo and die. As we were by the sea, I thought it couldn't hurt to at least go down to the beach and maybe that would help soothe him a little.

At first, our stroll seemed beneficial. Omar mellowed a bit. Then I thought that once we actually hit the beach, felt the wind, smelled the ocean, took in the scene, he would feel even better. But, as it happened, our destination didn't turn out to be ideal. In fact,

I later heard it had the distinction of being the only place in Italy that tourist guides recommended *not* visiting.

When we got down there, it was clear why. The beach itself was rocky and covered in seaweed, the air had a chemical stink, the water was oily, and cargo ships were stacked up about a mile off-shore. The only person in sight was a very fat man asleep on a huge rubber tube about a hundred yards out.

"Wow, look at this, buddy," I said, trying to put the best spin on it I could. "Could be worse, huh?"

Omar ordinarily would have shot back with some wiseass remark, but he just groaned. I flicked off my shoes and started rolling up my pants.

"Let's waddle in for a little," I said.

"No."

"Come on, it can't hurt."

"OK," he relented. "Whatever you want."

We sloshed out maybe fifty feet until the sea was up to our knees, and the water was surprisingly clear. Our idle chat petered out. For a while, we didn't talk. We were, basically, two guys standing knee-deep in sewage looking for some kind of connection. Then Omar spotted something in the water and reached down and picked it up. It was white and had the rough texture of a shell.

"Look," he said. *"Hobbanitza."*

"What's that?"

"You know, *hobbanitza.* Bone. Like fish."

"Fish bone," I guessed.

"No. *Hobbanitza.* For bird," he explained.

"Bird bone," I guessed again.

"No! *Hobbanitza!*" he shouted. "For bird in cage. *Hobbanitza.*"

"All right, *hobbanitza,*" I said, trying to end the discussion.

"How do you say, in English?"

"I don't know if we have any *hobbanitzas* in English."

"Yes, of course. It's a word. Tell me. *Hobbanitza.*"

"We just call it a fish bone."

"No! NO!!!" he shouted. "*Hobbanitza!* For bird, but not fish bone."

"Octopus. Squid," I guessed.

"No! It's a *hobbanitza,* not squid."

"What the fuck does it matter."

Angry, he shoved the *hobbanitza* in his pocket. He looked like he was going to break into tears.

That night I bought him dinner, but on the way home a car slammed into the side of another right in front of us, the first flipping over, and three teenaged girls hanging out at all the wrong angles. The fuel tank was ruptured, too, with gasoline spilling out into the street. Omar and I did what we could until the ambulance came, but later Omar lost it. He was making no sense, jabbering, full of questions, angry. He would demand my attention, and then just as quickly grow frustrated and start yelling at me.

My plan was to leave the next day, but that night he begged me to stay with him. "Don't leave me," he kept saying. I stayed, but the day after I absolutely had to go. I had Dina to worry about, my radio spots, and Vlado. When he realized I was going, he begged me to take him back to Sarajevo. "Johnny, I need to get out of here, now. I'm going crazy. Crazy!"

"Look, your job is to just hang in there," I told him. "Just relax, Omar. It's all gonna be good, and your only job now is to just take it easy and don't think so much, OK?"

I eventually calmed him down. Getting into the cab to the airport, I swore I would be back in ten days, no longer. That seemed to make him feel better, and he hugged me. I thought the worst was over.

After parting with Omar in Italy, I caught the next UN flight into Sarajevo and got back to the Nonoviches' around five. Nino and Ella were waiting for every detail about how Omar was doing. I didn't want to worry them, so I kept it positive, describing our trip to the seashore and adding a certain amount of picturesque detail.

"I miss him here," Nino said, touching his heart as Ella teared up. "My boy. But he is safe now, so it no matter how I feel." Then Nino added that Vlado had called a few times while I had been gone and left word for me to come see him. As always, that was the great news.

By then I had known Vlado for almost two months. For days we would hang together in one of his nests, and then suddenly he would disappear, either into the mountains in search of food or called away to an emergency in another part of Sarajevo. But always when he returned home he would call me and I would accompany him to one of his nests. There he would explain the art of antisniping, which came down to not being a world-class shooter but being a world-class observer.

Vlado was responsible for suppressing the sniper activity in a square mile of Serb-held territory, and he had in his head a mental sketch of every detail in that chunk of real estate. If some Serb sniper out there moved even a single brick or nudged open a window to get a better line of sight, that sniper was dead. Coupled with what Slobo had told me about him, I began to realize just how lethal he was to the other side.

Although I knew by then a lot about antisniping, in many ways I knew less about my main subject, Vlado, than I did the first night I met him. I knew some things about his past, that he was a successful businessman before the war, wore Pierre Cardin suits and drove a Beemer, and that he was a hippy as a teenager in the seventies, but I could never get any deeper than that. Just as a conversation seemed to be leading someplace interesting to me, he would always steer clear into another subject. But I kept at it because I was certain that someplace in Vlado was not only a great story but something else I had been looking for for a long time. It was like he had something I wanted.

When I had been depressed, especially during those episodes

when I was clinical, completely overwhelmed by it, I lived in a world that seemed meaningless. When life seemed a fool's game, nothing made any sense. During these episodes I was nonetheless compelled to figure out a meaning to it all because I felt that if I could do so, find that one key insight, it would provide that bridge back to a normal life. I think that was what had come to intrigue me about Vlado. In the darkness of his existence he had found a reason to keep on going; life had not lost its meaning to him and I wanted to know how it was he kept going.

Out of everyone I had met in Sarajevo, Vlado existed in the bleakest place of all, yet he had this hidden inner core that kept carrying him forward. He knew something and even said as much to me that first trip to his perch. I thought that if I could just get access to that core myself, maybe I would finally find that golden nugget of wisdom I had been looking for. Despite a daily dose of Zoloft, I was still searching for something. That's why I considered it always good news when Vlado called.

When I got to Vlado's that night, he greeted me at the door by putting his arm over my shoulder. "I wait for you to return before I open," he said, holding a half-gallon jug of moonshine. "It's pure, perfect."

Once inside, he poured two healthy shots. We clinked glasses and cheered each other, *"Shivoli."*

For half an hour or so we small-talked as usual, me answering questions about Omar in Italy and my life back in New York while he filled me in on the latest war news. After I was a little liquored up, I asked him a question I always eventually ask someone from Sarajevo: Did you see the war coming? Vlado told me, no.

"Really? Come on, everyone tells me that. You *never* saw it coming?"

"Of course, never," he said. "It was 1992. I live in Europe. Fly to Rome. London. I drive BMW. I ski with family, here, nearby, on Olympic mountain. Friends and me, see Rolling Stones in concert. Everyone have good life here. Why war? Only crazy man can see war come from that." He finished off his remaining booze. "Of course, crazy man was smarter than the rest of us," he said. "He plan for war, while normal man sleep."

For the next few hours we drank and shot the shit, completely ignoring the war raging outside. It was the first time we ever had a totally normal conversation, and most of that time he talked about his former business. I sat there and learned the art of designing plastic pens, stick shifts, and soda bottles. Normally this wasn't my idea of fun, but by that time I was loaded. Plus, Vlado was really into it. But the party ended when the bird door bell went off and in walked Vlado's wife, Majda, who began talking, in rapid-fire sentences to her husband. Vlado just nodded along, and when she was through he started straightening up: emptying the ashtray, issuing us clean new glasses, folding a blanket that was out, tucking away his grenade in a drawer. I didn't have to ask because I knew the drill, but I couldn't help anyway.

"What did she say?"

"Ahhhhhhhh," he moaned. "My wife, I can't do anything right."

I laughed my ass off, and Vlado couldn't help but cut a grin himself. Here was this guy, the devil to the devil, the scourge of every Chetnik sniper, being henpecked by his wife. It was hard to imagine Genghis Khan astride Samarkand being forced by Mrs. Khan to straighten up his yurt, or else.

The next morning Vlado and I went back to business as usual, hiking up to his nest atop Building B. For an hour or so he chatted with his partner, looked through the notebook, and scanned the Serbs' side of the line. Finally, he moaned, "Ehhhh, shit." Then turned around and said, "Johnny, come with me."

We walked down the hall to the elevator and sat in some rubble, where he lit a smoke. "So strange," he said. "Nothing there. No sign of any Chetnik snipers."

I was still hungover from the night before, so I just sat there, a lump on rubble. For the next minute, we didn't say anything to each other, until he finally broke the silence. "Johnny, you ever see the film *On Golden Pond?*"

"Not really. Why?"

"That was my favorite film," he said. "Favorite film of all time. Purrrfect film. Fonda . . . what's his name?"

"Henry Fonda."

"Ah, yes," he said. "Henry Fonda. And Katharine Hepburn, the actress. We loved her here in Yugoslavia. Now that was a star, that woman."

"That was your favorite movie?"

"Of course, why not? I saw it many times. Before war, that's how I saw my life."

"Whatya mean?"

"I mean, me and wife, work hard when we are young, raise family, save money. Then we get older, grow tired, settle in the mountains, in woods, near Sarajevo, in beautiful home, on lake, like in movie. Forget the troubled daughter in film. Not important. What *is* important is me and wife together, end of our lives, and *our* daughter come to visit us with her family. That would be something . . . but anyway, never mind, just dream."

"War's gotta end, right?"

"Of course, war can't last forever. We will grow tired someday. Johnny, sometimes I don't think I will survive. I know I won't. Me and just a few others are left. It is quiet now, but won't always be."

"You really think you won't live?"

"Who cares about me? But what of my daughter, my wife? They are what's important. Even if I do live, so what? That life is gone, forever. Everything from before is gone, here."

"I'm sorry," I said.

"It's hard, very hard," he continued. "I was just a normal man. Family. Work. Vacation. Had drink with my best friend on weekend. Too busy, I never thought of politics. Maybe I was just stupid.

Maybe I am stupid man. But this war, not normal war. It is ugly. Too ugly. And it took from everyone, a part of their heart, no matter."

Then he stopped talking and just stared at me, hard. I held it for as long as I could, but finally looked down at the ground.

"You know what normal people don't know?" he now asked. "Don't know about war?"

"No."

"It is easy to kill," he said. "It is too easy."

"I'm sorry."

"Well, I do not need your sorry. Everything I have done, I did, and I would do it again. I remember once, over year ago. It was May 1992. The first big action for us, our line, biggest of the war. Chetniks attack our sector of city with everything: Praga, APC, tank, many, many Chetnik soldiers. Too many."

"Was that around the thirteenth?"

"Never mind the day. But yes, you are right, on thirteen May. And we fight hard, lose many on our side but kill many more of them. The next day, on fourteen, we are at our positions, waiting for new attack. Our leader, Juka, has given me body armor taken from dead Chetnik. Only body armor we have then. I am nervous. Very nervous. Cannot see anything. Maybe enemy right out there. So, I make mistake. I put head out of bunker to look and then, bang. Chetnik sniper shoot me. He watching the entire time. And feel like I am hit by Volkswagen. Fly in air across bunker and hit wall. Oh, the pain. It hurt. Another soldier check me for wound but plate in vest stop bullet. Broken ribs, but nothing more. I am lucky, very, very lucky."

"Could you walk?" I asked.

"Yes, after while. And I go back home, in basement of building. Majda and Diana are in shelter in basement, whole building hiding in basement. Majda cry when she see me. Not know if I dead or alive. Diana cry, too. I cry. We all do. And I look at them. That Chetnik almost took me from my family. I never get angry in life before. Never hurt anything, anyone before. Why hurt anything? But that day, oh, I hate. Feel it in me, like volcano, Vesuvius. And that night, watching my wife and daughter in shelter, Diana crying, scared, I make promise to myself in head: I kill that man, that Chetnik sniper. And next morning, before I go, I find that Chetnik's bullet, now flat like coin, in pocket of vest and give to my daughter. I don't tell Diana for what, that is talisman, but she know. Already she getting older. Then I get my rifle and go out."

"Was this the first time you hunted a sniper?"

"Yes, the first. But I do not know what to do, so I go slowly, quietly, building to building on our side, looking for perfect position to look down on where I think that sniper shoot me from. Hour, maybe two, and then there he is. He shoot few time, two hundred meter away, from inside what was doctor's office. I watch and wait. Later, maybe three hour later, he come out of back of medical building. He is in uniform, normal-looking man, holding sniper rifle. But it is him. I put rifle on him, and pull trigger.

"He fall down. Not like in movie, roll. Just falls, right down. He is dead. I leave position, and go back home to Majda, Diana. When Majda see me, my face, she ask, 'What is wrong, Vlado?' I am crying. I am crying, you see. Hard. Never cry like that before. I hurt inside. I tell her, 'Majda, I just kill a man.' She cannot understand. How can I tell her, make her understand. Oh, you see, that night was hard. My head. My head was filled with a thousand whys. And so, now, maybe I, too, am crazy man."

He snuffed out his cigarette under the heel of his shoe and picked up his rifle.

"Come on," he said. "It is time I go back."

sixteen

Prozac's for You

After I asked my mother to "please help me," she had said, "Don't worry about a thing. You're going to be fine, John." At the time I thought she'd gone crazy, too.

"How do you know, Ma?"

"John, there's an answer out there and I won't rest until I find it. Trust me. Your life is going to get better."

About four hours later, my mother came up to my bedroom and told me she had just gotten off the phone with Dr. John Atchley, the same Manhattan psychiatrist who had finally turned my little sister Sara around years earlier. "I told him it was an emergency," she said. "And you have an appointment with him tomorrow morning."

"An emergency? Oh, come on," I moaned, trying to save even a little face. Whatever I felt, no matter how bad, the shame was worse: I didn't want anyone, even the doctor, thinking there was something wrong with me.

The next morning my mother drove me into New York City for the appointment. Growing up, even in my worst nightmare, I never saw my future like this: I was a twenty-three-year-old shut-in being hauled off to an "emergency" session with a shrink by his mother. All that was missing was the straitjacket and padded room. Who cared what happened next? I don't think I did. On that ride in, my thoughts were all over the place. One moment I felt humiliated, the next a little relieved, then a lot anxious. But what if he said I was just unredeemable? As we got closer to the city, more and more, it was just pure self-loathing, the shame again. Here I had been given everything in life, all the advantages one could ask for, but I was such a royal fuckup that I couldn't even make it out of bed in the morning anymore. While others somehow intuited that life was a gift, something to be savored, I slinked into adulthood a totally self-absorbed, naval-gazing, whining ingrate. I don't think I exchanged even a hundred words with my mother on the drive. I was completely lost in my feelings and racing thoughts. The world passed like a strange gray whirl.

We got to the office early and sat in the small waiting room outside Dr. Atchley's office. There I buried my head in my hands while my mother calmly read *National Geographic* as if she had no doubt that salvation lay just on the other side of that door.

About five minutes later, the door opened and a middle-aged man walked out of Atchley's office. He looked straight out of a Brooks Brothers catalog, and as soon as he saw us he put his eyes on the floor and hurried out into the hallway as if we had just busted him coming out of a brothel. I knew exactly how he felt. Then, a minute later, Dr. Atchley came out to greet me. Obviously an über-WASP, he looked sixty-something with his long face and patrician bearing. He was dressed in tweed. This was not the guy I saw myself connecting with.

Inside his office, I took a seat in a wooden chair. He sat opposite, opened a notebook, took a pen out of his jacket pocket, and there I was.

"So, why did you come here today?" he asked.

"I guess the best answer is, I'm miserable."

"What do you mean?"

"I don't know. Miserable. Really unhappy. It's hard to explain."

"Try."

I held up my hand, reached into my back pocket, and took out my copy of *A Portrait of an Artist as a Young Man*. My ability to focus was so compromised by that point, I had taken the book along with me just in case I found myself at a loss for words. I just never expected it would have happened so quickly, but nonetheless I flipped open to one of my underlined passages and read:

> *Nothing moved him or spoke to him from the real world unless he heard in it an echo of the infuriated cries within him. He could respond to no earthly or human appeal, dumb and insensible to the call of summer and gladness and companionship.*

"OK," he said. "But let me hear you tell me in your own words."

"I don't know. I mean, like the guy said, dumb to the call of summer, gladness, friendship. Everything fucking sucks."

"You're sad a lot?"

"Oh, yeah."

"You feel hopeless?"

"All the time."

"Have you been going out, seeing friends, doing things with people?"

"No. Not in a long time anyway. I can't explain it, but when I go out it feels like my skin's burning. I just get really nervous, like I got to get out of wherever I am. So, no, I don't."

"Not working?"

"No, and *it's a fucking disgrace.*"

"Well, tell me, do you do anything during your day that makes you feel happy, gives you pleasure?"

"No. I mean, I read a lot and sometimes that helps. But no."

"John, do you fantasize about killing yourself?" he asked, matter-of-factly, like he was asking the time.

"Yeah."

"How long?"

"A year, maybe more. I don't really believe I'll do it, but it just gives some relief when I need it. It's hard to explain, but knowing there's a way out if all, you know, if all else fails . . . makes me feel better for a little while."

"John, have you gone farther? Have you ever tried to kill yourself?"

"No. Well, I got a shotgun out of our attic the other day, but that was just to see it."

"What do you mean?"

I sighed, upset with myself for having brought it up.

"Well, just knowing it was there made me feel better. But again, I don't believe . . . I mean, I really don't think I would ever do it."

"That's not normal, you know."

"I know."

"How's your relationship with your parents?"

"Great. I mean, hard, of course, but it's not my relationship; that's the problem. I just know they're worried, and sometimes I get angry. But it's not them, it's me."

"So, you're miserable. You're unhappy. Why is it, you think, you feel this way?"

"Well, I've been reading a lot. Watching a lot of stuff, *Oprah*, PBS. Thinking. And the way I see it, there's a pattern to life. Something you need to know to live it right, be happy. Whatever. But the point is, maybe I'm depressed, but I think a big part of the problem is, I've got to figure something out. There is this professor on PBS, Joseph Campbell . . ."

"I've seen it."

"OK, well, his whole myth thing, like you have to know how to live life to do it right."

"Uh huh."

"Well, he talks about going on quests and stuff. But what I think I need to do is go through some kind of transformative experience, you know. Some ordeal or something, meet someone, something where I could figure things out and be free."

We talked for maybe another fifteen minutes, but when I started going in circles he shut his notebook.

"John, those are good questions to ask. It's good you think of these things. I have some patients, very successful, but their personal lives are a mess. They're very unhappy, some of them. I think maybe they should be wondering what you're wondering, but for now I want you to forget all that jazz."

"Really?"

"Yeah. You're a textbook case of what we call unipolar depression."

"What's that?"

"I've heard it described as a permanent low-grade fever of the spirit."

I sat up in my chair.

"So, you think that's what's wrong with me?"

"I *know* that's what's wrong with you. This runs in your family. You are suicidal for no reason I can see. Nothing major, bad, ever happened to you."

"Yeah, but sometimes I think maybe that's the problem. Maybe my life's been too cushy."

"Well, that's bullshit. You've probably been this way since you were a young teenager. The point is, it's chemical. There's some imbalance in your brain, but these days there are medicines that can correct it."

"You really think it's that simple?"

"There's nothing simple about it. But listen, here's what you're going to do for me. I'm going to give you some pills now, Prozac, and a prescription. For the next six weeks, I want you to take these pills and then you're going to come back. Between now and that time, I don't want you to think. I don't want you to try to figure your life out. Your only job for the next six weeks is to take the pills, relax, watch TV, just take it easy. Can you do that?"

"Yeah."

"All right, now go out there and send me in your mother."

I never thought I'd be happy to be certified a nut, but when I left Dr. Atchley's office with an actual diagnosis, my inner tank was full of hope again. Part of me still felt that taking an antidepressant was cheating, but I trusted Dr. Atchley—and then again what choice did I have? For the next six weeks, I did as I was told, or tried to. I took the meds, plopped down in front of the tube, tried to clear my mind, and waited for deliverance.

What that would actually feel like, I didn't have a clue. When I had asked Dr. Atchley, "How will I know the Prozac's working?" he only said, "You'll just know." Would I just suddenly be happy? Feel hopeful? Atchley's answer had been vague, leaving everything about me subject to miraculous change. I found it hard not to wonder. Maybe I'd hit the trifecta of brain chemistry and wake up not just happy but as some kind of kick-ass dude.

Most of the time, to soothe my soul, I watched Woody Allen's *Hannah and Her Sisters,* which I must have seen twenty times. Part of the reason was that I identified with the character Allen played in the film, a guy who is in a race against time to discover the meaning of life. He studies the great philosophers, explores Catholicism, takes up Wonderbread and mayonnaise, and even chats up some Krishnas in Central Park. In the end, he gets nowhere in his quest, finally giving in to the belief that life has no meaning. Unable to live with that, he takes out a rifle and tries to shoot himself in the head. But he misses, and so, distraught, slinks off to a movie theater that is showing *Duck Soup* starring the Marx Brothers. There, he has his epiphany: Maybe life *is* meaningless. *But so what?*

When Allen's character accepts that, leaves that big why behind, he's freed from that prison he had built around himself. He concludes that the goal of life is to enjoy it, here and now while you can. And by the end of the movie it all works out perfectly for that character. If Prozac could effortlessly transport me to that place, too, I was all for it.

"How you feeling?" Dr. Atchley asked when I returned six weeks later.

"Worse," I muttered. *Worse* was actually a mild choice of words considering I was now as low as I had ever been, including the day with the shotgun. I finally had asked for help and what I had secretly always feared came true: for me, there was no solution. I really was unredeemable. I was going to be stuck on the outside of life forever. Everything hurt worse now because I had actually let myself hope.

"So, what do you think we should do now?"

I shrugged.

"Listen to me. They're coming up with new medications all the time, many in their trial runs right now. I promise, something will work with you. I've been in this profession for a long time, seen everything, and you are a textbook unipolar depressive. No doubt."

"But for how long? I mean, my life's pissing away. I've lost too many years already and I'm really tired. How long am I going to be this way?"

When I had first laid eyes on Dr. Atchley six weeks before, I had no hope that this guy could understand me, despite my mother's faith. To me, he appeared to be the stuffy, high-handed shrink I always feared was waiting for me. Yet, once I started to speak with him in his office that first session, things changed. He was down-to-earth and didn't treat me necessarily as someone who was sick or crazy, but rather as a young man with a fixable problem and some valid questions about life. He performed one magic trick that first day: he took away a good part of that intense self-loathing. I trusted him, so on that second visit I believed him when he told me that to get some semblance of a normal life going while I waited for the right medicine, I should attend this self-help seminar in Manhattan called the Forum. He was just buying me time, but the way he made it sound like if I threw myself into this seminar with all I had, just maybe, I could feel better, medicine ar not. Dr. Atchley was a real pro and knew exactly who he was dealing with in me.

"You really think things will make sense again, or I'll just feel alive, or . . . ?"

"I do," he told me. "I really do. The way they say it at the Forum: When you get 'It,' you get 'It.' And when you get 'It,' I'm telling you, you're going to be a much happier young man."

What did I have to lose?

The Forum promises "Transformation" and those who get "It" during the seminar leave with something called a "moment-by-moment approach to being alive." The Forum is held over three days, fourteen hours each day, and ends with a three-hour evening session dubbed Graduation Night. On that final night, participants are supposed to invite friends and family to witness the big event. But as excited as I may have been to attend and finally experience my own life transformation, there was no way I was inviting anyone to witness anything, whatever happened. I had already decided that.

When the big day arrived, I had my father drive me into the city so I could get to the site early. After checking in and being issued my name tag, I went into the large hall where the Forum was set to take place. As I was one of the first to arrive, I had my choice of little plastic seats and parked myself in the front row. On the stage in front of me was a microphone stand, a black director's chair, and a table with a box of tissues on it.

Over the next fifteen minutes about a hundred other people walked in—a perfect cross section of New York: white, black, Hispanic, Asian; young and old; rich and not so rich. Some were chatty, but most were like me, careful not to catch a stranger's eye. It was comforting to see so many people looking for answers, too.

Right on schedule the door at the back of the hall opened and in walked a short, intense-looking dude in a sport shirt and black slacks. He strode straight up to the stage, spun himself into the director's chair, and welcomed us. His name was Peter and there was not a self-conscious bone in his body. He was our Forum leader.

The first order of business were the rules: If you wanted to be "acknowledged" then you had to raise your hand; if you were late returning from a break, you wouldn't be allowed back into that session; and if you had to use the bathroom while the Forum was on, you forfeited "the right to expect the result." Finally, to "get It," you really had to want "It." Sitting on your hands wasn't going to be enough. The key to getting the result was to stand up, be acknowledged, and "to share." This last part made me nervous, as talking to anyone had become very difficult for me over the past year, and now I was being asked to discuss my life with a room full of strangers.

For the better part of the first day we were given a run-through of the Forum's take on the human condition, the reason why so many people were screwed up and unhappy. It's not that humans are born with any limitations, but that we choose our identity and then get imprisoned by it. As kids we make a few key decisions that become "our stories," which define us and dictate how we interpret and interact with the world. These stories imprison us in lives of limited expectations, groundless anxieties, and fear. It's all a vicious cycle, where our past dictates our future, keeping us from lives of possibility, robbing us of true happiness.

The first step in working your way out of this vicious cycle is to discover your "Rackets," the set of complaints you tell yourself over and over again that keep you from doing things. It's that little voice in the head that says, "No, I can't do x because of y."

When we were sent home at the end of that first day, I still hadn't gotten "It," but some others obviously had: they'd thrust up their hands, get acknowledged, and then openly discuss their story and Rackets. The sincerity was obvious and often these testimonials would be accompanied by tears. When it was done there would be a hearty applause from the rest of us, initiated or not. Walking back to my hotel room that night, I was nervous that I would be one of those unlucky few, like with Prozac, who never could get it.

When we started up the next morning, a guy asked to be acknowledged and for the next twenty minutes engaged Peter in this back-and-forth about his life that grew quite intense. He wouldn't admit the obvious: he was so unhappy in his life because his father had died young and this guy was so uptight in his life that he was still trying to save his father. Then at some point in the exchange a block gave way in this guy's head and he doubled over and started sobbing.

When he came back up for air, he looked years younger, like he just took a deep breath for the first time in years. After we all finished applauding, Peter asked the audience, "Who else wants to share?" I shot up my hand.

"My name is John, and I'm twenty-three," I said into the mike. "I'm from Long Island and for the past year I've been living in my parents' attic. They say I'm depressed because I can't get out of bed, do anything, without having these panic attacks. Most of the time I just sit there in my room, reading, trying to figure out the meaning to it all. Like if I can find a meaning, then I can go on, figure out what it is I want to do with my life."

"There is no meaning," Peter declared.

"I know. I know now. But that's my Racket. If I don't know why, then I can't move forward. And since I never know why, now I don't do anything. I was even put on Prozac but that didn't help."

"Depression's just another story we tell ourselves," Peter declared again.

"I know. And all this crap, my Racket, it's what making me miserable. I even tried to volunteer for the Gulf War so maybe I'd change over there, or maybe lose an arm or something, have something real to struggle against."

The entire crowd let out a big, "Ohhhhhhhh."

"Oh yeah. I just wanted something to justify how I was feeling. Something real, like cancer, I could fight with. And now I get angry, very angry. My parents, God bless 'em, are always there for me but I'm a prick to them. Once I even made my mom, my 'there-for-me-no-matter-what' mom, cry. *Oh God, I'm such an a-hole.*"

I was surprised to find myself choking up and tried to fight back the tears, but they came anyway.

"Keep going, man," a guy next to me said. "You're great."

"No. I'm an asshole, even to my little sister. She tries to help, but I tell her to fuck off. But no more. No more whys. No more feeling sorry for myself. It started when I was twelve, but no more."

When I handed back the mike I received a big round of applause, but I didn't need it to feel better. It felt as if someone had just lifted a Buick off my chest. Finally, something had worked *for me!* I had gotten "It," and "It" came with a sense of liberation and an incredible self-acceptance. After years of banging my head against myself, I thought I was free.

During the break period, I signed up for the advanced course and afterward went out into the hallway to hang, where I received a lot of congratulations. There was this one guy who hadn't shared yet who came up to me. I had met him on break during the first day, but dismissed him as a pussy because he had once taken part in an Iron John outing, that male-bonding ritual I had seen on PBS. But now that I had "got it," that self-inflicted wall between us was down.

"Looks like you got it," he said.

"Yeah, I think I got it," I told him. "You get it, yet?"

"No, not yet."

"To get it, you got to speak up," I advised.

"I know," he said. "I just hope I'll get it before this is all over."

"You'll get it, man."

"You think so?"

"Absolutely," I told him.

We parted with a solid yet reaffirming hug.

Graduation night came upon us before I knew it as so much transformation was packed in so little time. Before I started, there was no way I was inviting anyone to this event, but when the night came I had in the audience my parents, my sisters Christine and Sara, and a buddy from home, Tom. About an hour into it, we, the new graduates, were given a chance to share with the audience what the Forum had done for us. I was the second one to go.

"Man, before I came here I was doing nothing with my life. Just sitting on my ass, waiting for life to start, waiting until I knew what it was exactly I wanted to do. And you know what? I was doing nothing. But now. Wow, I feel free for the first time in as long as I can remember. I can't wait to walk out of that door and dive back into life."

Big round of applause.

"Also, I want to apologize to my guests for being such an ass-hole over the years. Sorry, guys. And especially my mother. Mom, would you stand up?"

My mother stood up, clutching her pocketbook.

"Look at this woman. Look at that face. This is the woman I made cry because she was so worried about me. Can you believe that? Well, never again. I know that."

After I sat down, I got a lot of backslaps and, when the ceremony was over, it took me a while to work my way to the exit, as I had a lot of hugs to issue. My biggest one was reserved for our Forum leader, Peter.

"Thanks for everything, man," I told him. "Love ya."

"Love you too," he said.

When I finally did make it out into the hall and reunited with my family, they all looked this side of pleased, except, that is, for my father, who had a smile frozen on his face but all the same looked as if he'd just witnessed his son get married in Madison Square Garden along with five thousand others.

"Dad, it's over," I reassured him. "All that crap is over."

"That's great, kid," he said. "I'm really happy for ya."

seventeen

Stranger on a Train

As much as I wanted to hang with Vlado now that he had begun to open up to me, I couldn't, as I had to get back to Italy to check up on Omar, and more important, find him a new place to crash. Money was a big issue, and I couldn't afford to keep him in that pension forever. When I left the Nonoviches' for Italy the next day, I left with two love letters for Omar from his parents, a few pairs of the kid's underwear, and—I don't know how the hell she pulled it off—a foot-long pepperoni sausage, courtesy of Ella. That made me probably the first man history not only to leave a siege *with* food but actually to import a pepperoni sausage into Italy.

But when I rolled into that pension in Ancona a few hours later and asked the girl behind the desk to ring for Omar Nonovich, room 204, she just shook her head.

"Mr. Nonovich not stay here for week," she said.

"What? You gotta be kidding me," I said. "What do you mean, he left? Did he leave a message?"

"No. No message," she said. "Sir, do you need a room, or no?"

That entire day I walked around Ancona looking for Omar: the beach, the restaurant, the piazza d'what the fuck. I asked strangers, cops, taxi drivers, anyone if they had seen him: a tall, skinny kid. "Looks like Balky, on *Perfect Strangers*? TV? You know? Big hit show?" I might as well have been speaking Arabic. It was hopeless and by that night I was in a real panic.

"Nino, dude. Sorry, I lost Omar, but I swear, I know what I am doing now. Trust me, I won't lose Dina."

It was around seven that evening and I was in the bar of the pension, slowly poisoning myself with what was at hand: Jack Daniel's, cappuccino, Marlboro Reds, and a plate of Italian pastries. The bar was in the lobby, though, and when the night clerk came on duty she saw me and came over to my table.

"You Johnny, American reporter?" she asked.

"Yeah."

"Here," she said, handing me a light blue envelope. Inside, there was a note, dated from a week before:

Dear Johnny,
It is Omar. I meet a man from Sweden. Make movie. Very nice. He have sister, Monica. Monica live in Italy. I go there to her. All good, but come as fast as you can.

Omar

On the other side of the letter was this Monica's address. She lived outside of Bologna, a city about two hundred miles to the north. The next morning I caught the early train and headed up. I was relieved. Omar sounded like he was in good shape. Plus, I assumed, he had, at least temporarily, solved one of our major problems by scoring himself a place to stay. My plan was to spend maybe a day or two with him, make sure everything was kosher, then drop some bread on him and split back to Sarajevo.

After pulling into Bologna's main train station, I got a cab and about twenty minutes later was dropped off at the entrance to a long dirt drive in the middle of rolling green hills dotted with stucco villas and grazing cows. It looked like little old Omar had scored a place in a postcard.

I walked down that dirt road for about a quarter mile until I heard some voices coming from behind a high stone wall. Whoever they were, they were speaking Italian, but I thought at the very least they could read the address I had and help me find this Monica woman. I walked over and hoisted myself up so I could see over the wall. *Oh, fuck!* I thought. *Why me?*

There was a man in a T-shirt and linen pants with curly long hair taking pictures of another man, a hairy man, a large man, maybe six two and two hundred and forty pounds, who was dressed in fishnet stockings and a purple lace teddy. He was sprawled on the hood of a red Volkswagen Beetle and trying his best to look seductive, but he looked more like a plumber who had gone totally insane. But I had an open mind. *To each his own.* Then I caught sight of Omar wearing a black beret and silk ascot, hosing down this plus-sized transvestite with a garden hose. Omar was the only one facing toward the stone wall and soon spotted me. He didn't make a peep, just gave me that look as if to say, *Why did I listen to you?*

"Hey buddy," I yelled to him, again trying to put a positive spin on things, but he only raised his chin at me.

"John?" the photographer asked.

"Yup."

"Hey, look Omar, your friend has come," the photographer said to him.

Omar huffed.

"Come in," the photographer told me, all excited. "The gate, it is right over there."

When I walked into the compound, I shook hands with the photographer, whose name was Mauro, and was then introduced to the model. While this was going on, Omar just stood there with a blank look on his face, looking really uncomfortable. I was still unsure what the hell I just walked into, and only when Mauro and his subject went off to talk did Omar smile, rushing over and giving me a hug.

"Omar, what the fuck is going on?" I whispered. "Is everything cool here?"

"Please, don't be primitive," he said. "Mauro is great. Help me a lot. He live here, right next door to Monica. Come inside, let me show you."

Monica's house managed to pull off the impossible by being even more offbeat than her driveway. It was well furnished, antiques mixed in with upscale IKEA, but from every rafter hung these puppets. Not little ones, either. Giant puppets. A four-foot Pinocchio. Five-foot yellow bird with human teeth. A washing-machine-sized purple orb with red eyes, top hat, and holding a walking stick. And dangling above Omar's bed on the second floor was a four-foot-high black crow.

"You sure everything's cool, dude?" I asked him when we were up there, alone. "You like it here? If you don't, just tell me."

"No, Johnny," he said. "I do, but it is hard for me. Everyone is so nice. They talk to me, but I cannot talk to them. They don't understand."

"Oh."

"I know how to live in the war now," he said. "Understand me? But I feel like alien here. I am serious. You must help me."

Reaching into my backpack, I took out the gifts I had brought along from his parents. I handed him his underwear and the two letters, but when I took out the pepperoni sausage and said, "From your ma," he burst into tears.

My plan to stay for one day eventually turned into ten. We did nothing special, just laid around, watched soccer on the tube, sometimes talked, sometimes not. But it was clear: If I was around,

he was relaxed. Whenever I got up to go somewhere, he always followed me. When I didn't pay him enough attention, he would flick
my ears or throw paper balls at me, and I had to keep reminding
myself that he was only eighteen, a war refugee who was supposed
to be nothing more than a pimply-faced twelfth-grader.

Monica, whose house it was, was even nicer than advertised,
blond, thirty-something, and cute. When I offered her money for
Omar's room and board, she refused outright.

"Omar is so nice," she said. "He has been through so much . . .
I am just happy to help in any way."

So, when it came time to finally head back to Sarajevo, I left
with peace of mind. Omar was in good hands. As usual, though,
there was some separation anxiety on his part when the day came
for me to go.

"What will I do?" he said. "You got to understand me, Johnny.
Sometimes, I think I go crazy. I want to go back to Sarajevo."

"Omar. Listen to me," I said, parroting back what my shrink
once told me. "You only have one job right now. That's to relax,
enjoy yourself. That's it. Nothing more. Run around the fields here.
Play with the fucking puppets. But I'll be back soon, then Dina,
and before you know it everything will be fine."

Except for a brief visit back to check on Omar in Italy, I spent
the next month almost exclusively with Vlado. By this time, Sarajevo was no longer the news hot spot it had once been. Rwanda,
Somalia, and Chechnya all were drawing attention, to the point
where more than half the press corps in Sarajevo had moved on. For
someone looking for a breakout story, hanging with an idling antisniper may not have seemed the most efficient use of time. But I
wasn't just after a story. He seemed to me to be going somewhere
when we talked, circling something, and when he got there I
wanted to be there, too.

Sometimes we would visit his perch, but most of the time we

spent in his apartment drinking coffee, smoking, and chatting about old times, his. He was big on visual aids—photo albums, maps, Italian shoes, political buttons, memorial prayer cards, car keys, trophies, an unopened souvenir Coke can from the '84 Olympics.

Through these things I finally got my read on what kind of guy Vlado had been before the war. He had grown up the oldest of three boys in a working-class family in Sarajevo. Whether it was birth order, genes, or what, he turned out to be the responsible son: never in trouble, always the best grades, a talented artist, a top marksman at the local athletic club (a big deal in Yugoslavia), the apple of his mother's eye. But in the photos he showed me from that period in his life, early to mid-seventies, he looked more like a Deep Purple roadie than the BMOC, clean-cut type of young man he described.

In most of those photos he was with two guys named Misho and Slavko, his best friends and teammates on his shooting team. The photos were classic seventies: all three guys were pasty and unhealthy-looking with long shaggy hair, tight bell-bottom jeans, skintight T-shirts, like they all had been smoking dope in the back of a van for a month.

"Good-looking crew," I joked.

"Of course," he said, totally missing the implication. "We were something, no?"

But everything wasn't so hunky-dory at home. The old man drank too much, and money was always an issue. When it came time for Vlado to go to college, he couldn't, even though he had won a slot in a prestigious art school. Vlado's father told him he couldn't afford it, so Vlado would have to go to work in one of the grimy factories that ringed the city.

"I wanted to be an artist," Vlado told me. "Paint nature. Make album covers, Rolling Stones, whatever. I was very sad, and angry. Very angry. But my mother come to me then and say, 'Vlado, don't be sad. Remember, anything you do with your hands can be art. Paint. Plastics. It's not what you work with, but how much of yourself you put in.' And you know what I discover? My mother is right."

Eighteen years old, Vlado found himself working as an apprentice lathe operator in a factory that made optics for the military. Like a Communist Horatio Alger, he threw himself into his work, pulling extra shifts on various machines for no pay so he could learn more. His buddies, Misho and Slavko, but especially Slavko, a world-class slacker, thought Vlado was crazy to work for nothing.

A year later, Vlado married his high-school sweetheart, Majda. He was nineteen, she was eighteen. Everyone thought he was nuts for marrying so young. As Slavko put it, "One woman for rest of life. *Think.*" Only his mother understood. "I loved Majda," he told me. "She was in my heart. Why wait?"

In the years that followed he continued to work his ass off, and then in the mid-eighties he caught a lucky break. The Yugoslav version of Communism softened a bit, and he was able to take his hard-won skills and start his own private enterprise, a one-room plastics factory in a village outside Sarajevo. At first, he filled orders for all those little plastic things everyone tosses away: toothpicks, clips, swizzle sticks, bookmarks. Then he branched out into pens, bottle caps, and lighters. By the early nineties he was filling orders for Volkswagen and well on his way to what he called "my American Dream."

"American Dream isn't just for Americans," he told me. "I wanted to work hard, give my family more than I had. And I was starting to, and that was really something for me. Nice things for my daughter. Benetton. Vacations with friends, Slavko, Misho, his family. Money for my wife. BMW for us. But then, of course, this war came."

By the end of that month, Sarajevo was enjoying the first city-wide cease-fire that held since the beginning of the war. More and more people were out on the streets, even venturing down Sniper

Alley every now and then. Vlado, now off-duty, began to take me on tours of some of the sites he had talked about: the shooting club, his favorite restaurant, Slavko's old bachelor pad. Most of these places were either burned out or, like Slavko's place, had been taken over by refugees, but that didn't stop Vlado from talking about them not as they appeared but as they had been. On these walk-abouts through his past, I was finally able to piece together what Vlado needed *from me.* It dawned on me that I wasn't just a reporter to him or his buddy, but I was his "stranger on the train." He was trying to make sense of something, understand something, make peace with something that had happened. I was sure of it. And he didn't want to go there alone.

A few nights later, I pinched a half bottle of moonshine from Nino and brought it over to Vlado's. As usual, we set up shop on his kitchen table: cigarettes, lighter, bread, ashtray, two water glasses, the booze on the floor. We had a few drinks, during which we talked about the current cease-fire and whether this one meant the end of the war. Vlado didn't think so. "Too much fight still left on both sides," he said.

At some point, I asked him to get out one of his photo albums and he had, his favorite, the one from the mid-seventies, which was stocked with his best friends and shooting buddies, Misho and Slavko. As he began to flip through the pages he got quiet, rubbing his finger over each photo as if he was reading Braille. He went deep in his head, far away, although, to be polite, he occasionally muttered something like: "This picture was taken after we won a competition in Banja Luka." Then, midway through the album, he stopped on one photo and just stared into it, completely gone. I didn't know where it came from, but I pieced it all together right there.

"Vlado, I once asked you, way back, who was the hardest sniper you ever had to hunt, and you told me, 'They all were hard.'"

"Yes," he said. "I remember."

"Well, I'm just curious," I asked him. "Thinking about it, was there one, one sniper out of all of them, looking back, that was maybe the most difficult?"

"Ahhhhh," he groaned, leaning back in his chair. He clasped his hands behind his head and looked up at the ceiling. Then he looked back down at me and said, "You never asked me like that before."

"So, there was one?" I asked.

"Yes," he told me. "There was one, of course. Everyone must pay a bill."

Then he told me this sightly circuitous story, which began a little over two years earlier, on February 25, 1992:

It was about forty days before the war would start and Vlado had been working late at his plastics factory overseeing a contract for Volkswagen. He got home around eight that night, and when he walked through the door he found Slavko, Misho, and Majda sitting around the kitchen table. As Misho and Slavko were always over at his place, Vlado didn't think anything of it. He simply said hello and went into the bathroom to wash up. Majda followed him in there and broke the news: Vlado's mother Kate had died that afternoon. Vlado sat and cried for a long time. He was always very close to his mother, and now she was gone.

A memorial mass was held three days later in a Catholic church and about two hundred people showed up, many of them people Vlado had lost touch with. There were the Nonoviches, workers from his factory, old coaches, childhood friends, even the old Meister from his first job at the optics factory who tapped Vlado on the shoulder and whispered, "Your mother was a good woman." The mourners were from every ethnic and religious group in the city—Serbs, Croats, Muslims, Catholics, Jews—but no one took notice of this except for the priest who commented, "Before the eyes of God, we are all the same. We are all God's children in God's eyes on the Final Day. I'm sorry for your loss but dear Kate, your mother, your friend, she is in heaven now, in peace. Take comfort in that."

That afternoon they laid Kate to rest. Fifty mourners were in the procession, most carrying floral arrangements with condolences attached. Slavko, an orphan, who regarded Kate Sarzinski as a sort of surrogate mother, carried one of the biggest arrangements, which read: *To Mama Kate, The last good-bye. Love Slavko.*

By the beginning of April, the situation in Sarajevo started rapidly deteriorating. Neighborhood thugs had thrown up barricades, and teenage gangs and heavily armed men in black masks roamed the streets at night. "I wasn't too worried," Vlado told me. "I thought it was like your riots in Los Angeles. The police would handle it."

In early April, forty days after his mother died, as was custom, Vlado took a bus out to visit her grave. Because of troubles on the street, he left his BMW and his family behind, leaving flowers at the grave and apologizing to his mother for not bringing the rest of the family but swearing to return.

Over the next few days, the situation grew worse, especially at night, when firefights broke out all over the city. It was even too dangerous for Vlado to go to work, but he tried to maintain faith in the authorities. Not everyone was so trusting: Slavko called from somewhere outside the city, offering Vlado, Majda, and Diana three plane tickets out of Bosnia. When Vlado turned him down, Slavko offered him canned food.

A day or two later, Vlado received a surprise visitor at his apartment. It was the gangster Juka, who had come for help. Juka was putting together a neighborhood self-defense force, and knowing Vlado was an expert shooter, he wanted him to join.

"I was a businessman, a family man, and Juka was a gangster, street guy," Vlado told me. "What did I know of such things? I told him no. The police and army will restore order."

"You're a fool," Juka told him. "Who do you think is shooting at us? The world you live in is gone."

For the first time since the crisis began, Vlado's neighborhood started taking shelling. The army was on television telling the populace to remain calm and that they would take care of whoever was attacking them. They also requested that all citizens turn in their weapons. Remembering what Juka said to him that night, Vlado took his binoculars up to the roof of his building where he had a clear view of the airport. What he saw turned everything upside down. The army claimed to be holding the airport against some unnamed enemy, but Vlado saw the opposite: the army had its guns turned on the city and was firing away with all they had. The next day, after consulting with Majda, Vlado went down to offer his services to Juka. He refused to carry a gun but said he would help in any other way he could.

A few days later, Misho stopped by Vlado's on his way to the airport, where Slavko was waiting for them. Misho was flying out with his family to Serbia and wanted to borrow a liter of gasoline so he could make it to the airport. Vlado was dumbfounded that his friend was cutting and running. He wanted to know why. "I'm Serb, my wife is Muslim," Misho had emphasized, saying it was just too dangerous, but telling Vlado not to worry because he was a Croat. Hearing this, Vlado interrupted, reminding Misho that both his wife and daughter were Muslim.

"What are you saying, Misho? My wife is Muslim, my daughter is Muslim," Vlado reminded him. What got to him was he had never heard his friend use such language before, carving people up according to the group they belonged to.

The day after Misho left town, several people were shot within in the neighborhood. A witness told Juka's men that the gunshots came from Vlado's building, and three guys were sent to investigate. Before they went around door-to-door, they got Vlado, who knew everyone. The guys were particularly suspicious about the old Meister, Vlado's old boss at the factory (who had attended his mother's funeral), as he lived in the only apartment that hadn't been searched yet. Vlado vouched for him, but when they came to the Meister's door, he got testy when they insisted on coming in, claiming they were discriminating against him because he was a

Serb. When he looked to Vlado for help, Vlado told him, "You must let them in."

Behind a false front, under the oven, they found an AK-47 that had been fired recently. After they took the old Meister away, Vlado and another guy searched the apartment further. In a book, they discovered a receipt for an AK-47 issued three years before by the Serb Nationalist Party in the name of the old Meister. Along with it was a list of other Serbs who had received guns, including many who lived right in Vlado's neighborhood, some of whom he knew, too.

It was now that Vlado realized Juka was right. The life he had lived before was an illusion. *The government. The army. The police.* All of those institutions where he had put his faith had betrayed him. His neighbors, colleagues, the old Meister had been plotting for years for this war. And worst of all his friends, Misho and Slavko—two guys he had known since he was twelve—whom he never regarded as Serbs or anything else but his brothers, were now gone. Misho was in Serbia, Slavko—God only knew where.

For the first time in his life, Vlado felt utterly alone. If he wanted to escape, he had a brother in Austria, but he wouldn't run. His thinking was, if everyone runs, who defends those who can't? The Serb nationalists wanted to ethnically cleanse Sarajevo—murder the men and rape the women—but if no one stood up to that evil here, then where? Where does it stop? And who stops them?

All the same, that didn't mean Majda and Diana couldn't go, but when he told Majda she must leave she said flat out, "No. The family stays together. Otherwise we're not a family."

"I was so angry at her," he told me. "But I also never loved her so much as I did at that moment. She was something."

Then, in mid-May, the troubles really began as the Serbs, with the army's help, launched a full-scale offensive on Vlado's neighborhood, hoping to slice it off from the rest of the city and then "clean" it. Vlado was shot in the chest, saved only by the body armor, but it was that next day when he killed his first sniper that he retreated into Majda's arms and cried all night.

When the Serbs failed in their attempt to overrun the neighborhood, they switched tactics to what they called "Fry the Brain," a terror campaign meant to drive residents out. The Serbs shelled the area day and night, ringing the neighborhood with snipers, who killed everything they saw, especially women and children. They thought that killing kids would make the women, and ultimately the men, take flight.

The people quickly learned to live with the shelling, but the snipers were a whole other issue. People panicked and begged Juka to take action. Without heavy weapons, he couldn't blow the Serb snipers out of their nests. The only real weapon he had was Vlado. So Juka sent his star out with orders not only to kill the Serb snipers but to train a class of antisnipers to take his place when he was killed, which seemed almost certain. Already Juka's unit had suffered over 50 percent casualties: antisniping was the most dangerous job of all.

Over the next three months, Vlado and his men hunted down and killed over twenty Serb snipers. Vlado committed himself completely, learning from everything he did and building up his own system for "taking" snipers. He learned to live with the idea of killing: "Simple," he told me. "Either him or me. That is war."

And then, around mid-July, just when the tide looked to be turning in favor of Vlado and his group, a new Serb sniper staked out the neighborhood.

"This one was different than all the others," Vlado told me. "He shot from extremely far away, an expert shooter. Must be. Four, five hundred meter. And from that distance he never missed, always hitting his target in the head. Consistent. Always in head."

Vlado began doing some detective work, trying to piece together a profile of this sniper, where he liked to shoot from, the time of day when he operated—any clue that could give him an edge. He read through the spotter's log book, visited places where the victims had been shot, tried to calculate the angles, and interviewed witnesses. Finally, speaking to a medic who had examined one of the victims, he caught a break: the guy had somehow recovered the bullet, a 7.92mm, quite unique. A week or so later Vlado was on the line when this sniper struck again. Vlado didn't see anything, but the report from the rifle was unmistakable. "Special sound," he told me. "It could *only* be one rifle."

Vlado, Misho, and Slavko had competed as a shooting team for almost twenty years. In the beginning, when they were teenagers, they used air rifle and small-caliber guns, caring for their guns like babies. But when they got older, in the mid-seventies, they graduated to a larger-caliber rifle, specifically the Mauser 98, a German rifle dating back to 1898, which used the now rare 7.92mm cartridge. (In 1988, in their last competition as a team, they set the national record for the Mauser 98 at three hundred meters.) Because of the length and shape of its barrel, the Mauser had a unique boom that set it apart from any other rifle. When the war broke out, there were sixteen Mauser 98s in Sarajevo, fourteen of which Vlado could account for. Misho's was one. But Slavko's was one of the two unaccounted for. When Vlado heard the report of the master sniper's rifle, a thought occurred to him—a thought he didn't want to consider.

"I couldn't believe it," Vlado told me. "I didn't want to believe it, but still, I had to stop whoever was out there."

In late July, the sniper finally made a mistake, coming in close, closer than ever, taking up a position in a small building only two hundred meters behind the Serb lines. But, as he was taking up his position, one of the spotters saw him and notified Vlado, who quickly took up a position overlooking the building where the sniper was waiting. Vlado cooled his heels for hours before he heard the unmistakable boom of the Mauser 98. A few minutes later, a figure darted from the back of the building and started running across a path to cover.

Vlado didn't have a second to think. He pulled the trigger and shot the man in the chest. He dropped to the ground and lay there twitching. The spotters with Vlado started to scream: "Shoot him, take him."

But for the first time in his life, Vlado couldn't pull the trigger. For almost a minute he kept his rifle trained on that body out there, but he couldn't do it. And then, from behind a wall a grappling hook at the end of a rope flew out and landed on the body and hooked him. Whoever was at the end of that rope two hundred meters out there started dragging the body toward the wall. Still Vlado couldn't shoot, and then the body disappeared.

Vlado didn't tell a soul that he believed the sniper to be a man he considered his brother. How could it have come to this? Vlado put out the word that he wanted to talk to any exchanged prisoners who may have been in his area on the Serb side of the line on the day he shot the sniper. A few weeks later, he was told of a man named Amir whom the Serbs had held as a prisoner since the start of the war. When Vlado asked the man to describe this sniper, Amir described Slavko perfectly. He went on to say that, yes, he had been shot and that he had died.

Vlado thanked Amir and turned to leave, but before he could get out the door Amir asked, "Hey, don't you want to know his name?"

Before Vlado could say no, Amir smiled and said, "Slavko."

Vlado was in tears, hurting hard. Except for Majda, I was the only other person in the world he had ever told.

"It is hard," he told me. "It is so hard to live with. If he was out there, he was a monster. But he was also my friend, my brother. I can't forget that. He was that close to me, closer than blood."

I didn't know what to say, so I just nodded in sympathy. All the time I had spent with Vlado, I had never seen him like this.

"I have this dream. I think of time after war and I am here, alive," he told me. "Then Slavko comes to me. Not the sniper Slavko, but the Slavko I knew. My friend. My brother. And we talk, just old times. We laugh. Talk of women. But then I ask him, What did you do in the war? And he says, I was a sniper. Where, I ask, and he says, around here. Then I tell him, Slavko, open your shirt. And he does, and right in the middle of his chest is a scar, a large scar, just where I shot him."

Vlado stopped there.

"Then what do you do?" I asked.

And he said, "I kill him again."

eighteen

Back Through the Looking Glass

When I graduated from the Forum late in the fall of 1991, I felt that I had turned a real corner. I came away with a sense of transformation, as if I finally understood what it was that was holding me back from that precious feeling of being alive. It was my Racket, my damn need to understand the essence of everything before I did anything; hence, I hadn't been doing squat, just lying in bed complaining to myself about the meaninglessness of it all. *What a fucking jerk-off I was!*

With this newfound sense of liberation, I started cobbling together a semblance of a normal life just as Dr. Atchley had planned. For the next few months, I commuted from Garden City into Manhattan to my telemarketer job, started hanging out with my friends in town, and even accomplished what I never thought would have been possible: I attended my fifth-year high-school reunion and even a had a good time. But by the beginning of the new year, that buzz I had enjoyed, that feeling of finally having a definitive road map to life, started wearing off.

I went back to the Forum to attend its advanced courses, but gone was that sense of being on the doorstep of salvation. As with my unfounded faith in all else I had tried, reality eventually got in the way of my belief in Rackets, too. By February 1992 I was holed up in my bedroom again, sleeping my days away, staring up into the stars at night and daydreaming of suicide for relief.

This time around I was smart enough to keep my thoughts of suicide to myself because to do so meant losing control over my life again. I even stopped seeing Dr. Atchley once a month, telling him I was really doing OK, just keeping my powder dry until the right antidepressant came around. He called every so often to check in, but I never totally opened up to him again about how I was really feeling. I was a hard nut to crack.

I kept my dreams of self-annihilation to myself because I didn't want to worry anyone. I'd already done enough of that; I had already put everybody through too much. But some things don't have to be said. It was clear I wasn't functioning at all, and my very presence in the heart of my family was poisonous. My mother was so consumed with worry, she barely slept. My father, trying to hold the whole show together, was at his wit's end. Then circumstances intervened: my mother became very ill and had to undergo serious back surgery, and my father's business was struggling. They decided they had no choice but to sell the house. Needless to say, my attic sanctuary was going to go with it. I was about to lose my last mooring.

Despite my condition, my father had talked me into applying to graduate school for the fall semester of 1992. "You got to go. You got to make it work," he told me. "For yourself and for your mother. You've got to make a life for yourself." His desperation was as plain as the fact that he could no longer watch what my illness was doing to my mother.

I knew he was right but I was terrified, in pain, literally, at the thought of losing the one place in the world where I could feel not comfortable, really, yet at least protected. But then again, my father was right. This couldn't go on. I had to get a life. Plus, the damage I was causing to those closest to me was ratcheting up my rediscovered self-hatred. What finally made me agree was my father's conviction that if I went to school and really applied myself, great things were bound to happen. As he spoke, I could almost see what he envisioned. I wanted to believe in his dream, too, but I had wanted to believe in lots of things.

"You sure?" I asked him. "You sure about this?"

"Absolutely, kid," he told me. "Trust me, I know what I'm talking about."

Always a sucker for a new beginning, I bought into my old man's vision as best I could.

In the fall of 1992 I found myself down in Charlottesville, enrolled in the graduate program in foreign affairs at the University of Virginia. Upon arrival, my only priority was to find the right place to live. I didn't care about the location or amenities. The only thing I gave a damn about was that my new home had bookcases, enough space to hold the two hundred and fifty books that filled my car. These books were my security blanket, and I eventually found a room that had once been the library of a big, old Victorian house right off fraternity row.

Once I had moved in, I spent a week decorating: arranging the books by subject matter; taping a pheasant-patterned fabric to the box spring of my bed to make a dust ruffle; centering my desk in front of the bay window; scouring the local Salvation Army thrift shop for just the right furniture; tacking up Monet and van Gogh posters along with a school banner; and topping it all off with a Persian rug knockoff and an array of Boston ferns and philodendrons. Up to that point the verdict was still out, this whole enterprise was still all possibility, but it had to start and my energy was actually kind of surprising.

Dressed in khakis and a button-down oxford, I attended my first round of classes, a week late, and quietly collected all the handouts I had missed. Back in my room, I organized them on my desk, took a hot shower, got dressed, poured a cup of coffee, rolled up my sleeves, sat at my desk, and got down to work. The first of the Xeroxed documents was a survey of the ethnic makeup of southeastern Europe. Bulgars. Roma. Magyars. Romanians. Serbs. Greeks. Turks. Croats. Bosnians. Something called a Slovene. It took only a page for me to start panicking: *What the fuck am I doing? What's the point to all this? Where is this going to get me? What am I doing here?*

It was odd but I was back where I started, pretending to be normal to anyone who cared to inquire but privately living in a nightmare. My parents called every day when I was down in Virginia, and every day I told them everything was going great. But four months after I arrived in my new home in Charlottesville, that is, in January 1993, I was holed up in that old library turned bedroom. By then it was the start of the second semester, but the truth was I had never finished the first. Two months into my return to academia, I was barely hanging on. Some days I was so defeated and down I couldn't even scrape together a decent reason to move—not for class, bathing, or food. Other days I would make it out the door, but not actually to class.

When I did make it, about half the time, I never said anything and these were graduate classes, chock-full of people who were supposed to be passionate about the subject matter. Not only didn't I give a shit, I felt like a seven-foot, four-hundred-pound, eight-legged alien in a human's mask doing my best to remain undetected. I lived in abject fear that one of these professors would call on me and find me out, which, of course, eventually one did.

"Mr. Falk, we haven't heard from you yet. Maybe you'd like to give this a try?" the professor asked one day, referring to something he had written on the blackboard.

By that point in my life I had felt like an Other for over ten years. My sense of alienation had grown so intense that it had consumed everything in my brain. When that professor asked, "Maybe you'd like to give this a try?" all I can say is I felt like the whole world, all six billion people, was looking at me. I didn't move a muscle.

"Mr. Falk, maybe you'd like to give this a try?" he asked again, as if I hadn't heard him.

What he was asking was actually not that complicated, but I just couldn't speak, even to say no.

"Come on, give it try," he said.

I starting sweating. I felt it beading on the back of my neck. My heart was racing. I barely managed to shake my head.

"You sure?" he asked.

I lowered my head.

"OK," he said. "Maybe someone else would like to give it a try?"

At the end of class, the professor asked me to see him in his office. Walking over there, I thought I was totally screwed. I didn't belong in that school. I didn't even know what I was doing there, but if I got booted, I couldn't even imagine where else I could go. At least here, I was still alive on paper, technically doing something. So, when I finally got in there and he told me to take a seat, I was expecting the worst.

"Do *you* want to be here?" he asked straight out.

"Look, I don't know," I told him. "I wish I could tell you absolutely yes, but I can't."

"Then why did you come here?" he asked.

"I mean, don't get me wrong, I'm interested in this stuff," I said. "Look, I don't know if this means anything, but a while back someone diagnosed me with depression and maybe that, maybe that has something to do . . ."

He held up his hand, shook his head, and said, "Don't say any more. That's all I needed to know. Depression is a serious illness, and I'll work with you no matter what it takes. You're in this school now, John, and we'll all work with you."

I was amazed at his empathy. As soon as he heard me say "depression," he felt he had his answer. He hadn't told me I was crazy or trying to shirk something. This professor, this perfect stranger who owed me nothing, somehow intuitively knew that I wasn't so much a graduate student as someone who was just holding on for dear life, and having him say in so many words, "Don't worry, I'll help you," meant everything. It was a little bit of light at a very dark time.

So that January, the start of the second semester, I was a quasi-graduate student: going to class, but not taking exams. Most days I just sat in my room, staring out the window or watching videotapes of the history of Poland between the world wars. These tapes infuriated me because these Poles were fighting back and forth, shedding blood and arguing over all these fine points of government, national identity, economy, religion, and for what? I felt like yelling at the television every time I watched one, "You're fools. It doesn't matter. In a few years, the Nazis are going to show up. Then Stalin. It's all meaningless."

Before Virginia, I was in one of my deep episodes where I couldn't even get out of bed. I wasn't eating. I wasn't sleeping. All I had the energy to do was imagine my own death. About three days into it, with no end in sight, I reached out to my mother. She was in her room, folding laundry. As soon as I walked in, she tried to give me a smile but it was obviously forced. She was as desperate as I was.

"Ma, what do you believe in?" I asked her.

"What do you mean?"

"I mean, why do you do what you do?" I asked. "What do you believe in?"

She took a seat on the bed and took a deep breath. "I believe . . ." she thought for a second. "I believe in being good, that we all matter."

"What does that mean? All matter? How could that be?"

"What don't you understand?" she asked me.

"All of it."

"John, life is short. It can be hard, trust me. But we all matter to other people. What we do matters to other people. At the end of the day, that's what matters. Being a good person."

"But that doesn't make sense," I said. "Why does it matter? Who cares?"

"John, it does matter," she said. "It's the little things we do for each other that make life. Maybe it doesn't make sense, but it matters. Let me ask you: What do you believe in?"

"Nothing."

"What do you mean?" she asked.

"I mean, I don't believe in anything."

"Nothing?" she asked, shaking her head, almost as if she didn't believe me.

This anger, this pure venom, just welled up in me and I screamed, *"Ma, I don't believe in anything!"* And as I yelled that, I whipped the phone against the wall, shattering it. My mother put her head in her hands and wept. I put my hands to my head because I knew I had become a monster. I leaned down and hugged her, and she seemed so small and frail.

"I'm sorry, Ma. I'm so sorry," I said. "I would never hurt you."

"John, just tell me, even if you have to lie, just tell me you'll be all right."

"Ma, I'm gonna be fine," I lied. "Trust me."

In truth, by then I had actually come to believe in something but I didn't want it to be true. Life was just brutal. It wasn't fair. No one was promised happiness. Virtue wasn't necessarily rewarded, vice punished. It was all just a crap shoot. Some lost, some won. And for whatever reason, I had lost.

Sitting in that room down in Virginia that January, in that carefully reconstructed replica of my attic, that was how I pretty much had come to see it. I was defective. There was something wrong that prevented me from simply living. But deep down I didn't think it was depression per se, some faulty chemical interaction in my brain. It was *my* fault. I was the only person living my life, making the choices I made. I was the one who had built this prison for myself, a prison no one else could see. Most others couldn't understand, which made it all the worse. Who the fuck was I to feel this way, anyway? I had nothing to complain about, yet that's all I did. Everything was negative. Empty. Without value. I was on this planet sucking up resources but producing nothing. I was excess baggage. If I had it my way, I would have been dead already.

One day, I remembered that box I found in the crawl space off my attic bedroom when I was a kid. I thought of the kid in the cowboy outfit who turned out to be my uncle Robert. I remembered my mother's sad words when she described him: "On the edge of other people's lives." He never had anyone; his own mother had abandoned him to his fate. He had died alone "on some stupid beach in Eureka," as Mom had put it.

"On the edge of other people's lives." That was me and this was now. In Virginia, I didn't know anyone well anymore. I had made no friends. I didn't make plans with anyone. I had a cousin who lived only a block away—a star athlete at UVA whom I had been close to growing up. But I never saw him. I had friends from home who had younger brothers at school down here. I never saw them. The point was, I didn't want to see anyone. When I did get caught, I would always do just enough to ward off any questions and then disappear back into my cocoon. Back there, safe and alone, I would find myself envying Robert. *"Dying alone on some stupid beach in Eureka."* That sounded nice to me. I wanted to be that lone photo stashed away in someone's attic. I wanted to disappear. But if I took my life, the pain I would inflict on the very people pulling for me, believing in me, would outweigh the intense misery I experienced every day. And that's the only reason I chose to keep my heart beating at this time. I had truly been beaten because I finally gave in for good: I was never going to be part of the world.

Before I left for Virginia, I had asked my mother, among other things, not to worry about me. A ridiculous request, and, of course, she ignored it. She stayed in touch with Dr. Atchley, mostly to keep him up to date on how I was doing and keep abreast of any new developments. As luck would have it, around that time a new anti-depressant hit the market. In clinical trials, it had proved particularly effective with unipolar depressives like me. It was called Zoloft, and my mother called to tell me that Dr. Atchley, who had recently semiretired and moved up to Massachusetts, thought I should go to the student health clinic to get a prescription. As my parents and Dr. Atchley were the only people I still trusted completely, I did.

I went on Zoloft in January 1993 and for a few weeks nothing changed. When Dr. Atchley had put me on Prozac a year earlier, I had asked him, "How will I know it's working?" He had said, "You'll just know."

It was a few days before Valentine's Day, and I have no clear recollection of how I spent the night before. Probably like always, I was just lying in bed, staring at the tube, utterly alone, running through the same loop of unanswerable questions. I probably knocked off at my usual time, two or three in the morning.

When I awoke, it was after ten. With the pillow over my head, and still a little groggy, I remembered I had a class at eleven. Plus, I still had those damn Polish tapes in my possession, a good two weeks overdue. If I hustled, I could return the tapes and still make it to class. I rolled out of bed, and as I hadn't bathed in a few days, I took a quick shower. I put on some pants, an Irish sweater, a jacket, grabbed the tapes, a notebook, and ran out the door. I walked down the driveway, turned onto fraternity row, and headed to campus. It was one of those rare winter days, sunny and brisk. It was a quarter-mile walk to the video store and I don't remember thinking that much in particular. But I'll never forget what happened as I was crossing over a little graffiti-covered bridge. I smelled wood smoke. It was as simple as that. I smelled wood smoke, and suddenly I had this feeling of being this little kid again, running home in the winter, through the snow, it's dark, my nose is ice cold, my hands in balls, but I know at home everyone is there, hanging out. It will be warm when I get home.

And that was it.

"You'll just know," Dr. Atchley had told me.

And he was right. I just knew at that moment that it was over.

I stopped and turned around and around and looked at everything. Nothing had changed. Everyone was just walking along as they had been. The only difference was, I wasn't on the outside watching. I was just simply part of it all, part of life. Nothing more, nothing less. I doubled over, put my hands on my knees, and let out a breath I had been holding inside myself for ten long years.

nineteen

Blessing in Disguise

I had known Vlado for just a few months, but in some ways I knew more about him than people who had known him his whole life. And the whole situation was making me crazy: I had finally found a great story—the tale of a normal guy forced to kill his best friend in the middle of this heartless, bloody war—and I couldn't use it. He had told me as a friend. He saw himself as a man who was literally waiting on death's door; he didn't know how much longer his luck was going to hold out. Now, suddenly, I was his confessor and this was a confidence I just could not break. In fact, I could never even bring myself to broach the subject of writing about what he had experienced.

Even though I thought that I could never publish Vlado's story, I still felt better than I had in a very long time—maybe ever. Vlado may not have panned out professionally, but I believed we had become friends, that I had gotten tight with someone special. And then there were Dina and Omar. I had set out to help them because I had grown to despise myself for living in their apartment and eating their food while they were suffering through a war. But when I crossed that bridge into their lives, I inadvertently tapped into something new. For the first time I wasn't searching for something, but doing something. I had a newfound vitality and sense of purpose; it was as if I was finally connected to something real.

By April 1994, Omar had been safe and secure in Italy for months, although I had to make frequent trips back to keep his spirits up. As for Dina, I was still working on a way to get her out of Sarajevo. On top of that, in March, Dina's aunt—a fragile woman who was clearly becoming more and more despondent, had asked me if I could help her daughter, Olja, get out of the country. What the hell was I gonna say? I knew Olja; she was a nice kid. How could I say, *No. Sorry, the ark is full?* So the situation was that by the beginning of that April I had taken on a lot of responsibility. I was also strapped for cash. Getting the passports and taking care of all the traveling details had made this into a money-eating operation, and—let's face it—I wasn't drawing in the big bucks. And there weren't new freelancing opportunities: the city was holding and the story was lacking in the kind of dramatic new developments that grabbed headlines. In other words: No blood, no news. No news, no cash. I was happy for Sarajevo, but wondering about my next move. But there were some developments that promised some work.

Something was simmering out in the hinterlands of Bosnia. Spring was coming, and the Serbs were bound to launch an offensive someplace out there in the countryside. If I could anticipate where the upcoming Serb offensive would strike, then I would be on the scene before anyone else. I could scoop what was left of the foreign press corps in Bosnia, do great journalism, and, more important, fill my empty coffers.

If necessity is the mother of invention, than desperation is the mother of hare-brained schemes. Way back when, Harald had introduced me to another American freelancer named Michael. In late

March, I ran into him again in Sarajevo. Michael was as hard up for a story as I was and he had money, $660 (a veritable fortune), but no ride. I was desperate for a story, had no money, but had bought a Russian jeep in the late fall when I was flush with cash after my MTV gig. I had bought it for fifteen hundred deutsche marks off a gimlet-eyed peasant under a bridge in Croatia, where I kept it stashed for forays into the mountains of central Bosnia. But I ended up driving it more often around the northern rim of the Adriatic on the way to Italy to visit Omar.

So, in the first week of April 1994, Michael and I rolled into Bosnia and headed up to the northern edge of an area called the Tuzla Pocket, the place we both agreed the Serbs were likely to attack in the coming weeks. We both thought we'd return by the beginning of May.

Three weeks later, I was sitting across the table from a man pouring a shot of moonshine into the knee of his artificial leg. As he prepared the cocktail, his beady eyes locked on mine. Islam was the local poet laureate, and the drink was one of his not-so-subtle tests of brotherhood.

Michael and I had made decent progress, but it had been tough going. The Bosnian army had morphed into a real army; it was no longer a loosely knit confederation of warlords, but a by-product of this professionalism was that reporters were no longer tolerated on the front lines. We were considered unnecessary security risks. So Michael and I did our best to work our way around this by making contacts with regular Bosnian soldiers in the field, guys we hoped would be willing to disobey their superiors and take us to the front lines. Slowly but surely, we were able to hopscotch our way up the pocket, from one contact to another, each one a bigger lunatic than the last.

Ultimately we had found ourselves holed up in this abandoned one-floor brick house with Islam and his strange crew: a giant troubadour in ski boots named Yeti, a fourteen-year-old alcoholic armed with a Russian pistol, and, most important for us, two combat medics nicknamed Seal and Hell Rider. It wasn't ideal, but we were only a few hundred yards behind the front line that, Michael and I believed, would soon be the site of the Serb offensive.

We had been drinking with these guys for twenty hours straight, trying to talk them into bringing us up those last few hundred yards. Somehow, their willingness to take us to the front lines became inextricably connected with our ability to drink superhuman amounts of moonshine. Now, with this whole prosthetic-leg-as-shot-glass routine, Islam was upping the ante. Having lived with Ella Nonovich's gruel for the past seven months, I had a library of gastronomical excuses (translated into Bosnian). But they were clearly inadequate to this challenge. After Islam topped off, he handed me his prosthetic chalice with about two shots of clear moonshine in the cavity that usually held that scarred knob that was his knee. A tiny slick of oil floated across the top as I brought it to my lips. It stank of sweat.

Islam and the others cheered as I downed it and patted me on the back. Steadying myself as my stomach churned, I began to sermonize about friendship, the power of the press, and how fucking important it was that they finally escort us up to the line. I was making progress. We were growing tighter, closer. Before long they were saying things like "I'll die for you" and "You can have my sister." I had done good, but it didn't matter because events were soon to make the trip to the front line irrelevant.

A little later, a stick-thin farm girl with a T-shirt that read EAT TO WIN stopped by, and Hellrider turned on the radio for a little mood music. That's when I heard the news: the Serbs had done an end around and attacked the southern part of the pocket. To everyone in the room it was a great relief: they weren't going to die in the next week. I was happy for them, but I had lost yet another big scoop. And, in the attack, the Serbs had cut the only road in or out of the Tuzla Pocket. This meant Michael and I were probably going to be marooned for several weeks. For the first time in over a year, I was going to have to go without Zoloft. I was already down to just a few pills—a three-day supply at most. I had my large reserve stash hidden in my tube sock back in Sarajevo, but that was a hundred miles and one very active front away from here.

The next day, Michael and I left Islam and his friends and headed back to the apartment we were staying in in the city of Tuzla to wait out the Serb offensive. For the first hour of the ride, I was pretty quiet, nervous about what would happen when the last of my Zoloft finally drained from my brain. God, I didn't want to go back there — the alienation, the inability to break out of myself, lose myself in anything. It was all a very bad dream by now.

But then I thought, maybe this isn't so bad. I turned back to the idea that my depression had been nothing more than a character flaw— the result of bad decisions I had made. Maybe now, after everything that had happened, I would be different. Maybe I was going to find out that I didn't really even need the Zoloft now. Maybe running out of the stuff was going to prove a blessing in disguise.

But, just in case, I had to prepare Michael. As we were driving over the Posavina Mountains back to Tuzla, I decided to come clean. I had no idea what was going to happen, but we had become friends and so—just in case I did retrograde into some unpleasant, less personable version of myself—I wanted him to know that he shouldn't take it personally. So, as we were cruising past some peasants working on a water pump, I told him about the Zoloft without going into too many unnecessary details.

"Oh, man, I'm sorry," he said. "I didn't know you were on anything."

"Nah, it's all right," I said, playing it down. "I don't think anything will happen, but if I become a little down or something, that's probably the reason. Just so you know, that's all."

• • •

The apartment where we were staying in Tuzla was in a complex of gray, eight-story apartment buildings near the center of the city. Middle-class Communist chic, it was comfortable but a bit dreary with Bulgarian couches, Yugoslavian appliances, oil paintings of snowcapped mountains, and a cheap Korean television. We had water and gas—a treat—but electricity was sketchy.

Upon our return, Michael headed out to look for new stories. I tried to get going on an article about Celic, where we had spent some time earlier in our trip. Celic was a small town of only a few hundred people virtually surrounded by the Serbs, who were dug in along the ridges of the hills that ringed the place. The people shooting one another there had once been neighbors. There was indiscriminate shelling. It was, basically, a Sarajevo-type situation but more intimate.

For days, I worked on my piece while Michael did his thing. At first, it was difficult finding some coherency in the chaos of my notes, but I eventually got going. In Sarajevo, the war was slightly more principled: a lot of the city people saw themselves struggling for an idea, a pluralistic society, and against a fascistic ideology. But in Celic, the fight struck me as more tribal, there was an Us vs. Them mentality.

About twelve days in, I found myself tearing up everything I had written. The coherency of the work seemed to me to have vanished. I just couldn't connect the dots anymore. As a matter of fact, I doubted for the first time that they were ever there. So I started over, in search of a new angle, a different kind of understanding, and I scribbled the rest of the morning away. But I realized it was just verbal spaghetti. In the afternoon, I tried again but made little headway because I started to recognize some fundamental problems.

Why was I writing?
What difference would another article on Bosnia make?
Who cares?

I couldn't concentrate, as these questions stood like sentries in front of any coherent thought. But I tried to push ahead. Michael had even left me his laptop after I promised I would put it to good use.

Three days later Michael snuck into the living room where I had set up camp to see how I was doing. He found me sleeping next to a pile of cigarette butts. I had a heavy five o'clock shadow lit by the glow of the screen and he assumed I had written myself into exhaustion. He looked over and read my story. It read: "Celic was a small town."

The following night, Michael started getting on my nerves. There was no newsworthy action in Tuzla, yet he was always writing dumb-ass stories in his room like his piece on the price of vegetables. He even had the balls to ask me to read his stuff.

I told him, "Michael, no one wants to read about this stuff."

"I don't care," he said earnestly. "It's good practice."

Michael was a good guy. He was easygoing, with a decent sense of humor. He had a likable vibe. All the same, as the days ticked away, he started getting under my skin more and more. It was like living with the Energizer bunny; he was always moving. And whenever I pressed him to clarify why he was writing stories no one would ever read, he would always say, "How do you know? Anyway, what else am I going to do?"

It got so bad I found myself wanting to toss the little girl scout off the balcony. As he worked away, the heavy taps on his keyboard pounded in my head like Morse code that read: *This is great. I can't wait until tomorrow. What are you going to do with the new day, chief?* I staked a heavy blanket to the beam above the doorway between the dining and living rooms. It worked like a charm. I no longer heard Michael gathering his nuts.

Safe behind that blanket wall, the obvious finally hit me. I was slipping back through the looking glass. How else to explain the sudden onslaught of intense loneliness? The need to get away? The need to know, down to the absolute, *why?* I tried to stay afloat by reminding myself that this was nothing more than the result of a misfire in my brain. But was it, really? What was the greater reality?

This or being heavily medicated? I slid lower and faster down into my prison than I ever thought was possible.

Eventually, I put blankets over the living room windows to shut out the world even further. Basically, I re-created my attic bedroom on Long Island and my one-room library sanctuary in Virginia. I did it out of a kind of second nature, like an animal going to ground. But at noon every day, like clockwork, that cheap Korean television reached up into the heavens and brought *Rivera Live* on the NBC Superstation down to my cocoon. From where I was sitting, he had some balls, I'll tell ya. I remembered back to the late eighties when he had opened up Al Capone's vault live on TV. *What the fuck was that about?* And now here I was again, hunched over the tube in my cocoon.

After an hour with Geraldo, my head would be spinning. *Who was this guy? How did he keep his TV gig? What was journalism coming to? Why did they even let the damn TV people in on serious stories?* I got angrier and angrier, but it was hard to nail down just what was getting my goat. But I was damn sure there was something wrong out there and Geraldo was right in the middle of it—up to his hocks. Michael got an earful. He was the only person with whom I had to discuss this crisis in journalism I was perceiving. But it was frustrating because he just didn't get the seriousness of the problem. Michael was basically turning into another damn Geraldo himself right in front of my eyes. And I wasn't having it.

"You think you can take me?" I asked him when he returned from one of his morning jogs. Little Mary Sunshine was wearing his ridiculous nylon jogging shorts. They were smug and pissed me off.

"Yeah," he said matter-of-factly as he untied his little sneakers.

I was taken aback as I took this not only as a personal insult, but also a glaring example of elitist arrogance. He was from Massachusetts. I hated fucking Massachusetts.

He looked at me and smirked. I was standing before him in a blue T-shirt and jeans, the same outfit I had been wearing for two weeks. They were stained with streaks of dirt, grease, and chocolate. I hadn't bathed either, so I smelled like the bottom of a gym locker. My face was ghost-white, covered in a bushy red beard stained yellow with nicotine. My greasy hair was sticking out in all directions. I had everything but the squeegee.

"How do you figure?" I asked him, truly interested.

"I'm quicker than you are," he answered.

Quicker? What a strange response, I thought. Then venom splashed against my skull like coffee against the glass knob atop a percolator. *He's fucking with me.* I wanted to rush across the room face first and take a bite out of him. Perhaps he saw in my eyes I wasn't so much joking around anymore because he didn't say anything, just backed out and went into the bathroom.

By the third week of that May, my depression was more intense than I had ever known it. Edgier. Lonelier. Angrier. Even more lifeless. What's more, sometimes I found my thoughts turning on Omar, Dina, and Olja. I was pissed at them and more so at myself. Waves of regret washed over me. I was nothing but a sucker—a stone-cold tool. These friggin' Bosnians had fleeced me for all I was worth. Nino had played me like a flute, and now I was stuck babysitting his kids. It was like I was at war with myself.

The Serbs were more predictable in Tuzla than they were in Sarajevo. They shelled more or less the same place at the same time every afternoon. So usually, after I had watched Geraldo, I would jump off the couch and run to the balcony when I heard the sirens blasting their warnings of an impending Serb barrage. There was usually a ten-second window before the shells started hitting; I heard them coming from the east, like freight trains barreling toward me. Because a nearby military headquarters was a Serb target, the shells would soon be right over our apartment building, ripping the air right above my head. Then there would be this silence for a split second, and then a huge detonation that shook the building. The danger was the only medicine I'd had in days; every new round gave me a rush. After five minutes or so it would be over, though, and the buzz would fade.

My memories of this period are fuzzy and disjointed. I remember, at some point, being naked and rummaging through the apartment looking for who knows what. From somewhere, I dug up some white sheets, so I wrapped myself in them, taking on the look of a depraved and deranged Roman emperor. I proceeded to the balcony, which overlooked an empty parking lot. Below me a group of kids played soccer with a patched-up ball. *That's pathetic,* I thought to myself. *Those poor little fucks don't even have a decent ball and they don't even know it.* I stared at them until one kid caught sight of me and froze.

"Hey, you all ought to be in school," I yelled at him. "Hit the books or you'll never get out of this dump."

They took off running.

Later that afternoon, I woke up swaddled in sheets on the couch as an artillery shell screamed over our apartment. It blew up the casino down the street. I was on the balcony in my toga just in time to hear the second shell rip the air above my head. More shells followed and I was riding a wave of joy. Each shell flew over me and exploded nearby with great force. The building shook. I cheered as they approached and held out my hand and opened my mouth to feel the air suck as they whizzed by. I wanted to touch them.

On the twenty-second of May, Michael finally scored a tank of precious gasoline from the commander of the United Nations base in Tuzla. We were finally free to go, and the next day he piled me into the jeep, and took the wheel, and we headed out. We both thought the worst was over.

In the last town before we exited the Tuzla Pocket, we were arrested for spying. By then, with my big red beard and Pigpen style, I looked as if I had been living in the woods since, like, the dawn of time. The mere sight of me was enough to alarm a Bosnian counterintelligence guy who hauled us in. We were interrogated for a while with Michael politely handling their questions. Then, having had enough of the bullshit, I snapped. I essentially told the bastards that if they thought we were spies then they should shut up and shoot us, and if not, then let us go. Michael looked anything but thrilled by this development. But in the end they let us go. Sometimes it pays to be a little crazy.

That night, for our protection, we camped out outside a Swedish outpost in the woods. I slept in the jeep while Michael—*fucking nature freak*—slept outside on the ground. Around nine, he knocked on the window.

"You know today is your birthday," he said.

"Fuck, I'm twenty-six," I told him.

"Well, you want anything?" he asked. "A present for the big day."

I had run out of cigarettes, so I asked him to bum a few from the Swedes. He left and returned with four smokes, which he passed through the window into the jeep.

"There you go, big boy," he told me. "Happy birthday."

"Thanks."

"So Mr. Falk," he added. "Growing up, is this how you saw yourself spending your twenty-sixth birthday?"

It took a while to make it back. For much of the ride, I was comatose, locked away in my own skull. Basically, I didn't give a damn about anything, so when Michael would suggest making detours to check on this possible story or that, I just shrugged. We got arrested again, then again, drove into a mammoth mud slide, were shot at and shelled. Then the jeep broke down. Finally, I caught pneumonia. Michael had to drive me to a Doctors Without Borders office to get help. Two weeks after we left the Tuzla Pocket,

I finally made it back to my tube sock full of Zoloft. All in all, the trip had been a disaster.

As soon as I got into the Nonoviches', I went right for that tube sock and swallowed a handful of the blue pills, about 300 mg, 100 mg more than usual. I wanted out of this prison fast. Day after day I munched away, and about two weeks later I awoke once again in a different world. Suddenly, I was free again. But what struck me this time, maybe because I had been through it once before, was the subtlety of the transformation. It wasn't as if the clouds parted and angels sang as I ascended into the sunlight. The change was really just a sort of small tweak of consciousness. When the Zoloft reached a certain level in my blood, it wasn't that I suddenly felt one with the world. I had a sense of self but it just wasn't all-consuming, all the time. When I did something, I could lose myself in it. And the more I did, the more I would want to do. Before Zoloft it was the complete opposite: the more I did, the less I wanted to do; every endeavor seemed to reinforce a sense of separateness, of being alone in the universe. The medication opened up the *possibility* of living to me. For the first time, I really took it in: I had a problem. It was serious. There was no way around it. I was a depressive.

It was now mid-June, and as my mother had miraculously succeeded in getting scholarships for all three of the Bosnians, that left only two short months to get Dina, Olja, and Omar to New York in time for the start of school. From that point forward, that's all I focused on—getting those kids out.

When I had first offered to help get the kids out of Sarajevo, I thought the most difficult part would be getting them out of the city. And it was. Omar's departure had proved to be a bit tricky, and Dina's looked like it was going to be even harder. After she had received her scholarship papers and then her passport, the UN had stopped issuing those coveted press passes to locals. I didn't know how else to get her out, so in a moment of desperation I asked her to marry me, the only guaranteed way I knew of getting her out.

"John, I would rather die here than marry you," she explained.

"Dina, I don't mean marry, marry, like I love you. I mean . . ." I tried to tell her.

"No. I don't want to hear any more," she said. "Getting married may be a joke to you, but it is serious to me, no?"

Dina had come to see me as a giant fuckup machine, but I didn't hold it against her. She was Miss Perfect, straight As, president of the class. She seemed absolutely flummoxed by the fact that by some cruel act of fate her future had somehow landed squarely in the hands of the kid in the back row with his finger up his nose— in other words, me.

But in the end with Dina I didn't have to do anything. She, as was her way, took matters into her own hands and somehow secured for herself and her cousin Olja two seats in a refugee convoy out of Bosnia. So by mid-June, everyone had their passports, was safely out of Sarajevo, and held bona fide scholarships. All that was left to do now was get their visas to the United States.

I thought this step would have been the formality, and for kids from Germany, Saudi Arabia, or Japan, it would have been. But in a classic case of bureaucratic catch-22, the more desperate a student was to study in America, the less likely they were to be issued a student visa. In 1994, there was no more desperate class than Bosnians. And to make matters worse, it was a one-shot deal. Once refugees had been rejected, they entered the database and their fate was sealed. This wasn't my little secret, either. It was pretty well known among Bosnian refugees that they weren't exactly welcome in many places. Dina especially hounded me, wanting me to ease her worries, but all I could tell her was, "Just trust me, it's gonna work out." That never helped matters, but the truth was I knew it would.

Back in college when I decided to play Mr. Normal again, I

had interned for two senators. I can still remember sitting at my desk in D.C., thinking, *There's got to be more to life than this.* But I did come away from that town with one clear impression: democracy works. Many of those senators' staff worked on what was called "constituent matters," basically interacting with the public, either in person or, more often, via letter, clarifying a senator's position on an issue or helping a person address some problem. My plan was to fax a letter to a handful of senators and representatives outlining the kids' stories and the fact that they had scholarships. What I asked my mother to do was to go down to D.C., meet with everyone, and plead our case in person. In late June, with my father behind the wheel, that's just what she did.

I had faxed my letter to four senators and one representative, and over the course of that day she visited every one. They were expecting her. The first four offices she visited were those of three senators and representative Henry Lantos—all were moved by the stories of these kids' plights and agreed to help. But my mother really hit a home run with the last stop of the day: Senator Joseph Biden, a big wheel on the Senate Foreign Relations Committee. His staff was very proactive and arranged with her to notify them at least twenty-four hours in advance before each kid arrived at an embassy for their interview. In that twenty-four-hour window, the senator's office was going to fax a letter of support to the ambassador. My job when I showed up with each kid was to make sure that that letter got attached to their application.

In early July, Omar, Michael, and I left the puppet villa outside Bologna in my Russian jeep and headed down to Rome for Omar's big interview that afternoon at the American embassy there. Omar was a bundle of nerves. I kept trying to reassure him, and it wasn't just cheap talk on my part, either. With Omar's application in my lap, complete and triple-checked by Dina, and with the senator's letter awaiting us in Rome, I considered it all but a done deal. We were running a little past schedule, though, so an hour outside of Rome, Michael stepped on the gas of my Russian jeep to make up for lost time. We were up to about sixty when the jeep threw a rod. It bucked, swayed, and then two fists of black smoke poured into the jeep through the air vents. We rolled to a stop on the side of the highway.

"That didn't sound good," Michael said. When the smoke cleared, we saw a baseball-sized hole in the top of the engine. Omar was freaking and, as we attempted to calm him, a flatbed truck with flashing lights on top pulled up. A man got out and started hooking the jeep to a winch. In a few minutes, we were all heading back down the highway. But, because of the language problem, we weren't exactly sure to where. Twenty minutes later, the tower dumped us in a junkyard in the middle of nowhere, and left.

It was a nightmare. That jeep was our only mode of transport and it also had been my only asset. After the Bosnians were safely off to the States, I had planned to sell it to stake my trip to whatever war zone I picked next. I wasn't in the greatest of moods, but no matter how I was feeling, it was nothing compared to Omar's terrible disappointment. I knew, without a doubt, that if we didn't make the embassy this afternoon we'd make it tomorrow, but for an eighteen-year-old who was living day to day on a precarious edge, snafus were catastrophes. As with Dina, Olja, and most other refugees I had met, there was no sense of proportion because everything in their lives was so fragile. Any little screwup could feel life-threatening, so instead of bitching I focused on reassuring Omar.

About half an hour later we found a bus stop and jumped on the next one. By that night we were in Rome, where the three of us shacked up in some skanky hotel Michael paid for. The next morning, Omar and I left for the embassy. Up to that point, I hadn't been nervous. I knew everything would be OK, but when we stepped into the embassy and made our way to that interview room my nerves started popping.

When Omar was called before the bulletproof glass for his

interview, I went with him as his sponsor and slid the application to the counsel. She was a young woman in her early thirties. At first it didn't look good. She was hemming and hawing over little details: Where exactly was Omar going to be living? Who was going to pay for what? Then I asked her about the fax from the senators. She had no idea what I was talking about, took Omar's passport and application, and disappeared through a door. Half an hour later we were summoned back to the glass and right there she handed Omar his passport, complete with an American visa.

We didn't celebrate until we were safely outside. For eight months, I had been telling Omar, then Dina, and finally Olja, "Don't worry. It's all gonna work out." But they never quite believed I could pull it off. But it was done now, with big help from my mother. I had a part in changing someone's life for the better, and it felt great. Omar actually gave me a big hug and said, "Thank you, thank you, thank you, thank you."

Two weeks later, when it was Dina's turn, we took a train down to Rome and within ten minutes of entering the embassy, we were back out the door with an American visa stamped in Dina's passport.

"Well, John," she said. "I never believed you could do it, but you did it."

She stuck out her hand and gave me a hardy handshake. Two down, one to go. Ultimately, Olja's case went off without a hitch.

It was early August and we were all back at Monica's villa. Finally everything was set: the kids had passports, scholarships, visas, and ultimately three plane tickets from Rome to New York City. They were due to leave in ten days, the eleventh of August. My plan was to hang with them until they left, and then return to Sarajevo to rebuild my career and reload my wallet. As I hadn't filed any radio since early April, when I had ventured off into the Tuzla Pocket with Michael, I was going to have to win back my radio gigs from whoever held them now. Also, as my only asset—the jeep—blew up and I had borrowed pretty heavily over the past four months to support myself and the Bosnians, I was seriously in debt, owing Michael six hundred dollars, Harald four hundred, and over three grand to American Express.

If I was successful in getting my radio gigs back, and if there was enough news from Sarajevo to sell, I was figuring I could be back in the black in a few months. After that, I would need to earn another three grand, enough to fly back to the States to host a fund-raiser my parents were organizing for the Bosnians in Garden City. With what remained, I planned on flying off to cover the blood-baths in east Africa for round two of my life on the road. Although I hadn't achieved what I wanted to in Bosnia (I was still a lowly freelancer with no great story to his credit), there still was an upside. I now had experience and solid contacts.

As we had no money, the Bosnians and I pretty much hung around the villa for those ten days watching the tube, talking, and going for walks with the photographer Mauro's dog. Every so often, for a change in scenery, we would venture down into Bologna and stroll around. At night, Dina and Olja would make dinner, and when Monica returned home from her job in a bookstore we'd all sit around the kitchen table to eat pasta, occasionally drink some wine. As a nightcap, we sometimes went next door to Mauro's to look through his photo albums.

But on the Bosnians' part, underneath all that normalcy, there was still this whirlpool of fear swirling around. I could see it in the number of cigarettes they smoked, the way they always were moving about, the bandanas they still wore to use as tourniquets in case they were wounded, the questions they peppered me with about what would happen to them once they landed in America. The war was obviously still very much in their heads, and the people they loved and left behind all still in mortal danger. I knew I had no idea what they were experiencing, but I tried to do my best to make them believe that everything was going to work out great. I took a page straight out of my depression handbook and conjured up this picture of the magical future I felt would be theirs.

When it was sunny, we would sit around a picnic table underneath a pine tree. There we would all light up and, just like when I was a kid and my father would slow down on the Long Island Expressway as the Manhattan skyline would come into view, I would describe their new home, the buildings, how the tallest office towers in Sarajevo would be mere midgets in midtown Manhattan. I told them how New York had eight million people, twice the number of inhabitants as all of Bosnia had before the war, and how many of these people were new to the country and had come from every conceivable corner of the globe: Russia, China, Ghana, Bulgaria, Mexico, Brazil, Vietnam, Korea, the Caribbean, Eritrea, the former Yugoslavia. They were white, black, and every shade in between, Christians, Jews, Muslims, Hindus, Sikhs, Orthodox of every kind, pagans, atheists, punks, anarchists, bankers, lawyers, taxi drivers, actors, models, students, drug dealers, billionaires, working-class, homeless, straight, gay, those left wondering, bike messengers, limo drivers, diamond dealers, Yankees, Mets, launderers of both clothes and money. There were clubs for any interest, literally thousands of restaurants and bars, traffic everywhere, people everywhere, a city that literally never slept. I was trying my best to paint a picture of a place in the world that was brimming with life, energy, a place where everything was possible. They never told me as much but I knew each of them had to have some dream buried away inside them, and I wanted them all to feel that there was no better place in the world to realize those dreams than New York City.

It wasn't puff on my part, either. I believed every word of it, and more so, knew that the three of them were perfectly cut out to make New York work. They were hardworking, disciplined, honest, brave, but, above all else, they still believed in life. Even in the war, Dina would get up every morning, clean her room, and pedal off through mortar barrages to work two jobs, neither one of which she got paid for. She studied for classes that didn't exist and even fell in love. Omar made new friends and was also always out there doing something, too, like when he applied to that art school that only existed on paper and then miraculously got in. It wasn't that they were brain-dead. They were cognizant of the fact that they were screwed, targets in a human shooting gallery, but like almost everyone in Sarajevo, they didn't give in to that.

Before we knew it, it was August 10 and time to say good-bye. One of Monica's friends came by the villa that morning and drove us to the station so Dina, Olja, and Omar could catch the train to Rome. When we got there, Monica's friend stayed in the car while we all went in and bought the tickets with some money my parents had wired us. After that, we headed out to the platform to wait for the train. It was all business: checking tickets, passports, other paperwork. I reminded them what my parents looked like so they would recognize them at the airport in New York. And then the train pulled in. As I was due to see them in a few months anyway for the fund-raiser, we all just gave one another quick hugs and then they got on board.

They never saw me standing out there watching, but I could see clearly as the three of them walked into their compartment on the train. I couldn't hear anything through the glass, but Dina was obviously telling Omar to put their luggage up in the racks. Wisely, he started to do so. Olja asked Dina something, and she shook her head. Then Olja sat down. Dina then asked her something and she got back up. As Olja was checking her pockets the train started pulling out. The last thing I saw was Dina's face as she was still standing. She was looking down, and she was anxious about something. Then the train hit a slight curve in the tracks, enough to obscure my view. And that was it.

It was strange watching them go, but stranger still that I was wishing I was on that train with them.

twenty

Good-bye to All That

I stood on that bridge there in friggin', prepped-out Charlottes-ville, Virginia, for another minute, just taking it all in: the chill in the air, the sun on my face, the breeze flowing over my scalp. That wonderful wood smoke, which I snorted through my nose as deeply as I could, was so rich, so full, so real. I was *there*.

I ran my hand across the top of the concrete rail on the bridge, which was covered in old paint, rubbing the chips that cracked off between my fingers. They were sharp on the edges and brittle. I heard a girl laughing with her friend as they passed by. My wrist had goose bumps. The tip of my nose was cold. I wiggled my toes in my boots. It was the same world as before, but now it *felt* com-pletely different. Instead of interpreting everything, I was sensing it, taking it all in. Twelve years before, my senses had been powered down during the course of one night, and now suddenly the micro-scopic engineer in my head had hit the On switch. "Ho-leee shit," I whispered to myself. "It's working." I kept thinking, *Thank God. Thank you, God.*

Instead of rushing off to return those Polish history tapes, I spent what time I had before class just walking around in this new world. *The trees. The way the students were dressed. A mountain bike chained to a lamppost. A mud puddle. The dilapidated state of the frat house across the street. The way the sun warmed me. The kids hustling into the building down there.* None of these things had whys attached to them anymore. I wasn't compelled to ruminate. It all just was, and that was good enough. *Thank you, God.*

I made my Yugoslav history class on time, but instead of hiding away in the back of the class, I sat smack in the middle. A few minutes into it, the professor, the same guy who had once been so kind to me, posed a question and I put up my hand.

"Mr. Falk," he said, genuinely surprised. "You wanna give it a go?"

"Sure," I told him, and went into a long-winded answer regarding the political differences between rural and urban Serbia. A few months earlier when I had been called on in this class I had felt like the whole world was watching me. I was so intensely self-aware that I couldn't even speak. Now, although I knew people were staring right at me, wondering what the hell was going to come out, I could still think and function. Unfortunately, I didn't have the slightest clue what I was talking about.

"You make some good points, Mr. Falk," the professor said graciously. "But I was looking for something else."

After class, I met up with the professor in his office. It had been less than three hours since my breakthrough, but I was confident enough to declare myself cured and ready to get on with things.

"You feel better?" he asked.

"Absolutely," I told him. "It was like a miracle, and I want to thank you for all you did. But the point is, I guess, I'll be ready in a few days to take those finals."

After that meeting, I returned the tapes and then headed back to my room to call my parents to break the good news. Already home from work, my father picked up the phone.

"We guessed," he said after I told him.

"What do you mean?" I asked.

"About five days ago, both me and your mother agreed, something was different about you, your voice. No edge. You didn't sound angry. It's hard to say exactly, but we both recognized it."

"My voice?"

"Weird or not," he said. "All I can tell from this end is, Thank God. Here, say something to your mother."

"It's working?" she asked.

"No doubt."

"Oh, thank God. So, how do you feel? I want to hear it all."

"I don't know," I told her. "Like when I was a kid, I guess. Like myself, if that makes any sense."

"That's so interesting. Last week I told your father that you sounded to me like you did when you were a little kid."

"Really?"

"Yes, just like I remembered. You were a great kid. Always up for anything, and I could always talk to you. Then you withdrew. But you put up such a good front, it was impossible to get through. You wouldn't let anyone in, and you never came back. And it was very painful for us because you kept going farther and farther away into yourself."

"I don't know. All I can say now is, I remember liking doing things and now I want to do things again."

"Well, I love you and I couldn't be happier for you."

"Ma, I'm sorry for everything," I said. "I wish I was better, had been a stronger person."

"John, you did all you could do. You kept fighting, and that's a lot. You never gave up."

"Yeah, but come on," I told her. "I put you through so much. Both of you, so much b.s. I just wish I could take it all back."

"Well, that's not how life works, is it?"

We talked for another few minutes, during which we covered what I planned to do next. Obviously, I was going to keep taking the Zoloft. I would see the shrink at the university, as my mother advised, and I intended to finish out my degree by May and then go look for a job. After those bases were covered, my parents probed a little deeper to make sure I felt as good as I sounded.

"It's amazing," my father said when he got back on the phone. "It's true, you sound like the kid I remembered."

"Well, I feel that way."

"Amazing," he reiterated. "Just amazing. And thank God. All I can say is, I love you and couldn't be happier for you, believe me."

I hung up, sat back in my chair, and thought back over the conversation I just had, how odd it was. Here I had spent twelve years locked away in my head and now it was just over. *Very odd,* I thought. *This is all very odd.*

To make sure I wasn't suffering some placebo effect, I looked out the window at the night falling across the yard: the wind hitting the bushes, leaves swirling, the neighbor's light coming on, the sound of some far-off dog barking. For the next minute I sat perfectly still, waiting for anything to change. *Tick, tick, tick.* As I kept looking out that window into the yard, listening to the wind and that mutt, nothing I saw or heard made me feel like an Other. I picked up the phone again to share the good news with another person.

My history with the opposite sex had unfortunately dovetailed perfectly with my depression. I awoke that morning back in 1981 overwhelmed with that sense of alienation and uncertainty. But the depression never impinged itself on my burgeoning lust. As with most teenaged boys, girls weren't only a complete mystery to me but were intimidating. They didn't just look older but acted more mature. I was driven by something more powerful than fear, however—hormones, you know—and whenever I got the chance I put my neck out there and tried to win some chick over.

My first girlfriend was a cheerleader, beautiful and full of life. Unfortunately, she got bored after three months and dumped me for an edgier kind of guy. Little did she know. Anyway, I rebounded pretty quickly and by football season my senior year things were better, but there was always a problem. No matter who I tried to date, no matter what kind of girl, I could never connect. *Be myself?* That seemed impossible. I was always playing a part and was hyper-conscious of whatever I was saying. So, after a while, I would bail before I died from overexposure.

I always just assumed that, over time, I would either meet the right girl or click back into things, neither of which happened, of course. The further away I got from my first, brief relationship, and the deeper I fell into my depression, the shorter each subsequent relationship became. By college, it was essentially all one-night stands. I had the script down for that, could front a lot of energy and vitality for brief sprints, but as to relating to a girl over the long run, I knew that wasn't possible. I felt too under scrutiny. I never felt completely relaxed unless I was on my own.

After college, it got even worse. As I wasn't blessed with a model's good looks and didn't give off the faintest whiff of Future Lucrative Employment, I was dead in the water as far as women were concerned. That's what made Ann Moran so remarkable.

After my father talked me into attending graduate school, but before I left Garden City, he pushed me out the door one night into the arms of some of my old friends. Naturally he was a little worn out by the sight of me sitting around the house in advanced existential reveries. It was the last thing I wanted to do, but I felt like I owed it to the old man to play along until I could retreat back home. My friends and I were driving up to a local bar when I spotted a girl walking in. She was beautiful and way out of my league, but something happened in that bar. I got drunk and, with the confidence of eight beers under me, finally approached her and started talking. When I told her I was headed off to graduate school to study foreign affairs, she replied, "Perfect."

What was perfect I didn't know, and it didn't matter. I called her the next day and asked her out, although I was terrified about sitting across from a stranger and making conversation. Luckily, as it happened, Ann Moran was a depressive's dream girlfriend because, basically, she never shut the fuck up. It was one story after another, an endless stream of words and, even better, most of the stories were pretty good. All I had to do to play along was to say every now and then something like, "No way," "What a bitch," or "So then what did you do?" This was a role I could handle.

The problem was that after two months, even my small role seemed too much of a challenge. I was going to lose her one way or the other. So I came clean.

"I don't know what it means, but some doctor diagnosed me as depressed," I told her. "So if I have seemed to be moody or not with it . . ."

"Ohhhhh," she moaned, giving me a big hug. "My poor baby. Why didn't you tell me earlier?"

"I didn't want you to think," I mumbled, not wanting to admit my actual fear, *I didn't want you to think I was lame.*

"Well, don't you worry," she said. "I just wish you had told me earlier."

After I left for school a few weeks later and she left for her junior year of college in Baltimore, we kept on dating, long-distance, mostly. Again this was fortuitous. Distance was my preferred form of intimacy. But with even this limited exposure, I continued to feel like an Other around Ann. Whenever we were together, I was always playing the part of me. It was like trying to hold up a picture on the wall during an earthquake. But I thought I loved her.

After the Zoloft started flowing, I wanted her to know I was a changed man. When I finally called and told her the news, Ann didn't detect any difference in me. Still, she sounded genuinely thrilled, and we made plans to meet up in Charlottesville that coming weekend. *Just getting better and better,* I thought.

But by the time Friday night rolled around, and I was sitting in my room waiting for her to arrive, I had become a nervous wreck. This was going to be our first date, really. I felt myself now, something I had never felt around her. How was that going to affect us? I knew one thing for certain: I didn't want to lose her. She was sweet, funny, and hot. But in many ways love was just a word, an abstract to me, and I knew it. I was *guessing* I loved her. Now that I felt different about me, would I feel differently about her, *us*?

But the second she opened that door and jumped into my arms, I ceased wondering and worrying. All I cared about was kissing her, holding her against me, nibbling on her ear. I even whispered, "I missed you." She called me a "love fag," but instead of making some stupid comment like usual, I fell back into my bed with her wrapped around me. There was nowhere else in the world I would have rather been.

Usually when Ann visited we spent a lot of our time alone, but on this trip I wanted to make sure she had fun. I had called my cousin Burt to arrange something, so about an hour after she got to Charlottesville Ann and I headed downtown to the Biltmore Bar to meet up with him and some of his friends, a few of whom I already knew from Garden City.

The Biltmore was always packed with lacrosse players, frat guys, and the kinds of girls who majored in business and summered in the Hamptons. Before the Zoloft, and unless I was really drunk, a scene like this would have most likely set off an overwhelming, heart-pounding panic attack. I would have walked in with the sweat rolling off me, hyper-self-conscious, overcome with a sense of my overall deficiency. Even a minimal conversation would have been impossible. The moment I walked into the place, I would have been conspiring to get back to my room where I could be alone.

But none of that crap even entered my head on the evening in question. Ann and I picked up some beers at the bar and joined Burt and his buddies at a table. We were there for hours, and most of the time I just shot my mouth like the others, busting on this guy, telling bullshit stories. I really listened to what was being said, genuinely laughed when I thought it was funny, and shook my head when I thought it was stupid.

But it was the damnedest thing. Sometimes, when some story was going on too long or I just had the urge, I would pull back from what was happening. Not physically, but in my mind, and I would think: *If this had been even a week ago, I would never have come here. If I had I would have been completely aware of feeling alone, of being a completely separate entity from everyone at this table. I would have made as many trips to the bathroom as I could get away with to grab a few precious minutes of alone time to recharge before going back onstage again to perform the role of me.*

The odd thing was, not one person at that table recognized anything different about me. No one had the faintest clue that a few days before I had for all intents and purposes been commuted from a death sentence. No one leaned over and said, "You seem different. What's up? You lose weight or something?" To everyone there, I was the same damn guy I had always been, and that was testimony to how successful I had been over the years jiving people, creating that silhouette of an intact guy out there along the edges of their lives. Except for my parents, no one actually knew me well enough to get that things with me weren't quite right.

As for Ann, nothing had changed between us, outwardly. I was enjoying her company more than ever. I listened to her stories with even greater interest and, instead of running out of social energy, I found myself not wanting her to leave. All was well. Until Saturday afternoon when she got thirsty and we drove down to a convenience store together to pick up some diet soda.

The store didn't have its own parking spot, so you had to either park in the private lot in the back, which cost a few bucks, or take the risk and park the car for a few minutes in a tow-away zone out front. We chose the latter.

When we came back out of the store with the soda, there was a cop putting a ticket on Ann's Golf. She ran up to the police officer and pleaded for him to take back the ticket. When that didn't work, she started crying. He didn't care. Ann being Ann, didn't care that he didn't care and all but insisted he take the ticket back. It was getting ugly, and the cop finally turned me and said, "Do your friend a favor and get her back in her car before I arrest her."

"Arrest me?" she shouted. "For what? You can't arrest me!"

"Come on," I said, trying to gently tug her away. "It's not worth it. *Come on.*"

Ann had a bit of a lead foot and had been pulled over for speeding on pretty much every road she ever went down. I knew she was scared that this ticket would push her over the edge and she'd lose her license, but I wasn't concerned. This was a parking ticket, not another speeding violation. But when she finally got in the car, she started going nuts.

"Fuck," she screamed, pounding the steering wheel. Ann still had baby fat in her cheeks and looked as if butter wouldn't melt in her mouth, but I had been around her long enough to know she also had a little temper.

"Fuck, fuck, fuck!" she yelled, tears rolling down her face. "Fuck, this can't happen. Why did you let me park here?"

If this had been a week ago, I would have probably said very little, other than some comforting words. I wouldn't have known how to react: Was she justified in being so pissed? Was she overdoing it? I would have also been terrified of saying the wrong thing and losing her. But now, without thinking, I said what I felt. "Ann, it's no big deal."

"Yes, it *is a big deal*!" she shouted.

"Ann. This is nuts," I said, then enunciated. "It's-a-par-king-tick-et. Christ almighty, it's not that big a deal. Let's just get the hell out of here."

There wasn't a sound. Ann just sat there, confused, and then looked over at me as if to say, *Who are you and what did you do with my boyfriend?*

We managed to patch things up that night, and the next morning we exchanged presents for Valentine's Day. But three days after she left, I got the call. "John, I've been thinking a lot about this, but maybe it's best if we see a little less of each other. Maybe we're better off as just friends."

I was devastated and drove up to Baltimore that night to

plead my case, but I might as well have saved the gas. She was a tough cookie, and no matter what I said or promised, she left little doubt that we were history.

Driving back to Charlottesville, I was confused, upset: *Just when I feel myself, she dumps me. . . .* I tried to think of anything but Ann, but I couldn't. I kept picturing us together: snuggled up on her couch watching *Saturday Night Live,* taking a tour of the Rotunda on campus, the time she shot-gunned a Pabst Blue Ribbon and bounced the can off my head. I missed her, missed her *bad.* When I hit the strip malls near Mechanicsville, I lost it and the tears started rolling. I mopped them up by rubbing my face against my shirt sleeves. "Fuck! Fuck me!" I growled, smacking the steering wheel.

When I got back to my place that night I felt no better and I had a lot of trouble sleeping. The next morning, exhausted and alone, I wanted to just wallow in my misery, but I didn't have a choice. I had promised my professor that I would take those exams that coming Monday, so I had to study. I managed to pack up my books and walk over to the library, where I hid away in the basement stacks and worked well past nightfall. The next day, with still a lot more material to digest, I returned to the stacks and did it all again.

It wasn't easy because little snippets of Ann kept forcing themselves back into my head. Wondering what had gone wrong, rehashing our last weekend together, I would always go numb. But when I tried to concentrate on the material on my desk, I was usually able to reclaim my brain. In the past, unless under extreme duress or completely bombed, I had little control over my mind's eye. No matter where I was, who I was with, what I was doing, I was always detached, observing, and left compulsively wondering, *why?* But here I was in control, able to focus at will. Yeah, I was in pain, but realizing I suddenly had the power to manage it took a bit of the sting away.

That Monday I took those exams, and I didn't need the professor to grade them to know I did really well. Every question I understood, and I was able to marshal the information I had crammed into my head into coherent, persuasive answers. Walking back home that night I stopped on that bridge again, the first time I had done so in two weeks, and looked back on all that had happened already. I talked in class, had some good times, got dumped, drove up to Baltimore, returned in real pain, was managing it, and now had caught up with my schoolwork. Admittedly not the stuff of Napoleon but, knowing where I had just come from, it felt that way.

In the weeks that followed, my life fell into a routine. With student loan money running out, I got a job as a gardener on the estate of a German car-wash magnate. I got to work at six in the morning, an hour early, digging right in, weeding beds, digging holes, and carting around mulch. By eleven, I was usually done and heading home covered in dirt and sweat. I'd shower, put my books in my knapsack, and head off to class. After a few hours of lectures, I would find myself a nice quiet spot in the library to study. There was a lot to do. I had to complete that semester's work and I was planning on taking my competency exams at the end of May so I could graduate early. Even though I found I enjoyed the material, I wanted to get the hell out of Charlottesville, out of school. I wanted to start my life out in the real world.

My parents and I still talked nearly every day; it was clear they were still keeping tabs on me. In early April, with my mood still promising, my dad instigated a Father and Son Talk, hoping to find out what I was planning to do when school ended. The way I saw it I had two options: stalking the halls of Congress for a position on a congressional staff or finally pursuing this crazy-ass dream life I had given up on years earlier.

A few years before, when I had literally walled myself off with my books, my father had, warily, made one of his after-work trips to check up on me. Usually our chats didn't go so well, with me pontificating about my recent insights into life and him trying his best to take me seriously. Usually our face-offs ended with me flipping out, telling him he just didn't understand. The night I'm remembering, however, he came up looking exhausted, sat down, and asked a provocative question: "If you could be anything, I mean anything in the world, what would that be? What, if you had the power to do anything, would you do?"

"If I could do anything, I would be a freelance foreign correspondent."

"What?" he asked.

What he didn't know was that many of the books stacked next to my bed were by war reporters, including *Shooting Wars, Means of Escape, Ways of Escape, Dispatches, A Bright Shining Lie.* They brought me into the unpredictable worlds of guys with balls who just got up one day, packed a few things in a bag, and headed off to find experience. They were free agents who answered to no one and lived each day like it was their last. I got charged up by the tales of firefights, mined roads, hostages, bad drugs, whorehouses, the corrupt and the noble. Villains. Heroes. By going out to the edges, these reporters saw life raw, up close, in ways normal people never would. I was twenty-three and spending my pathetic days in my childhood bedroom and I would have given anything to live at a hundred-mile pace like these writers did. I just didn't see how I could pull that off.

"Let's do it then," my father said.

"What do you mean?" I asked.

"I said, 'Let's do it.' It's not what I thought you'd say, but if that's what you wanna do, then let's do it."

My father had a unique way of injecting hope into me, and he called it "bucking me up." It wasn't just his enthusiasm. Even in my deepest valleys, I trusted him. So when he said, "Let's do it," and then cobbled together a plan of action right there on the spot to make it happen, my spirits lifted.

"Really? You think that will work."

"Absolutely, kid," he said. "You just got to get there, get that foot in the door, and the rest will take care of itself."

The next day I drove my father in to work so he could pump me for what I had to do. When I dropped him off at his office in Manhattan, he kissed me on the head and wished me luck and I drove back to Long Island nervous as hell but resolute. The plan was for me to drive over to a local newspaper chain, Anton Press, and volunteer my services. After a year or so covering whatever assignments they gave me, I would then take my clips and secure a paid position with a regional newspaper. After a few years padding my résumé and learning the business there, I would then be in a position to ship out and see the world as a foreign correspondent. When my father and I sketched the plan out the night before, it all sounded not only logical but eminently doable.

Everything was fine until I parked my car in the tiny back lot of the newspaper's offices. Instead of getting out and walking in to offer my services as planned, I just sat there, staring at the glass door with ANTON PRESS emblazoned on it. Just like that day a year earlier when I had tried to drive down to D.C., I got lost in my head. I envisioned myself twenty years out, forty-something, still working here and snapping pictures of some old bags showing tulips at a town flower show. The little bubble of hope my father had managed to inject in me exploded. I gave up.

Now, two years later with Zoloft coursing through my blood, my father and I were once again back at it, cobbling together a career plan.

"I haven't thought about this in a while," I told him over the phone. "But you remember when I told you I wanted to be a free-lance foreign correspondent."

"Oh Jesus," he said. "Tell me you're not thinking about that again?"

"Hey, you were all for it the last time."

"I was desperate," he told me. "I didn't care if you wanted to collect roadkill."

These days, though, he was pushing me toward a job on Capitol Hill. With my pending degree in foreign affairs, with two internships during college, snagging a job up there was at least a possibility. And the more we talked, the more excited I became about it. Then I realized something.

"Dad, I gotta explain all the time gaps in my résumé. What am I going to say I was doing?"

"Well, you could tell 'em you were managing Leo's. Or you could say you did a thorough rehab job on your parents' attic."

The last time I had headed to D.C. I never made it. That day I had started with a vision, a carefully crafted vision of myself living in D.C. as a hardworking, hard-playing young man on the go. I thought that if I could just assume that identity, play that role, somehow all the pain I was in would go away.

This time when I set out, I didn't have all my hope tied into a new identity, never got consumed with self-doubt, and, except for a quick pit stop at a Wendy's, the drive was a straight shot. As I approached D.C., I turned the radio off and rehearsed my pitch. Then I headed up to Capitol Hill to sell myself.

All day I walked the halls of Congress handing out résumés and chatting up office managers. In some of those offices I had scheduled appointments, but for a lot of them I simply strolled in and announced myself. It was awkward, but since I was there anyway I figured it couldn't hurt. And I did all the little things right, too: I remembered to be polite to the receptionists, looked my interviewers in the eyes, and conveyed a positive attitude. By the end of the day no one had offered me a job, but then again no one had treated me as if I was radioactive, either. Walking back to my car, I believed I had at a minimum two semi-promising leads.

But there was one slight problem. I realized that, as the day progressed, as I had walked around hustling myself, I had heard two small words sounding off in my mind, repeatedly: *Fuck this!* This reaction wasn't triggered by just one thing, but a compilation of impressions: the "kill me now" look on the faces of some of the staffers; the "toss me the ball again" eagerness of the others; an Ansel Adams photo pinned to the wall of one sterile cubicle; the forced peppiness of the receptionists; the sound of the keyboards crackling. I had gotten well to suddenly get boring?

Since my breakthrough, this trip to Washington was the first time I had seen the world around me as flat and senseless. It wasn't the overwhelming sense of alienation I'd known before, but it was something that was definitely sending me a message. And that message was: *Run!* Having been locked away in my head for so long, why would I now, when I could do anything, force myself, into a life that I couldn't feel part of? I remembered a book I had read called *Something Happened,* the story of a middle-aged executive waking up one day to find himself a person living a life he couldn't understand. I had promised myself that I wouldn't let that happen to me.

On the way home from D.C., I was too excited to eat. Somewhere out near Front Royal, Virginia, I made a key decision: I would become a freelance foreign correspondent. No matter what I had to do, I would make it happen. I had lost too much time already.

I drove back to Charlottesville exhilarated. I had made a conscious choice to break away from all that confusion and alienation to find a place where I could feel alive.

By the time I pulled into my driveway that night, I had decided on Bosnia as my destination. It was the major international story of the day: war in Europe again; concentration camps; ethnic cleansing; an Olympic city under siege; and talk of U.S. military intervention. Like Lebanon in the seventies and El Salvador in the eighties, that's where the action was. Also, I had just spent months studying the topic in school and there was an inherent appeal in going from the intellectual study of Bosnia, late nights in the library spent wading through Xeroxed academic papers, to actually dropping into the place to see and feel it all firsthand.

For the next week, I did my gardening shifts in the morning, attended classes and studied all day, and then at night pulled my books about foreign correspondents out of my bookcases. Instead of trying to peer inside some alternative life far from my own reality, this time I read looking for clues. How does one become a freelance foreign correspondent? The answer was, there was no one way. The only prerequisite there seemed to be was to have the drive to get there and when you arrived to have in your pocket a permission slip, a letter from a news outfit stating that the bearer of the note was a professional reporter acting on their behalf. It was called a letter of accreditation.

But how does one with zero professional experience, absolutely no qualifications, and no contacts talk a news outfit into writing them a letter of accreditation? My answer was volume. I would approach as many newspapers as I could and simply ask them. After all, I only needed one hit.

That Sunday I spent in the school library, going through phone book after phone book writing down the names and phone numbers of regional newspapers across the country. With about twenty-five in hand, I skipped class that Monday and called all of them. But when I asked about accreditation they unanimously replied, "We just can't accredit freelancers. Sorry."

But I wasn't deterred and went to my books. I realized that war zones, like any big event, had gatekeepers. Often it was the military, sometimes even guerrilla groups, but the main gatekeeper in Bosnia was the United Nations. Switching tactics, I called UN headquarters in New York and simply asked, "How does one get into Bosnia?" The answer was, "Call this number." After being handed around five times, I was finally referred to the United

Nations Press Office in Zagreb, Croatia. The woman there, obviously in a rush, gave me the number of the Croatian Foreign Press Office. When I told her that I didn't speak Croatian she said, "No one does." And hung up.

With little left to lose, I called and thank God a woman with an Australian accent picked up and I shot it to her straight. "I have no experience as a reporter whatsoever. I mean none, but I want to work in Bosnia as a freelancer. How can I do that?"

The woman turned out to be a wannabe freelancer herself, and she understood exactly where I was coming from. She told me that she had left the dullness of her life back home in Australia in search of something more and that many others had done similar things. There was a whole community of freelancers out there. She gave me the names and phone numbers of several American freelancers with apartments in Croatia.

I talked to two young American freelancers that day, a guy and a girl. They knew each other and had both arrived in Europe in the summer of 1990. Together they started an English-language newspaper in Prague, and when the war broke out in Yugoslavia in 1991, they essentially accredited themselves, soon picking up gigs with major magazines like *Time* and *Newsweek*. Now they were fully established foreign correspondents. That's exactly what I wanted to be, and when I asked their advice as to accreditation they were both quick to say, radio.

"Most freelancers start out in radio," the guy told me. "That's definitely your best shot."

I had never considered radio, but as luck had it many of the major news radio networks had their offices in Washington. The next day I called the headquarters of the Associated Press Radio Network and told the assignment editor there that I was headed off to Bosnia soon and would like to stop in for chat. The next day I drove up to see him, believing I was now only a few hours away from that golden letter.

When I walked in, I met the assignment editor in the lobby

and he escorted me back into the newsroom, where I was introduced to a few editors and technicians. To one guy he even said,
"Soon you'll be talking to this guy from Bosnia." On the rounds, he
told me I had a good radio voice and it was a bonus that I was also
studying the conflict in graduate school. When the tour was over,
we sat down at his desk and he offered me coffee. I passed as I could
already sniff the accreditation, but when I brought up the subject
he shook his head. "Oh no," he laughed. "I can't do that. We don't
accredit freelancers."

By early May, I had hit on every newspaper in central Virginia,
all the big regional newspapers in America, and all but one radio
news network. That last network was NBC Radio located in
Arlington, Virginia. Down to one last shot, I decided to change my
tactics. This time when I called the assignment editor, I stated flat
out to her that I was already accredited by something called *The
Charlottesville Observer* but that I would soon be leaving for Bosnia
and I would like to meet her as I was planning to do some radio
work on the side.

When the elevator doors opened, I walked into the lobby of
NBC Radio in my suit and tie and told the receptionist I was here
to see the assignment editor. And, yes, I had an appointment. A few
minutes later, a woman in her forties walked out, shook my hand,
and escorted me around the newsroom, introducing me to staff.

"So, you're going to Bosnia," she began. "And you're a newspaper reporter?"

"Yeah, down in Virginia a way. Charlottesville."

"Sure, beautiful country," she said. "But I didn't know smaller
papers like yours could afford to send people to cover big foreign
stories."

"Well, I've wanted to cover this story for a long time. So, I'm
gonna be sharing some of the cost. No other way, but that's why I'm
going to be doing some radio."

"Have you ever done radio before?"

"No."

"Well, you've gotta deep voice, that's good. Anyway, what is it you need from me?"

"It's a little thing, really. I'm going to be based out of Sarajevo."

"Oh great. We could always use someone else there."

"Yeah," I said. "But the only way to do stories for you from Sarajevo is to use a satellite phone run by the United Nations. I'm already accredited, so it's not that. It's just to use those phones to file stories for you I need a letter saying I'm going to be reporting stories for NBC Radio."

Right there she banged it out, and then got up to fetch what she had just written from a nearby printer. While she was gone, I sat there staring into her cubicle, at the framed photos of what I took to be her kids, the plastic travel mug, the Far Side cartoons she had taped to the monitor, praying she wasn't really coming back with two goons and a letter reading, YOU GOTTA BE KIDDING ME!

"How does that look?" she said, handing me the letter as I nodded my approval. "So, when can we expect to hear from you?"

"I figure six weeks, maybe a little more."

With that I got up, said thank you, and, no, don't bother, I'll find my own way out. When I got in the elevator with that letter in my pocket, and those doors closed, for the first time in my life I really almost swooned.

Four weeks later, at the end of May, after completing all my course work and successfully passing my competency exams, I had only one chore left to accomplish before I could move on. As I was about to head off into a war zone, a place I was assuming had no working pharmacies, I was going to need a large pile of Zoloft to bring with me. So I stopped by the student health clinic to renew my prescription, this time for a year's supply. The last time I had been to this clinic I spoke with a young psychiatrist and when I explained to him that Dr. Atchley had advised me to go on Zoloft, he wrote me a renewable prescription. But this time I was sent in to see someone else.

"Hello," the psychiatrist said when she walked through the door of the examination room. "John Falk, right? What are you here for today?"

I gave her a rundown on my history, that I had been depressed for many years and then recently went on Zoloft.

"How do you feel it's working for you?" she asked.

"It's a miracle. One day I felt dead, the next I feel alive. What can I say?"

She wrote something in her notebook. "So, since you say the Zoloft worked for you, have you been active? Would you say you've been enjoying things again?"

"Absolutely. Sure, sometimes I feel like crap, you know. My girlfriend dumped me. But that's par for the course, I guess."

She wrote in her notebook again, and then asked, "You miss your girlfriend?"

"Not really."

"OK," she said.

"Listen, the reason I'm here is, I'm about to go overseas to work as a reporter, in Bosnia. I don't know how long I'll be there, but it will probably be six months, maybe a year. So what I need is a prescription for Zoloft for at least six months, hopefully longer."

She nodded along as I talked and jotted down notes. This time when she spoke, it was in an even softer voice. "John, you *are* aware that depression is an illness?"

"Yeah."

"And that you've been through a terrible, terrible ordeal."

"Okay."

"And that you suffered horribly."

"Yeah."

"And that this suffering has impacted you in ways, negative ways, ways you may not realize?"

"You're not goin' to give me the prescription, are you?"

"I can't, not unless you are willing to work with me."

"What do you mean? What are we looking at?"

"No," she said. "If I give you the prescription, you must be willing to stay here and see me in person on a regular basis. Two, three times a week."

I rolled my eyes.

"John, to truly get over depression, yes, antidepressants are important, and they're effective, too. But just as important is understanding what you have just been through. You have a lot of work ahead of you and you need time to heal, to learn coping skills, and you should know that that is okay."

Brushing aside the fact that she was talking to me as if I was a four-year-old and as fragile as Humpty Dumpty, the point was I had just spent the past twelve years analyzing myself to death, compulsively searching for answers and meaning. Now here was this Joni Mitchell knockoff, who looked to me as if she could use a few pills herself, telling me that I needed to do it all again. Instead of diving into life, getting out there on my own to feel and experience things I had never been able to, this woman had all but declared that I was not only too wounded to swim, but the only hope I had of living normally was to strap on some water wings and ease into the shallow end of the pool with her.

"Is there anything I can say or do right now, a cartwheel, recite the alphabet backward, anything where you would give me that prescription?"

"As I told you, as a professional, I can only prescribe you Zoloft if you are willing to stay here and work with me."

"All righty then," I told her. "Thanks for your time."

"So, what are you going to do?"

"I guess I'll find my own way."

∙ ∙ ∙

Short of dragging a shrink to Bosnia with me, how was I going to score a year's supply of Zoloft? It struck me as a cruel irony that the one thing in my life that was enabling me to finally do what I wanted to do, Zoloft, would prove to be the same thing that would prevent me. For a second I even thought about going to Bosnia without it, but just as quickly realized that wouldn't be such a hot idea.

Then in early June I remembered a woman I had met a few months before through my gardening work. We had been discussing the popularity of the new antidepressants and she had mentioned that her boyfriend was a doctor who had begun to prescribe Zoloft quite often. Out of embarrassment I had kept mum to the fact that I was actually on the drug myself, but now out of desperation I called her, came out the closet, and asked if she could hook me up.

I met the doctor for lunch at the Biltmore and ran through the whole sorry tale: the happy childhood, the years of depression, the hell in the attic, that day on the bridge, my dream of freelancing, the letter of accreditation, and finally my encounter with the shrink at the health clinic. When I was done, I asked him if he knew any way I could get my hands on a load of Zoloft. "Man," he said. "I wish I had your balls. Sure, I can help you. Why not?"

That afternoon I followed this doctor in my car over to his office. Later, after he'd given me what amounted to a physical and asked a few more questions, he unlocked a storage closet and gifted me with the medicinal equivalent of the cave of Ali Baba, presenting me with a generous supply of samples he had stored away to hand out to patients, and throwing in a prescription should it be necessary.

I drove back home that afternoon with a year's supply of Zoloft in my trunk, and that night in the quiet of my room poured the blue pills into a tube sock. When I was done, I tied it up real tight and then started packing.

Ten days later, I was making my final preparations. A few days earlier I had returned to Long Island, sold my car to a teenage boy and his mother, and used the cash to buy body armor, radio equipment, and a plane ticket to Budapest. This left about a nine-hundred-dollar stake for Bosnia. My plane was scheduled to leave that evening. My parents and I had been talking this through for a long time. They, obviously, had their qualms, but I guess you could say they had finally given in. A few weeks before, my mother had called Dr. Atchley to ask his opinion. "He's not my patient now," Atchley told my mother, and then to my relief added: "But it sounds to me like John's about to do what a lot of people want to do but just don't. It's terrific he can now do it. Good for him, that's what I think."

After my mother told me what Atchley had said, she looked at me very seriously, then shut the den door behind her.

"I'm going to ask you to do me two favors," she told me. "And you're going to promise me you will do both. Just promise."

"How can I . . ."

"John, I've never asked anything from you. *Ever.* I've always been there for you, and I never stood in your way when you wanted to do anything. I always trusted you."

"I trust you, too, Ma."

"OK, then trust me and promise me you will do as I ask."

"OK, I promise," I told her. "Now what am I promising?"

"First," she told me. "If you manage to get into Bosnia, and I have no doubt you'll find a way, when you are there you will help someone. I mean just what I said. Really put yourself out to help someone. There will be many people over there in trouble, and I want you to do something for one of them. No matter how small, whatever you can do. You understand?"

"I'm gonna be a reporter and I don't know what's gonna happen, but . . . "

"No buts. There are always reasons not to do something, but you promise me you'll find a way, just once, just one person."

"All right, I promise, but why? I mean, I know why, but why do you . . . "

"Because it will be good for them, whoever that will turn out to be, but more important to me right now, it will be good for you."

"All right. What's second?"

"That you'll find the time, and no matter how you have to do it, you will apply to law school for next fall, one year."

I started laughing.

"It's no joke," she said.

"I know," I told her, wiping the smile off my face. "I'm sorry, it's just, I swear to God, I don't, I've never wanted to be a lawyer. I could think of no worse fate. Why would I apply to something I don't want?"

"Because in one year, you don't know who you'll be, that's why. Trust me, anything can happen between now and then. I know you think you know, but you have no idea what the next year will bring and I want you to have that option."

"All right. All right. I got it. A good deed and law school. You drive a hard bargain, but I promise."

When we walked back out of the den, my father wanted to know what we had talked about, but for whatever reason my mother wouldn't tell him. About ten minutes later, we all left for the airport. When we arrived at JFK, my father parked the car as my parents insisted on coming in with me.

Once inside, we finally say good-bye. A lot of hugs, a lot of "I love yous" and "Thank you for everything." I promised them I would keep safe and in touch, and they laughed when I asked them not to worry about me.

"You do what you have to do," my father told me. "And we'll do what we have to do."

And then that was it. I blew a final few kisses, and then they were gone. At first, I was too busy to think much, having to check my luggage through to Budapest, getting my boarding pass, getting X-rayed, and explaining to security for the third time why I was hauling around black body armor. After thirty minutes I found a nice secluded seat near the departure gate, where I planned to just relax and read the paper.

But I never really read very much or relaxed. Mostly I people-watched: a businessman looking through his briefcase; a mother corralling her kids; those tourists dipping into their fanny packs; that clean-cut group of guys and girls I took to be newly minted college grads setting off for a tour of Europe; that husband passed out in the seat next to his wife, who was nibbling on her finger while reading *Cosmo* magazine; the stewardesses wheeling their luggage onto the plane; and that guy three seats over doing a cross-word puzzle who finally leaned over to me and asked, "Where are you going that you need a flak jacket?"

"I'm a reporter," I answered. "Bosnia."

"Cool," he said. "Good luck."

I guess I should have been elated. I was finally doing what I had always wanted to do. But still it was bittersweet. I had been alone so long in spirit that I had not only learned to live without others but I had even grown to prefer it. When it came down to it, even after the Zoloft had done its magic, I only truly felt myself when I was alone. Deep connections with others had over time become a burden, something that took more from me than it gave. In a real sense, I just didn't understand what made normal people tick.

And that's what hurt. Not that I wasn't coming back to visit. Not that I wasn't going to keep in touch. Not that I wasn't even going to eventually end up living back in New York. It was that I would always be different in that way, walled off from those connections in spirit if not always in reality. And when I said good-bye to my parents before, I didn't have the heart to tell them that truth. That I wasn't just simply saying good-bye, but I was in a real sense saying good-bye to all they had hoped for me, an easier life, a normal existence, all that.

twenty-one

One More Thing

Even though I had grown close to Dina, Omar, and Olja, I was expecting to feel somewhat relieved when they rolled away on that train. I finally would be free to get back to work. Then I found myself wanting to be on that train with them—and *that* was unexpected.

Later that morning, Monica's friend dropped me off at the villa, where I would stay until New York verified that the Bosnians had arrived safely. Monica was at work and the photographer, Mauro, was off on a shoot, so the only conscious being around was Mauro's grumpy old mutt, Marta, whom I tried to coax out from underneath a pine tree for a walk.

"*Avanti, moja* pooch," I pleaded, but she was immune to my charms, so I grabbed the *International Herald Tribune* and flipped on the tube for background. After half an hour, I moved to the kitchen table and nibbled on some cold pasta Dina had made. Then, back outside, I sat under the pine tree with Marta. But nothing worked. I couldn't shake the memories: the kitchen where we fought over money and my lack of adequate planning; the spot in the driveway where Omar created that special moment by unexpectedly hosing down the transvestite; the sports page of the *Tribune* that I used to teach Olja about baseball. Now it was just me and Marta and all those times swirling around in my head. I was lonely. I wasn't content being alone anymore.

Later that afternoon, I plopped down on the bed in Omar's old room on the second floor. Dark and cozy, it was the perfect getaway. I took out a book that had nothing to do with anything—Japanese art of the fifteenth and sixteenth centuries. But I never got very far because that outsized puppet of a raven was hanging above my head, and every time I looked up at it I thought of Omar: Where was he now? Was he excited? Petrified? And of course there was the memory of that first time I had come into this room a few months before when Omar had been terribly homesick and panicked. Reverting to an old trick I'd used when feelings got a little overwhelming, I pulled a pillow over my head for a nap.

The next day I woke early, went for a walk, made myself breakfast, and reread the *Tribune.* Around noon, I took the phone and put it down outside the front door so I'd be sure to hear it and then sat down with Marta underneath the pine tree. Trying to use the time productively, I opened a book on post–cold war American foreign policy. Was I kidding? All afternoon, while trying to concentrate, I thought of home, imagining Dina, Omar, and Olja on Long Island with my parents driving them around. I envisioned their tour of Garden City. I thought of the large houses, the big cars, the manicured lawns, and I could virtually hear Dina in the backseat thinking, "I knew it. *Spoiled.*"

Although I knew both sides well, the Bosnians and my family were total strangers to one another. The last thing my parents ever thought they'd be doing was driving around with a trio of war refugees in the backseat. As for Omar, Dina, and Olja, it was a good bet they never thought they'd be huddled together in a Jeep Cherokee cruising through the suburbs. I could picture it: The jeep stopping in the middle of Cedar Place, in the shade of that big copper beech tree. My father pointing to the window of my attic bedroom and saying, "Up there. See, kids. Behind that window was John's room." Then the Bosnians would look up, dutifully nod, and then give one another the eye.

Sitting with Marta, I imagined myself, just two years earlier, locked away up in my attic bedroom: I peer out my window on a sunny, summer day just wishing I could die but torture myself by looking out at the big world anyway. But this time, I spot a Jeep Cherokee stopped in the middle of the street. Then I see a finger pointing directly up at my window, and three strangers in the back nodding in my direction. I freak because I've been spotted and drop the drapes and pull back into my sanctuary.

If someone had told me back in those old sad days that the Jeep contained not only my parents but three refugees from some place called Bosnia and that, what's more, I had put them together, I wouldn't have been able to compute it. Now here I was alone in this villa, sitting beside a mutt underneath a pine tree, having actually pulled that off and I was still not content. I realized that I would have given anything to have been the sixth person in that Jeep Cherokee. I wanted to be there with them. *This blows,* I thought, then focusing in on the phone. *Ring already.*

But the phone never rang that day. That evening, when Monica got home, I asked permission to call New York to find out what was happening. The only number I had was to my parents' new apartment in Manhattan. I got the answering machine. "Hello . . . Hello, it's me. Your son. *Remember me?* Anyone there? . . . Oh God. All right, listen. Someone please call me. I'm at Monica's still, waiting. Tell me what's up. Did you find them in the airport? Is everything OK? Please call soon. I'm goin' nuts here."

I spent that night in Omar's old room again, but I barely slept. I really was wigging out. My thoughts were out of control.

All night, I kept playing little newsreels in my head. At first, these scenes were strictly Bosnians-coming-to-America crap. But at one point it dawned on me that if it was now midnight in Italy, it meant it was six o'clock back in New York. Early evening. Back when I was really depressed, I hated that hour. To me, it was the hour of release from a hard day's work—happy hour, when people got together to chill. I used to hate that time most of all because, in my mind, it was so alive but I couldn't take part.

I started picturing my friends playing softball in Central Park, my buddies having beers in the basement of Penn Station, my brother lying on his couch, watching *The Simpsons* after work, guys with their ties undone putting four quarters in the jukebox at Leo's. God, did I feel lonely. Not homesick, lonely, though. The harder-edged loneliness of being left behind. Which was absurd, of course, because I was the one who had left that world behind and had sent the Bosnians away.

I was the one always scheming to escape, to find something more, some experience or place where I could feel more alive.

I finally fell asleep around five and awoke again at eleven. Monica was off at work, so I was alone in the house. I made some coffee, sat on the couch, and stared at the phone. As I waited there, this time I was visited by an old friend—the questioner. I started wondering, why? If I wanted to go back home so badly, then why the hell didn't I just go? If I had followed my gut all the way out here, why didn't I follow it again right now? Over the course of that day, if it was possible for a mind to be torn in two, mine was. Later that afternoon the damn phone finally rang.

"Ciao," I answered.

"John, is that you?" my mother asked.

"Yeah, it's me," I told her. "What the hell is going on back there? Why didn't anyone call earlier?"

"Everyone's fine," she said. "Relax. We just haven't had the time."

"What's been goin' on?"

My mother started filling me in, describing how she and my father met the Bosnians at the airport, my mother holding up a handwritten sign that read THE FALKS. DINA, OMAR & OLJA.

"We could see the relief on their faces when they saw us," my mother told me. "That someone was actually there waiting for them."

"That was Dina."

"Well," she said. "All three had huge smiles."

Then she told me how they all piled into the Jeep Cherokee and headed out to Garden City to have dinner at Leo's. When they got there, my father ordered them steak dinners and Cokes. They met my uncle James and aunt Mary. My father pointed out the caricatures on the walls. They had dessert.

"Was it all weird to them?" I asked. "What were they like?"

"They were very polite. Quiet," she said. "Mostly they were looking around. Dina told us it was exactly the way you had described it."

And just like I had imagined, after dinner my father took them by our old house on Cedar Place.

After that, they drove out to my brother's home farther out on Long Island. And the next morning my father took them on his grand tour of New York City: Brooklyn, Wall Street, the World Trade Center, Chinatown, Little Italy, the Village, the Empire State Building, Times Square, Park Avenue, Central Park, Harlem. They visited the New York School of Visual Arts, where Omar was going to begin his freshman year in a few weeks. Then they headed to Jersey to visit Olja and Dina's new school, Upsala College. When night fell, my father couldn't help himself and took them back across the Brooklyn Bridge to the BQE to show them the Manhattan skyline.

"What did Dad say?" I asked.

"You know, the usual," she said. "'Kids, have you ever seen such a fabulous sight in your life?'"

"What were they doing?"

"They were wide-eyed. It was a perfect night here."

And by the time they got back, it was too late to call.

When she was done, all I could say was, "Wow. That's wild."

"So, how are you doing?" she asked.

"Ah, tell you the truth, I'm a little lonely," I told her.

"That is because you are alone."

"I know, but it's not a big deal."

"Well," she said. "I have some good news for you."

"Really?"

"You've been accepted into law school."

To fulfill my promise to my mother I had arranged to take the LSATs in Croatia in the fall—and I had carried through. Fittingly, Mom had gotten the scores first. I had done well, well enough to apply to even Harvard, my mother's dream all along. That winter, with the deadline looming, she sent off the Harvard applications along with four others, which I had quickly filled out and mailed back. With my solid B average in college, I was comfortable in the knowledge that I wouldn't get into any of them. And I didn't. As far as I knew, all five had rejected me.

"Who accepted me?"

"The University of Virginia."

"Ma, how is that possible?" I asked. "I thought they nixed me."

"Well, they did," she told me. "But after your father and I drove to Congress for the kids, we continued on the next day to UVA."

"Why?"

"Well," she said. "I wanted to talk to the dean of admissions at the law school there. So I left your father in the parking lot and went up. I waited on a bench outside his office for an hour."

"Oh Jesus. Don't tell me you . . ."

"Oh Jesus, nothing. When the dean returned, I introduced myself as your mother and asked him if I could please talk to him about your application. He was very gracious."

"Ma, that's nuts."

"Well, he remembered you. And they all had been very

impressed with your trip to Bosnia, and especially helping the kids. It was your grades that bothered them, but I explained to him about your depression, and then he asked me if it was all right if he called Dr. Atchley to confirm that you had been depressed. He did, right there. Atchley told the dean that he had never seen such a remarkable turnaround in a patient before. He may have had a B average, Dr. Atchley said, but it was a miracle he finished at all. So this morning, the dean called and told me you've been accepted."

My first instinct was to simply say, Yes. I could suddenly see myself there—the classes, the new people, softball in the afternoon, even late nights in the library. It was as if my mother had called Italy with the perfect prescription for all that turmoil I had been ambushed with over the previous three days. If I wanted to come in from the cold, I could do a lot worse. It may have felt right, but still it was all very sudden.

"Ma, I got one little problem," I told her. "I don't want to be a lawyer."

"You don't have to be," she said. "But three years in law school will be good for you, no matter what you choose to do. The point is, you don't know. Maybe you'll like it, but you won't know if you don't try. School starts in a week."

"Why didn't you give me some warning?"

"How could I? Listen John, it's now or never."

"Oh Jesus," I said. "Part of me wants to, but Ma . . ."

Then almost as if she had been reading my mind, she said, "You've spent the past year out there. You've finally done that. Broken away. But now it's time to come home. You may not practice law but, John, this is the perfect way for you to reenter the world back here, to finally start your life. You don't have forever."

"Oh God," I sighed.

"I need to give the dean an answer."

"All right. Listen to me. I need two days. I have to go back to Sarajevo."

"Why?"

"I just do. There's one last thing I've got to find out."

The next afternoon I was flying back into Sarajevo aboard another C-130, and when we landed, as always I hitched a ride in the Egyptian APC across the Serb lines to the PTT building. From there, I walked directly to Vlado's. It never occurred to me to go to anyone else.

Inside my head I was always weighted down by this ever-present question: *Why?* But when the Zoloft kicked in, that compulsion to understand the reason behind everything just disappeared. I was finally free to take life as it was. Now that I had to decide between going home—that empty place it seemed I had always been running from—and continuing on out into the realm of the extraordinary, my old demon returned. It was as if that troll from *Monty Python and the Holy Grail,* the one who guarded that bridge over the Pit of Doom, was back in my head, holding up his bony claw to my face and saying with a grin, *"You still owe me an answer, big boy."* I still thought I had something to learn from Vlado, something that would free me even more, so I headed out.

I finally got up to Vlado's door around three that afternoon and rang the bell.

"Johnny," he said, smiling. He was dressed in jeans and a golf shirt; it was the first time I had ever seen him out of fatigues. I told him that I was back in town for a few days and that I had a few more questions for him.

"Questions, questions, questions," he said. "Of course. Why not? Come in."

As was custom, I took my boots off in the common area and then he led me over to the couch. He offered me coffee and moonshine, and I accepted both. While he was off in the kitchen, his daughter, Diana, came in, walked over to me, and held out her hand. Although that citywide cease-fire was still in effect after all these months, there was a lot of shooting going on outside.

"For you," she said, in careful English. "Present I make for you."

In her hand was a copper wire twisted to spell my name, "John."

"Jesus," I said. "Thank you, Diana."

"You are welcome," she stuttered, then ran out of the room.

When Vlado came back with our drinks, I showed him Diana's present.

"Oh," he said. "Diana ask me, 'Who is this man you keep talking to?' I tell her you are American reporter, nice man. She made month ago. Waiting to give to you. Also, she practice her English to speak to you. My daughter, something special."

Then he handed me my plum brandy, picked up his glass, and we toasted each other.

"So, what is it you want?" he asked.

I suppose I could have asked flat out what it was that kept him from simply surrendering to despair. But that seemed like something out of an Ingmar Bergman movie. I was embarrassed to be so self-absorbed, so I just started bullshitting. For an hour and a half we just chatted, but I was really circling around, looking for a thread of conversation that would lead me to the Promised Land without tipping my hand.

Eventually, though, Vlado, maybe sensing we were going nowhere, asked, "John, did you come to talk, or is there something you want to know?"

I told him there was something, but that it was a little complicated. Then he asked me if it was about Slavko. I said, no. Then he asked, "Are you going to write that as a story?"

"I didn't really think you'd be okay with that. I listened to that story as your friend."

"It's your story," he told me. "You do what you want, but it is a war story, ugly story, brother against brother. Maybe it is good people know. And I'm proud of everything I have done, so write the story if you wish."

I thanked him and told him that maybe I would. Then he asked me what I had come for then. I was as self-conscious as before, but it was now or never, so I asked the first direct question I could come up with. "Vlado, can you tell me, have you learned anything?"

"What do you mean, learn?" he asked.

"You know, learn. Learn something about life?"

"In the war?" he asked, looking confused.

"Sure, in the war. Before. Anything. About yourself."

"Aaaah," he said, then thought it over for a second. "I don't know."

"Come on. Has there been any change in you, how you see life?"

"Of course. How could that not be?"

"All right," I said, now excited. "What?"

He started listing things: that he was stronger than he ever thought he could be; that material things, money, aren't so important; that war changes everything, friends can become enemies. Then, as was his way before getting to the heart of the matter, he took a deep drag off his cigarette. "What did I learn? Here is something. I used to think, before war, I knew what love was. My wife. My daughter. But no. I didn't. In war, we stay together. We are strong for one another. We stay family. My wife stay with me. She fight, like soldier in her way. Strong for all of us. I love her more than I ever thought was possible, another person. That is something special. A power. Um, I cannot describe. How to say? Just love. Something special. That is something I learn."

After he was done, I could tell by the definitive way that he snuffed out his cigarette that he thought he had answered my question. But he hadn't. Or at least I didn't get it yet. I wasn't satisfied and kept pressing him. "What else have you learned?" "How have you changed?" "Why do you do what you do?" "What do you believe in, Vlado?" I drove him nuts, and about an hour into it, totally confused, he finally demanded, "What is it you want from me?"

"I'm sorry," I said. "It's . . . I don't know. I'm looking for something, and maybe why did you stay and fight?"

"Perhaps it's something in me," he said. "I don't know. Could be I'm a fool. But here, now, people killing women and children. I couldn't just leave. How? Maybe I am strange in some way, but for me I didn't have a choice."

"But why?" I asked.

"What do you mean, why?" he asked, increasingly frustrated. "Just me. I didn't have choice."

"But why did you do what you did? There must be some reason."

"Johnny," he said, chuckling. "Why? Let me ask you a question: Why did you help those kids?"

"I don't know."

"Exactly," he said. "But you do know. It was something you felt *you* had to do for other people. How many other reporters go through Nino's apartment while you stayed there?"

"I don't know."

"Four, five, maybe more," he said. "But no one else helps his children. And they shouldn't. Those aren't their kids. This isn't their war. Their people. But you help them. *Why?*"

"I guess it was something I thought I had to do."

"Yes," he said. "Something you *wanted* to do for other people. It gave you something, helping those kids. I can see that when you talk about them. But, Johnny, if you asked why, you wouldn't have done it. So John, don't ask me why. Because I don't know."

I apologized and dropped the subject, although I still wasn't satisfied. We had another drink and chatted some more. Then he asked me what I was planning to do after Sarajevo. That's when I told him about my option for law school.

"Didn't you tell me before that these schools not accept you?"

"Yeah, but my mother went down to one school and talked them into it."

"Mothers," he laughed, then added, "That means your mother wants you to go home."

"No shit," I said.

"So you go?"

"I don't know. Still thinking about it."

He nodded, like he understood. I thought that was the end of it.

And then it was time to go. But as we were cleaning up, he brought up the subject of law school again. "Please, I do not mean as insult," he said. "But I think you are crazy."

"Why?"

"I don't know," he said. "But to me, if I could leave here and go back to America, to school, that would be like dream. John, if you go far enough, long enough, you see enough. Enough things that may change you. Maybe enough where you can become like me. But, John, you do not want to become like me."

"What do you mean?"

He put aside the dish rag and put his hand firmly on my shoulder.

"You are a nice man," he said. "Maybe a very nice man. I like you, but I could never be friends with you, ever. With anyone. I cannot trust. That is something Slavko, this war take. The bill I had to pay. But that is something special, life, and I would give anything to have that back. So, you not ask me but I say, go home, back to America, to your friends, your family, go to your school, be a rich American. Why not? It is OK. But John, whatever you choose to do, I want you to promise me something."

"Of course."

"That after war, if I live of course, that one day I meet your mother."

"What?" I asked, taken aback.

"Just promise me, that after war, if I live, that one day I meet your mother."

I promised him, but all the same, I couldn't see how that could happen. He opened the door to the common area, where I started putting on my boots. He stood in the doorway just smiling. Part of me was hurt because he said that he could never be my friend. I understood why, of course, but that didn't make it any easier. Then I asked something I had been wanting to know for a long while. "Why did you talk to me that first time?"

"Eh, Nino told me a reporter helping his kids and wanted to meet a sniper. For Nino, old friend, I agree."

"No," I said. "I mean, why did you call me back that next day?"

"Every reporter I meet, first thing they ask, 'How many people did you kill?' Like that is most important. But you never ask me that."

"Oh," I said, finishing putting on my boots. But it was almost as if I couldn't let go. I needed to keep asking questions. So when I stood up, I said to him, "Maybe what I'm really asking is, why did you keep talking to me?"

He looked up at the ceiling and thought for a second.

"I thought I was going to die."

"You just wanted someone to talk to."

"No, not just someone," he said.

"Then why me?"

He sighed, almost as if I was forcing him to say something he really didn't want to say.

"I thought I was going to die. I guess I just wanted someone out there in the world, a stranger, someone like you, to know a good man once lived in this city."

twenty-two

Hello to All That

That day when I had walked into Vlado's, I was looking for a definitive answer. I needed him to say something that would really help me come to terms with what to do with my life. Vlado hadn't really come through in that way, but he had made me realize that he survived because he was doing what he was doing for other people. Because there were people he loved, the darkness had not completely changed him. He had already shown me that, despite impossible circumstances, a person should not ever withdraw from life, give in.

When I awakened that day in 1981, depressed but not really understanding what was wrong, the thing that had been most frightening was the sense of suddenly finding myself alone. Gone was the intimacy I had taken for granted. It was as if a tornado had blown through my room that night and carried me off into a space. Ultimately I resigned myself to a life lived out there on the edges of other lives. I was an aging photo of someone missing, waiting in the attic.

But I had the memory of what it was to feel differently. All the time I was sick, what I wanted most was to get back that sense of intimacy and connection. That was why I had fought so hard— because I could remember that feeling of home and being part of life. I wanted people back, wanted some sense of connection, of loving and being loved. But it never happened, and as the years went by, I turned my back on that dream. It just hurt too much to think about. Then the Zoloft worked, and I was tossed back in, but I had been gone so long, I never learned how to live.

In Bosnia, despite the odds, I had forged a new bond with life and made new relationships with people whom I now felt profoundly attached to. When I sent Dina, Omar, and Olja out of my life, I felt a loss. Not that old feeling—the unbroken isolation—but something different, the sense of missing people who were now far away and who had come to mean something to me. That was something new and when I felt that, I felt for the first time that the world need not be a cold and alien place. I could make it there, back to my old self, if I still wanted it. And that's the gift Vlado gave me. He was able to make me believe in my old dream again, of intimacy, of belonging, of being loved.

So that night after leaving Vlado's, I told Nino and Ella that I was leaving Family Nonovich for Family Falk. I was going home. I was expecting a tearful good-bye, and I got one. The next morning, after I packed my bags (except for the body armor, which I was leaving behind for Harald), I sat with Nino and Ella for our last coffee together.

"You always be in my heart, John," Nino told me, his big eyeglasses fogging up. "You always have a family here, too, with us. You are my boy, too. I mean, good boy."

We hugged, slapping each other's backs. Then Ella stepped forward. She put her hand over her heart and tapped it three times. Then she spoke the only English word I ever heard her say, "Love."

"My wife, she learn that word last night just for you," Nino said. I choked up, and I hugged her, too. I told them that I'd never forget them. With that, there was no more to be said. I grabbed my bags and left.

•   •   •

I had one last thing I had to do: go to the Kosovo hospital complex to see Laylo, Dina's boyfriend. He had been injured on the front line and was recovering in the rehab wing, perhaps the most depressing place in Sarajevo. Filled with young men missing arms, legs, eyes—whatever you could lose and still survive—the place stank of urine and formaldehyde. It was damp and moldy, the only illumination coming from the sunlight that managed to penetrate that milky plastic sheeting covering the windows.

"Johnny boy," Laylo said, slowly rising up on his cot when I walked into the ward. "Any word from Dina?"

I told him she was in America with my family and getting ready for school. Then I broke the news that I was leaving for home myself and that I'd be with Dina in a day or two. Did he want me to pass along a message?

"No one has to tell Dina to work hard, but tell her for me to relax sometimes, enjoy herself."

"I doubt that will work," I joked, and he laughed.

"But tell her anyway. And also say that no matter what happen to me, I will always love her. And remind her finally that I will get out of this place, this war, Bosnia, and I will find her again someday. Tell her that for me, just like that."

I promised I would, and then I left. After I was about a quarter mile away, a lone Katyusha rocket came screaming into the hospital complex and exploded.

Later that afternoon, as the C-130 that was taking me home took off from that battered airport, I looked out on Sarajevo to take everything in one last time. It looked the same as the day I arrived over a year before: tank traps, gutted roofs, blasted buildings—this was still a nasty place. Then the plane hit a cloud bank and it all disappeared.

Two days later, my parents picked me up at JFK and we drove straight out to my brother Quentin's house to reunite with Dina,

Omar, and Olja. As soon as I saw them in his kitchen, I was glad I had come back, not only for myself but for them. Around each of their necks were bandanas—their emergency tourniquets. Even safe in the suburbs of New York, they were still afraid it would come back. It was important that I was around, someone who understood a little of what they had been through.

"Popok!" Omar yelled when he saw me. He rushed over, kissed me on each cheek, and then tried to throw me into a head-lock. My brother's elkhound started barking.

"Omar, plappa noynavich!" Dina yelled, and Omar immediately withdrew. After reasserting control, Dina asked very formally, "So, how was your trip, John?"

"Fuck my trip. The question is, how are you guys doing?"

They never said as much, but the answer was that things weren't going so hot. I sensed their anxieties in almost everything they did. Sometimes when my family spoke to them, they were so zoned out they didn't respond. They moved together as this unit, as if all three shared the same hip.

At one point that first night, I took Dina aside and relayed Laylo's message to her about his undying love and romantic vision of finding her one day.

"Thank you," she said when I was done, like I had just passed the salt or something.

"And he also told me to tell you, above all else, to relax and enjoy yourself."

"John, *pleeeeease,*" she said, even cracking a smile. "You know me."

Before I left for law school, I tried to create as normal a few days as I could. We went to the beach where we smoked butts and swam in the ocean. We ate Chinese food and saw *Forrest Gump* together at the multiplex. And the night before I was scheduled to leave, my brother threw a big barbeque.

The next morning it was once more time to go, and Omar carried my luggage to the jeep. All three of the former Sarajevans were petrified. They had no idea how they were going to fare in this strange new world. But I knew them and enough of New York to know that everything was going to work out. But, realizing that only time and experience could show them that, I kept my thoughts and opinions to myself. I just reassured them that I would be back soon for the fund-raiser and then I was on my way.

My original plan was to take Amtrak down to school, but my parents insisted on driving me. I had tried to talk them out of it as I didn't want to roll into my new school with parental escorts, but I couldn't convince them. They were pretty determined. Adamant, actually. "We deserve it," my father said. To them, the drive down was a victory lap. No one ever said anything, but it was obvious I was back and finally set to get on with a more or less normal life, a full life—the one they had been pulling for all along.

It was a six-hour ride down to Charlottesville, and for most of it we chatted: how the Bosnians were going to do; the fund-raiser; law school; family gossip. By the time we hit northern Virginia we had been talking nonstop for four hours and finally the conversation just petered out. My father concentrated on driving while I stared out the passenger window and thought about the days to come, meeting babes, getting everything squared away, how I was going to pay for it all. For thirty minutes there wasn't a peep. Then from the backseat came a soft *"Damn."*

"What's wrong?" my father asked, without looking back.

"Oh nothing," my mother said.

Then I looked into the backseat. She was staring out the window.

"What's wrong, Ma?"

"It's just . . . It's just. I'm so happy for you. How things have turned out. It's where I always hoped you'd be."

"Then what's with the *damn,* Joanne?" my father asked.

"It's nothing," she said. "Really."

"Come on, Ma. What's up?"

She continued to stare out the window.

"It's just . . . " Then she took a deep breath. "It's just, damn. If Robert had only been born thirty years later, and I had been his mother, I could have saved him."

There's some unwritten rule that you're supposed to hate law school—the cutthroat competition, the tyrannical professors, the intellectual warfare—but I dug it. Maybe it was where I had been, but to me it was like a three-year sleepaway camp for twenty-somethings. Normally I would ease into the day with an hour of SportsCenter, usually two, then attend a few classes, tease the professors, and maybe learn some interesting things. Afternoons I played softball or racquetball. Nights I'd study a little or go out for some pops with my friends. As far as the women, it was rough going at first, but eventually I started seriously dating a fellow law student, Tara. By my third year, we decided to try to make a go of it. When I had everything set, she was going to join me in New York where we would live together.

After graduating in 1997, I passed the bar exam, and was admitted into the New York bar. Eventually, I got a job with a corporate law firm in Manhattan, and Tara moved up. Part of my job was putting together private placements for Internet start-ups. Like a lot of people back then, I looked at myself and thought, why not me? So I left my firm in 1999 to open a legal Web site. In March 2000, however, the bubble burst and the venture capitalists and wealthy angels stopped calling. My little enterprise went bankrupt. Again, like a lot of folks back then, I found myself destitute and unemployed. I tried to find legal work again, but except for some temp gigs, I didn't have much luck. I started panicking because Tara and I were planning to marry. Then I caught a lucky break.

That first year of law school, I had written up the story of Vlado and Slavko and sold it to *Details* magazine. Then two years later HBO made a movie based on the story. At that time, I thought that was the end of my writing career. But now, just when I needed it most, I fell ass-backward into a pile of money in the form of a Hollywood script I was commissioned to write. I just had happened to be in the right place at the right time. With that sizable loaf in the bank, Tara and I set the date for the wedding—July 2001. Afterward we planned to fly off to China on a three-week honeymoon. I had never been happier in my life.

By that point, I had all but forgotten that I had ever been depressed. Not that I couldn't remember it if I wanted to; it was just something that had once been and now was over. I was busy living with my life as it was. As to seeking therapy, I never felt the need. Sometimes life got tough over these years, but I never became overwhelmed. When shit happened, I dealt with it, grew, and moved on.

We had a very small wedding, but three weeks after my wife and I returned from our honeymoon we threw a big party in the backyard of my uncle Brian's house in Garden City. The night before, Tara and I went there to help set up, but mostly we drank beers while my uncle did the grunt work. The next morning a small army of caterers, bartenders, DJs, and riggers showed up and transformed his backyard into a setting for a summer dance at a country club: tent, dance floor, tiki lamps, flowers, twinkling lights. By the time they were done, there was seating for over a hundred of our nearest and dearest.

The party was scheduled to kick off at 3:00 p.m., but the first guest arrived at noon. He was a Belgian named Philippe and he was one of the first freelancers I had met in Sarajevo. He had flown in from Europe just for the party and that knocked me out. Soon others began to drift in—my uncle, aunt, cousins, friends from grammar school, my great-aunt Betty from the family's old neighborhood in Brooklyn. By two-thirty, Tara and I had our hands full with the meeting and greeting. Up the driveway they came: Michael, with a day's growth of beard and the world's tackiest wedding gift; Matt Bodden; Omar and his longtime boyfriend, a Wall Street financier; my tante Marie who greeted me with a punch; the boys from law school, still in their suits from work; Dina and her husband, Laylo, who passed along Nino and Ella's love and regrets that they couldn't be there; Diana, Vlado's daughter, now eighteen and starting her freshman year at Bryn Mawr on a full scholarship; my little sister Sara and her fiancé; my sister Christine, her husband, and their kids; Quentin and his wife; the photographer and publicist I had become friends with on the set of Vlado's HBO movie; the nice old judge who had married us in July and his wife. They kept coming until the yard was full.

By the time Tara and I returned to the party, everyone was already into their second drink and easing into the night. We cruised the tables playing host and hostess, and while we were out there the music died down as my father grabbed the microphone.

"I'd just like to take a minute to read something from Sarajevo, a letter. *Dear John and Tara, Majda and I wish with all our heart that we could have been there with you to celebrate this special day. We want to wish you every happiness in your new life together. With All Our Love, Always Your Friends, Vlado and Majda Sarzinski.*"

The crowd let out a big, "Oooooooh." Then the music cranked up again.

By seven that night, I finally got a minute to myself at the bar. Taking my Dewar's on the rocks from the bartender, I lit a cigarette and took in the scene. As I scanned that yard, I couldn't help but notice that it was an eclectic mixture, my uncle Brian in his Tommy Bahama shirt and silk Bermuda shorts talking with my friend Fritz, a Dutch photographer who looked as under the weather as I had on the day Michael managed to get me out of Tuzla. Omar and his boyfriend chatted with my grandmother and her sister. Dina and Laylo sat at the table with my parents. It was weird because now that I could see them all together in one place I realized something. There were two distinct groups of people in my life: those who had known me before I had become depressed—family and childhood friends—and they were mostly of a type. They were doers: bond brokers, salesman, businessmen, housewives, parents, weekend golfers, ordinary people who had never drifted too far off the path of convention. But the people I got to know on the other side of my depression were writers, photographers, reporters, artists, people who had fled that path at the earliest possible opportunity.

I was lucky. I had a foot in both worlds, and I was comfortable in both. My life was much broader than it would otherwise have been. But standing there, I couldn't help but notice another thing: not one soul in that backyard did I meet while I was depressed. Not one of these people first came into my life between my twelfth and twenty-fourth years. No one from high school. No one from college or after. No one from graduate school. It was as if I hadn't existed during those years. If there is a better way to explain what depression does to a life, I can't really think of it.

Standing there, I realized that if it hadn't been for my parents and the breakthroughs in antidepressants, I would have been Robert. There would have been no one in this backyard. And if I hadn't made that trip to Bosnia, met the people I had, everything would have still turned out very differently for me. Unlike many others I had been given an opportunity—and a second and a third cut—to take part in the blessings of the world. I remain grateful to this day that I had a chance to say hello to all that.

author's note

This is a memoir, filled with memories, personal observations, and opinions that are mine and mine alone. I have mostly used real names where I thought it was right to do so, but changed some others where I thought a fictitious name the wiser course. Not that they had anything to be embarrassed about or ashamed of, just thought they'd appreciate the privacy.

Half of this memoir takes place during a period of my life when I was an active journalist, during which time I took copious notes and/or recordings of conversations and events. The dialogue in these sections is either taken from those sources verbatim or checked for accuracy with those participants still living. In the places in the book where people speak to me in Bosnian, I didn't translate, nor did I use real Bosnian; rather, I wrote the words down as they sounded to me at the time they were said—essentially a blenderful of pure gibberish and Russian. The other half of the memoir takes place during my childhood and early adulthood, a time when taking notes and/or recording was the least of my concerns. As for the dialogue in these sections, I wrote in what I remembered and then conferred with others to check for accuracy.

When our recollections conflicted, we either came to some mutual agreement as to what was said or, failing that, I scratched the subject matter in question altogether.

Finally, in a rare few instances I switched around the chronology of events for dramatic effect. Otherwise, this account is as it was, and any mistakes and/or omissions are my fault and mine alone.

acknowledgments

Ten years ago, I first started toying with the idea of writing this book. And from that first inclination to these last words I'm now writing a decade later, I was never alone in my efforts. Whether we were in the middle of a game of chess, cruising along in a car, or taking in a *schvitz*, whenever I leaned over to a friend and asked, "You got a second for that book?" never once did they say no. Without those countless insights and the encouragement they provided, I never would have finished. So, in no particular order of importance, I would like to thank Philippe Deprez, Harald Dornbos, Scott Andersen, G. Blake Lee, John McLoughlin, LCDR James Perduto (USNR), Tammy Perduto, Anthony Borelli, Danielle and Barb Borelli, Marco Ireland, Andi Gitow, Craig Blankenhorn, Sue Nowak, Rev. Patty Love, Daniela Pestova, Maddy Falk, Katherine and Lauren Reidy, and Dr. John Atchley.

Also I would like to thank the people of Sarajevo. I came to see the worst, and because of you I saw the best. In particular, I thank the Kukic family for their generosity in first taking me in, but a special place in my heart will always belong to the Nonoviches and Sarzinskis.

To Francine LeFrak and the people over at HBO, it was a first-class job from beginning to end, so thank you.

Some of this material was first published in *Details* and *Esquire,* so to Will Dana, Mark Warren, and David Granger, thank you for the opportunity but more so for being pros. Without you, this would all still be just an inclination.

Thanks to my friend and literary agent, Stuart Krichevsky, who took in this lactose kid and despite everything made me believe in myself as a writer.

Forever thank you to my editor, George Hodgman. Placing my bet on you was one of the best decisions I ever made, professional or otherwise. Whatever happens, I'll always consider the day I shook your hand the day I hit the trifecta. And also a special thanks to Supurna Banerjee for all her hard work with each passing deadline.

Finally, thank you to my family, down to the last cousin. Never was a kid so blessed. In an age when families break apart all too often, having a big tribe to belong to was something special, my gift. Then to Q and Sherry, Christine and Patrick, Sara Cool, and Mr. Thomas Gustufson, thanks for your patience. But my parents—words truly aren't enough. I just hope someday I can give my own children a hundredth of what you gave me. If I could do that, then I will have considered it all a success.

about the author

Among psychologists today, John Falk is known as patient X and the story of his recovery from chronic depression is used to inspire hope in other patients. He is also a law school graduate and freelance journalist who survived the rough-and-tumble of reporting from the front in Sarajevo. An article he wrote for *Details* magazine, titled "Shot Through the Heart," became an HBO movie and won a Peabody Award for Best Cable Movie of the Year. His book originated with an article, penned for *Esquire* in 2001, titled "No Zoloft, No Peace."